TOWNS PRINTED BY LINDA SANCHEZ / HARDCOVER BINDING BY FRANK PAPP

PAUMANOK

PAUMANOK

Poems and Pictures of Long Island

Compiled and Edited by Kathaleen Donnelly

Cross-Cultural Communications
Merrick, New York
2009

Published by
Cross-Cultural Communications
239 Wynsum Avenue, Merrick, NY 11566-4725/USA
Tel: (516) 868-5635 / Fax: (516) 379-1901
E-mail: cccpoetry@aol.com
www.cross-culturalcommunications.com

Library of Congress Control Number: 2008936918

ISBN 978-0-89304-119-9
ISBN 978-0-89304-120-5 (pbk.)

First Edition

Printed by
www.superprint-bg.com

Cover Photo: *Green Reflection* by Bob Schmitz

Designed by Tchouki
Printed in Sofia, Bulgaria, 2009

In memory of my mother,
Dorothy,
her crossing-over left my world a degree cooler;
and to my son,
Keith,
who warms it up.

Gene Keyes

PREFACE

Paumanok, Long Island's original name, has many gifted artists. This book began with an idea, collecting beautiful images of our natural world, photographs no one had ever seen before, and never would, the ones that collect dust after being shared with family and friends. But the idea grew, inspiration coming from the many talented photographers in the Sweetbriar Nature Camera Club, and then the Photography Federation of Long Island (P.F.L.I.), which presents work from one end of the island to the other. The photography was elevated to art, and I discovered there was so much more to be found.

The idea grew when poet Claire Nicolas White, showed an interest and invited George Wallace, Poet Laureate of Long Island at the time, to tea. There the idea for the marriage of poetry and photography took shape . . . Long Island's life, through the verbal and the visual, through the eyes of the people who live or lived here. A year's worth, for journaling to also find its place. Letters found their way to the post.

The idea blossomed when the many made up for what I could not do alone, and so I became its guardian, nudging it along, making sure it progressed; writing, meeting, calling, collecting . . . going just short of mad!

Paumanok: Poems and Pictures of Long Island is not about the hustle and bustle of our harried, pedestrian lives, loss, or the disappearance of good things. It is about life on this island, the one we can find if we look hard enough, into the secret places all around, through the bramble and thickets of forests, deep into the pine barrens, in gardens and flower fields, along cliffs and rocky shorelines of the Sound, by river edges, near ponds, around lakes, and, often time, over the sandy dunes to the ocean. Even over the bridges to our beloved Manhattan. The island Walt Whitman knew, just yesteryear. It is about the beauty and wonder in our natural world, with us day in and out, just waiting to be explored.

And while exploring,
perhaps
there is paper and pen,
writing stone, camera or paint brush
and an idea,
inside of you,
waiting
to find its page.

—Kathaleen Donnelly

Ray Welch

SPECIAL THANKS

The Editor is grateful to the following:

The poets and photographers of Long Island who generously contributed some of their best work to this collection:

Aija Birgalis, George DeCamp, Ann Glazebrook, Ange Gualtieri, Richard Hunt, Kate Kelly, Jan LaRoche, Stuart McCallum, Ed Muller, Frank Muller, Russell Cameron Perry, Jim Pion, Susan Tiffen and Marlene Weinstein, who opened up their archives of photographs for the pickings, and members of the Sweetbriar Nature Camera Club: Laura Eppig, Ken Eastman, Kathleen Hervey, Gene Keys, Dr. Vidal Al Matinez and Sheldon Pollack, who did the same;

Linda Russo for her extraordinary talent in photography and photoshop which was of great help to this anthology;

Linda Sack for the many hours of assistance with typing and organizing text;

Rob Bonnano for his patience and helpful guidance at Color Images Laboratories in St. James;

Bob Harrison, who wrote bios for the poets of yesteryear and offered endless support;

Lynn Kozma and Ginger Williams, who patiently read through the text;

George Wallace, who helped kick-start and give shape to this idea, and Gladys Henderson who together with Ginger kept the inspiration going with their poetry readings at Cool Beanz Café in St. James each month.

Special thanks to Bob Schmitz, who assisted in the selection of photographs and was most generous with his own work, time, and support;

Stanley H. Barkan, Cross-Cultural-Communications, for his direction, expertise, and interest in this rather large project;

and lastly, most importantly, Claire Nicolas White, who assisted from the very beginning with the collecting of poetry and decision-making throughout.

DISCLAIMER

This book in no way represents all of the talented poets and photographers on Long Island; this is a small fraction of what is to be found.

Every effort has been made to provide proper credit for permission to reprint. In the event of any failure, the fault is due solely to myself, and will provide correction, if necessary, in a page of errata, and, if reprinted, in the text of a second printing.

—Kathaleen Donnelly

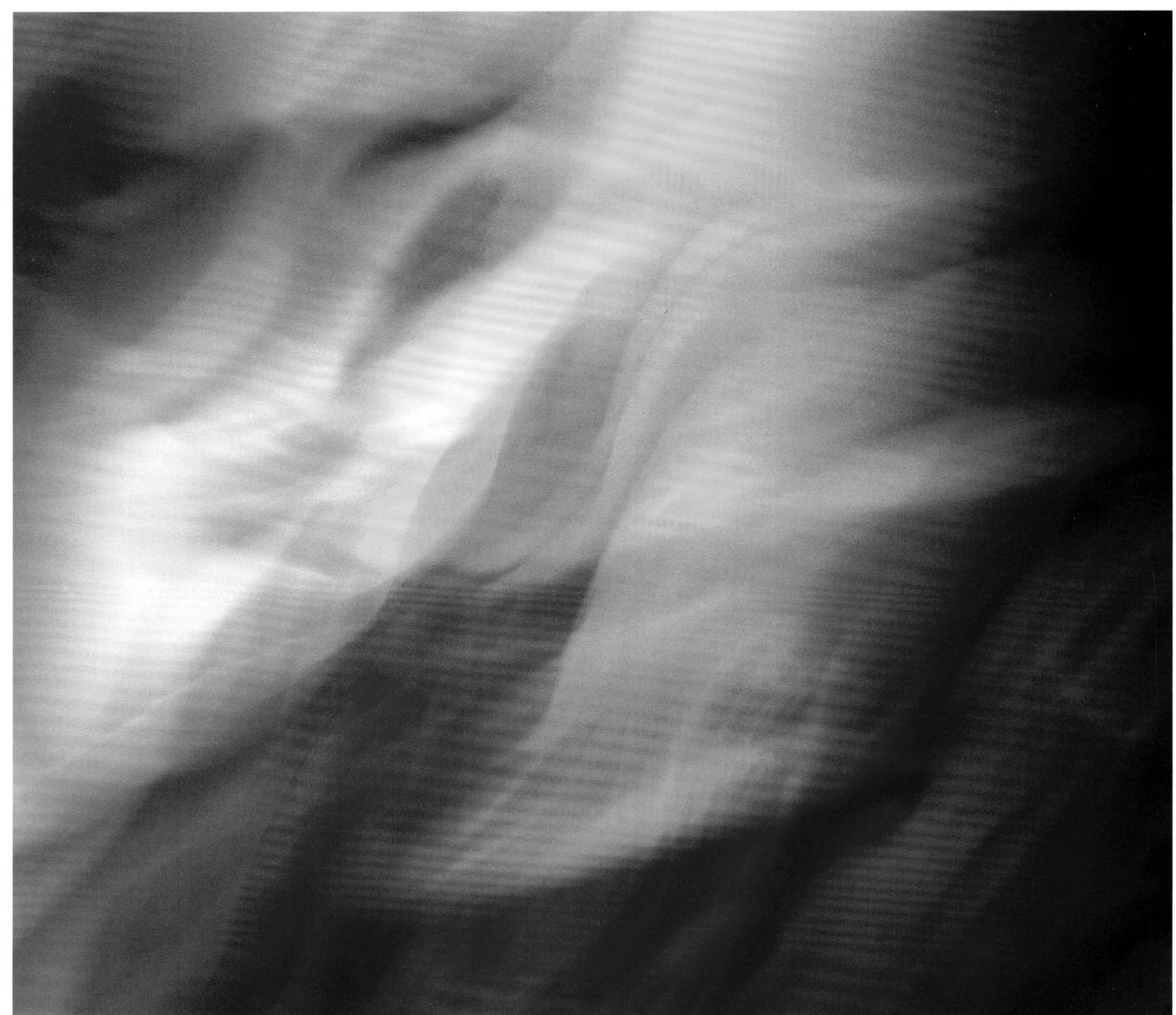

Jef Bravata

Have you reckon'd a thousand acres much? have you reckoned the earth much?
Have you practis'd so long to learn to read?
Have you felt so proud to get at the meaning of poems?

Stop this day and night with me and you shall possess the origin of all poems,
You shall possess the good of the earth and sun, (there are millions of suns left,)
You shall no longer take things at second or third hand, nor look
through the eyes of the dead, nor feed on the spectres in books,
You shall not look through my eyes either, nor take things from me,
You shall listen to all sides and filter them from your self.

From INSCRIPTIONS: "Song of Myself #2," *Leaves of Grass*
—Walt Whitman

◎

Poetry is the photography of the invisible.
—Graham Green
(not from Long Island!)

◎

Let the Spirit of Long Island ring forth
with the clarity of fresh, engaging language!
—Tom Stock

◎

It's a Short Life, But it's a Long Island.
—Allen Planz

CONTENTS

from
SANDS AT SEVENTY: PAUMANOK

Sea-beauty! stretch'd and basking!
One side thy inland ocean laving, broad, with copious commerce, steamers, sails,
And one the Atlantic's wind caressing, fierce or gentle—mighty hulls
dark-gliding in the distance.
Isle of sweet brooks of drinking-water—healthy air and soil!
Isle of the salty shore and breeze and brine!

Walt Whitman

January 1

William Duryea, Jr.

WINTER ON THE NORTH SHORE

I

The shrouded land
mirrors itself
a dark mass
of marsh in mist
its double image
swallowing
all sound

clumps of mounds
hirsute with reeds
still as sleep
bent on their own reflection
float on banks
of opaque light
beyond

III

There is no rhyme or reason
to the rhythm of the stones
along the shore
escaping counterpoint or pattern
they defy design
define the natural that can
erase the order we impose
on this chaotic randomness

We have clustered stars up there
to represent a scale   a bear
but should we rearrange the stones
to fit a scheme   the tide would come
at once to tear apart
the logic of our art

IV

In milky blue light
of winter thaw
ice floes capped with snowy crests
float by like swans
and creaking   break
opaque or thin as glass
quick waters ripple
wind their lively paths between
jostle   dissolve and trap
music inside their light

Birds flap and draw
their loops in tender air
weave longing cries with distance
then descend to settle
in colonies   still as prayer

V

No boom of waves here
no pretense at voicing
great messages
only this nibbling seeping
teasing brackish water
that creeps up and down
swallowing salt hay
lifting stones deposited
further   falling away
leaving us disorder and decay

VI

Pushed to the edge
we'll fall off into space
suddenly there is room
for wings
only gods walk on water
and though beaches obey
gravity
and coasts blur distance
it is the horizon
that incites to flight
that draws away
from this daedalus
this tangle of scurrying tracks
keeping traffic
locked inland

VII

Reaching the end
we meet the depth of air
and the cold bay
to explore further
would take gills
or anti-gravity

Water reflecting sky
locks its secrets
in this mirage
implies profundity
knows how to tantalize
with the unknown

Claire Nicolas White

* Stanza II omitted to fit the page with permission of the poet.

Frank Muller

IMPRINTS

The smell of wood smoke at dusk,
the feel, through laced boots,
of blue snow crust
breaking with my every step. Above all
the coming of night, and you.

And the earth's letting fall,
through a century-old wooded path
down to a seawall by the harbor,
the moonlight. Now add to that
the salt smell of winter.

There is nothing cruel in weather like this

despite our shared reflection
on the effect of ice, which creates
plated mounds where beach grass grew
with profusion in summer. There is nothing
cruel in the complacency of snowy hillsides,
deflecting heat from the sun all day,
though it may contribute to the cold.
For us, this winter night, what is true

and valuable is how we humans collect,
beneath a watchful moon, each to each;
how you gather yourself to my side.
Or how we walk together

in watchful silence along a frozen harbor.
Here, for example, where I take the imprint
of your body on mine. Here, where we measure
the pulse of a star's persistent warning. Here.

George Wallace

Linda Russo

January 3

THE AWL THAT THROUGH THE LEATHER PIERCES

The awl that through the leather pierces
a track of punctures for the thread
provides the seam that joins two pieces
to form one moccasin in which you'll tread,
with its opposite twin in step,
along the brambly, wooded path
that runs beside the aging stream
from this green place of tangled passions
to that darker, grayer place of peace.

The way you walk the wooded way
is all the cause there is to care for.
Whether you run headlong, heedless, blind
or take each step with careful ease
you'll reach the grayer place of peace
by the forceful will of time.

Recall the slow awl of the craftsman
that moves with sure, unhurried motion,
that pierces each hole so aligned
with the one preceding it
so that the thread, when threaded through,
is taut and strong and straight and true.

Steve Potter

from

INSCRIPTIONS: STARTING FROM PAUMANOK #16 / SONG OF MYSELF #39

On my way a moment I pause,
Here for you! and here for America!
Still the present I raise aloft, still the future of the States I harbinger glad and sublime,
And for the past I pronounce what the air holds of the red aborigines.
. . . .

Leaving natural breaths, sounds of rain and winds, calls as of birds and animals
in the woods, syllabled to us for names, . . .
. . . .

. . . charging
the water and the land with names.
. . . .

Is he waiting for civilization, or past it and mastering it?
. . . .

Wherever he goes men and women accept and desire him,
They desire he should like them, touch them, speak to them, stay with them.
. . . .

Slow-stepping feet, common features, common modes and emanations,
They descend in new forms from the tips of his fingers,
They are wafted with the odor of his body or breath, they fly out of the glance of his eyes.

Walt Whitman

January 5

Kate Kelly

ARRIVING ON PAUMANOK

Paumanok: "The island with its breast long drawn out." —W. W., Brooklyn *Standard*

A Midwesterner, an inlander,
a lover of the interior,
arrives on Long Island. "Paumanok!"
he whispers, savoring his Whitman,
local aborigine. "Paumanok," he says,
half aloud. He feels salt water swaying
on every side of him. He looks around
for the rows and rows of ripening
corn he'd sighted down since he was
pushed from the womb. None. Expressways.

"Paumanok," he repeats, looking
at a map. "Manhasset . . . Mineola . . . Massapequa,"
he reads. He picks out the red and green lines
looping the long breast. He turns them
on his tongue like strange herbs.
"Cutchogue . . . Patchogue . . . Ponquogue,"
he intones. "Wantagh and Wickapogue."

He feels a mist drifting in from the shore.
"Quogue and Nissequogue, Nesconsett
and Amagansett," he sings. He hears
the surf splashing nearer. "Commack
and Speonk and Setauket," he chants,
"Ronkonkoma, Ronkonkoma." "Shinnecock,
Peconic." In the middle of a fog
sliding inland off the sea like
the souls of the dead, he says, softly,
"Mattituck, Montauk." He whispers,
"Paumanok, Paumanok." He begins
to hear voices from the interior.

Norbert Krapf

January 6

Terry Amburgey

FOUR SPACIOUS SKIES

When I was small, this continent was mine.
Days when I felt expansive, I would
Spread the country all across the lawn
And lie on it, stomach on Kansas,
Toes dipped in the Gulf of Mexico,
Forehead pressed to the Canadian border.
Or I would straddle the phallic tip of Florida,
Stretching out my arms to stroke the coastlines,
Feeling for islands.
Wheat fields tickled me
And cities poked into my flesh like
Rocks under the picnic blanket.

Days when I was compact in my bravery,
The country grew, its edges reaching
To the corners of the neighborhood,
Until it took all afternoon to
Cross the tracks to Texas
Where the coyote of a hound dog
Bayed at the gas pumps and where
The ruffians leaned on the hitching posts,
Cursing, laughing, blowing at their beers.
I would pad through, red skinned and moccasined,
Chewing on dried beef.

At twilight I would double back across
The plains and forests, gathering
America's bounty: feathers, nuts,
Labels, nuggets of glass.
I would pocket them and

Wade through the Missouri,
Hurl myself across the Appalachian fences,
Run the open highway of the drive
And fall into my own backyard,
Clutching Long Island.

Susan Astor

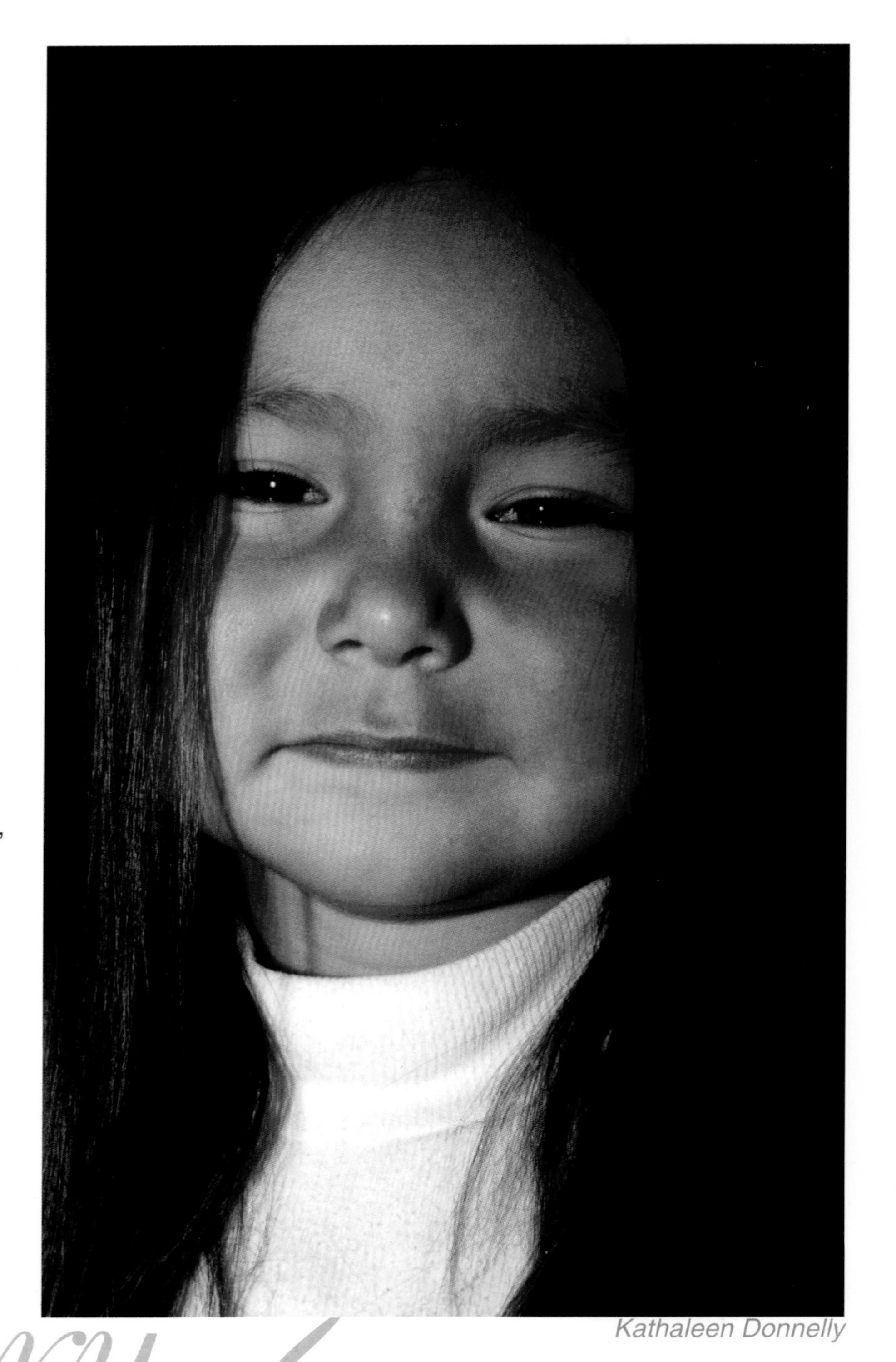

Kathaleen Donnelly

WESTBURY

No trace of Indian lives
Can be found among the houses,
Not an arrow has been uncovered
Even while digging for suburbia.
Of course there are no headstones
But neither are there tools or bones
Worthy of consideration.
Many crossed the Sound,
Fished the waters,
Trapped small game in the woods
North of here.
At this spot,
All trees are developers' creations.
What did the Indians know about
The greatest plains east of the Mississippi?
If they crossed this country,
They took their traces with them,
Holding their lives in their quivers,
Packing their shadows as they went.
On this earth we grow berries and asparagus;
Now beans and grapes grow full.
Massapequa, look for me in my dreams.
Tell me the secret of this forbidden place.

Arthur Dobrin

Ann Glazebrook

OCEAN OF SNOW

One year the snow rolled in so high
we thought we were an island.
Behind the pilings of the porch
waves crested almost to the sky
then stopped.

On shore, we rocked as merrily as sailors
thankful for our warmth
and our provisions,
watching the few masts
we could still see over the foam
flag in the wind.

When the storm subsided
we took our dories from the shed
and headed out
rowing up the hillsides of the waves
and coasting down
gleeful to be lost at sea.

When we were cold enough and wet
we climbed back on the pier
and hurried in to hear
the happy clap of dishes being set.
We drank and warmed our feet and sang
until we saw the ocean
finally turn blue.

Then, half-undressed, we wandered
back onto the beach
to hear the breakers crashing on our coast
to feel the fine intoxicating spray.
From a crow's nest far out in the dark
someone lit stars.

Susan Astor

William Duryea, Jr.

from
SANDS AT SEVENTY: FROM MONTAUK POINT

I stand as on some mighty eagle's beak,
Eastward the sea absorbing, viewing, (nothing but sea and sky,)
The tossing waves, the foam, the ships in the distance,
The wild unrest, the snowy, curling caps—that inbound urge and urge of waves,
Seeking the shores forever.

Walt Whitman

Ken Eastman

January 10

PSALM FOR A WINTER NIGHT

No cricket begs a place beside our fire
even the animal growl of traffic can't be heard—
the night sings only songs of stillness.

A pearly moon illuminates
smoke signals from chimneys
of houses with windows laced by frost
like those we used a heated penny on
to view the blizzard's work when we were young.

Winter has buried its secrets—
relentlessly the snow has sifted down
while windy drifts have piled sculptured
drifts between the tired trees.

What other world could ever be
so filled with such solemnity?

Joan Higuchi

Darlene Cunnup

ISLAND OF LONGING

Again and again, leveled by love,
I've come back down to
this island, considering the things
I might have done, all
the ascendant lives I lost
by not insisting that I am.

I've lived by longing quietly, an
island wherever I am, always
one of my letters silent,
dependent on the free, good will
of continents, the company of visitors
coaxed by a light to the land that is—

the long, low, retreating way I am.

John Kaufman

Bill Kreisberg

January 12

OFF SEASON

On Main Street at lunch time
painters, plumbers, carpenters
leave their lettered vans
and pick up trucks parked
with engines running, and line up
at the counter in the deli.
They pay the bill and buy
their lotto tickets with the change.
Then back to work
in someone else's mansion.

Away from the village, down
the long, wide street that ends
at the beach, there's a boardwalk
scoured by an offshore wind.
Not far away a solitary figure
swings a scanner back and forth,
back and forth, above the sand.
Imagine what his dreams are like,
filled as they must be
with all the precious things
the rich can lose.

Arlene Eager

JANUARY

Now the frost
covers the naked branches,
black against the gray sky.
Still as the eye of a hurricane,
the wind surveys its course.
Ice breaks like glass
down from the eaves,
scattered across the steps.
The door hesitates
against the pull of hands.
Nose pricked by the first
touch of outer air,
the man inches his way.
Enclosed in fur,
scarf flung about his neck,
ears reddened,
he thrusts himself
into January,
all the pine needles
sharp as the thought
of first emergence.

Stanley H. Barkan

January 14

Henry Mangels

GETTING UP EARLY

Just as the night was fading
Into the dusk of morning
When the air was cool as water
When the town was quiet
And I could hear the sea

I caught sight of the moon
No higher than the roof-tops
Our neighbor the moon

An hour before the sunrise
She glowed with her own sunrise
Gold in the grey of morning

World without town or forest
Without wars or sorrows
She paused between two trees

And it was as if in secret
Not wanting to be seen
She chose to visit us
So early in the morning.

Anne Porter

TOTAL ECLIPSE OF THE MOON

I mourn that giant orange
swallowed by the night
the pumpkin smashed to musk
the innocent immensity
of an eye suddenly closed.

Then awake before dawn
to the moon's full light
claiming my pillow
like some lustful
sleepless lover.

Ginger Williams

Larry Landolfi

ANNA'S SONG

Suddenly it isn't the day we thought it was.
Nor the day, nor the hour, nor the season.
I am dressed in gingham, you in close-knit flannel.
There are no appointments to keep. And so I leave
My dress at the edge of this day, beside your coat and trousers,
And I say, John James,
We are circling and circling—

Come stand with me on this shadowed incline.
The grass continues, so too the trees,
So too the stream and its talk of distance.
We will not be overseen. Come lie here prone
Where my loose hands cup your name,
Where the soil is dark and difficult and cold.
I'll tell you what's to come.

Jesse Ball

THE SEA COMES CALLING

Even if we were born inland
the sea calls us in our dreams.
We walk in a woods beside
a creek bed where clear water
slides by over sandstone. We
hear the incessant cry of birds
never seen in these woods.
Something circles high
above our heads, then dives,
and skims along a surface.
Something swirls above
our feet, and rises,
and stirs us to the roots.
We wake, look out over waves
breaking on top of one another,
feel undertow tug us back
home toward the depths.

Norbert Krapf

Kate Kelly

January 18

IN THE WINTER SILENCE OF THE WOODS

In the winter silence of the woods
Standing on a hilltop deep in snow
I gazed downhill and watched a grazing doe.
She hoofed the snow in search of still green buds.

Although she saw me there, she was not shy
Like she'd forgotten not to trust our kind.
Then, as if sent solely to remind,
An Air Force fighter jet roared past nearby.

Disturbed, I turned and looked to see it fly.
It was so swift it far outpaced its sound
And suddenly flew by right overhead.

I lowered my gaze from that cold blue sky
And eyed the silent doe on frozen ground.
She turned to the valley and fled.

Steve Potter

Eric Lohse

THE ICE POETS

All night it whispers
and collects, enclosing
each bud in a clear bauble,

sheathing branch and twig,
weighing down centuries
of growth.

Everything shimmers
and reflects: it is a landscape
made wholly ghostly.

* *

Ice orders sleep: almost all
obey. In darkened rooms
only machines stay awake.

But we remain outside
letting doors shut forever:
needing to prove our faith,

affirming an old allegiance—
and the ice sings to us:
Demon! First love!

My own true self! I make
the universe still for you—
this once.

Charles Adés Fishman

Drew A. Pantino

ANIMUS

Something waits
    beneath packed earth
        the measureless sea

waits within
    a clenched clam
        the hibernating eel

within a bird's breast
    a tree's heart
        the perennial fern

the gray grinding ice
    a curled leaf
        an exhausted moon

something waits
    unnamed, invisible,
        silent as snow

waits to spring
    waits impatiently
        in me.

Lynn Kozma

George DeCamp

January 21

WINTER TWILIGHT

On a clear winter's evening
The crescent moon

And the round squirrels' nest
In the bare oak

Are equal planets.

Anne Porter

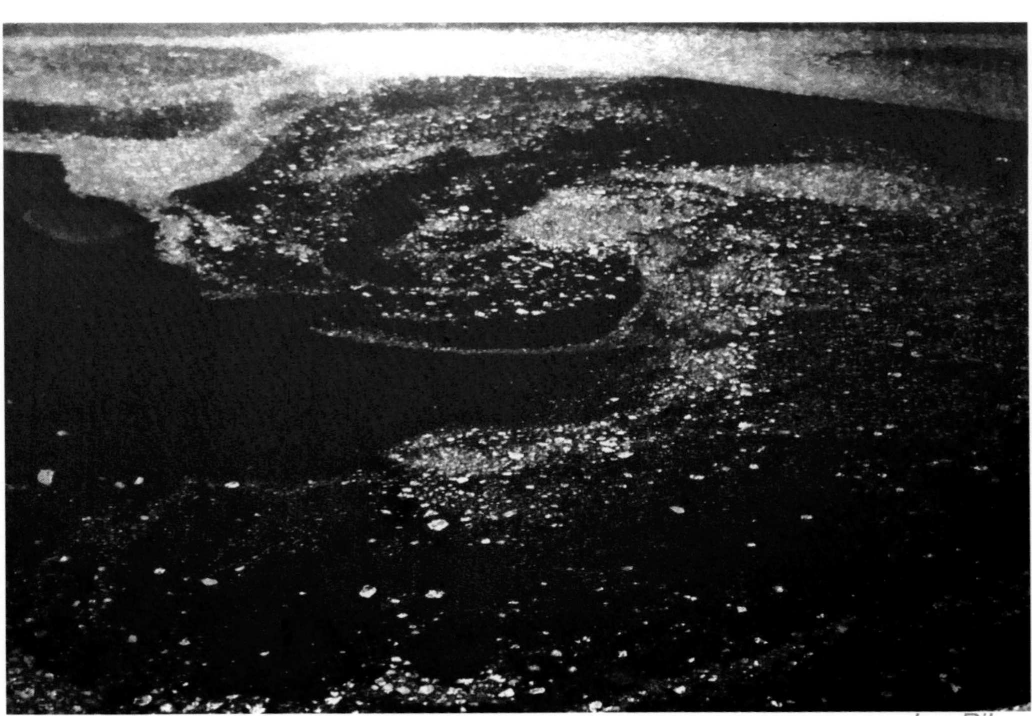

Joe Pihas

January 22

IF THESE BIRDS

If
these birds
could only know
how perfect they are,
how venerable.

Blacks and grays,
or browns against
a topsheet of snow.
Beneath a feeder
teeming with thistle,

Where goldfinches
work, clasped
to a short peg,
engaged in one more
dance with Winter.

They stab frantic
at what the finches
fail to hold, their
feet make starprints
upon the white.

Their struggle is
with the seasons,
unimpressed
with grace and
a defining silence.

Daniel Thomas Moran

George DeCamp

January 23

JANUARY, SEEN

In the air ten degrees colder
the birds, twice their normal size
—feathers fluffed to trap warm air—
gather in a tree.
I, at the stop sign below,
wait for their usual distress
but they, savoring their comfort
before necessity drives them
to forage and eat
move not so much as an eye or beak
so lost are they
in a mutual dream.

Charlene Babb Knadle

George DeCamp

NIGHT RISE

From where it has been night all day
The darkness comes
From storm sewers and wells
From one-eyed caves
From tunnels and the undersides of stones
From chimneys and pots
From drawers and boxes
From sockets, pockets, safes
Out of the coldest cavities of oceans
From the trunks of sunken ships
From the pores of coral
From the mouths of fish
Out of our own dilating pupils
From knotholes, worm holes, root holes
Out of cocoons and pouches
From the hollow cells of bees
From subways, cellars, crevices
From boots inside the closet
From the space between the molecules
From the space between the stars

Susan Astor

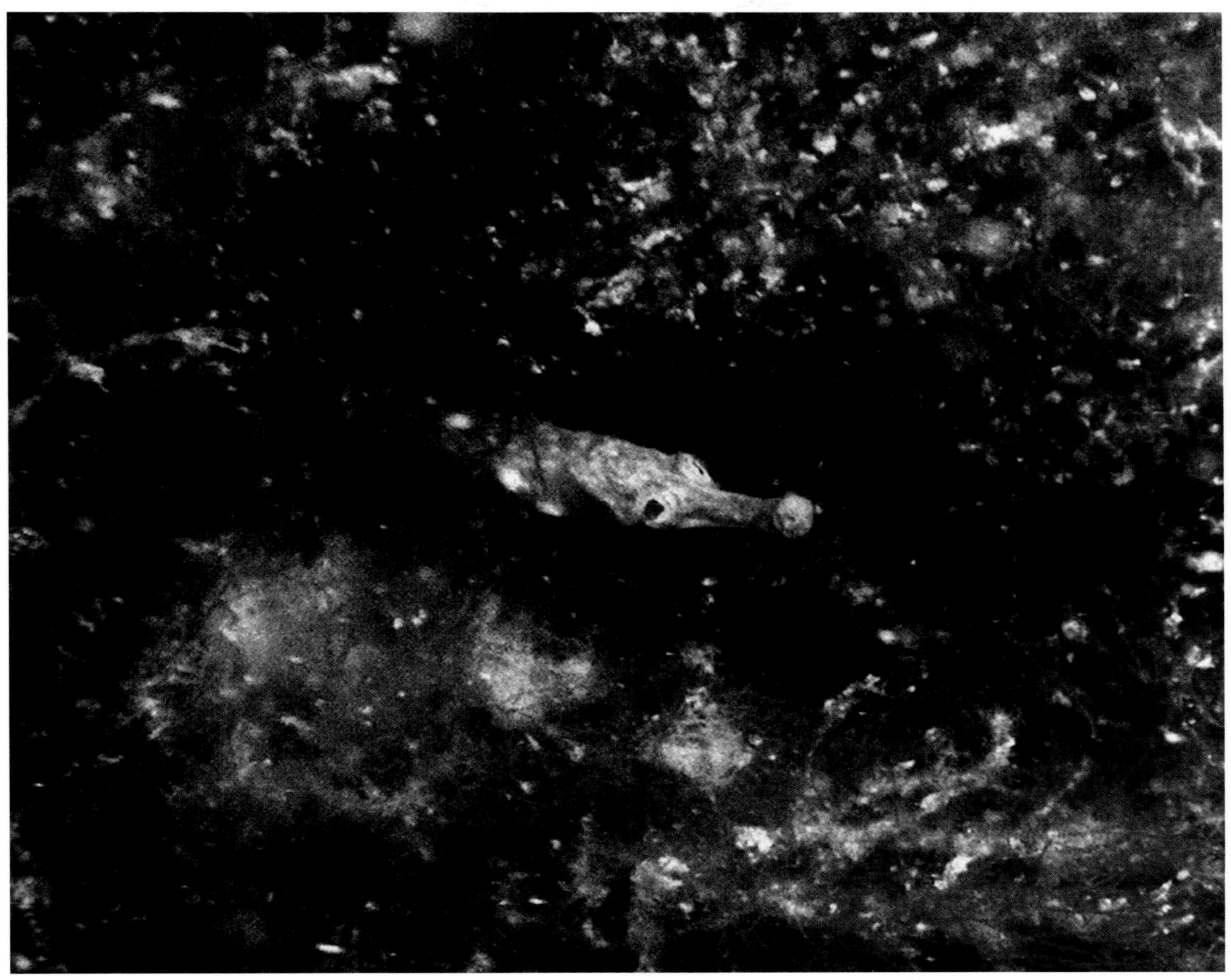

Peter Brink

AT LINDELL SCHOOL BULKHEAD

witnessed on water of Reynolds Channel
wrinkled patchwork patterns
artfully impressed
on the surface of the water
a canvas depicting
massive clouds
raked in ridges by
variable gusts of winds

Toby Lieberman

Frank Muller

CALL 911

what is needed
is to sing along
listen to rain on the roof
eat lasagna and apple pie
read a seed catalog in January
complain about the weather
take a long walk
believe in the magic of rainbows
finger a pocketful of totems
when drafts of cold air
shudder your spider-web strands of being

give now
there's a life to be saved

Beverly Pion

CARDINAL

Hurled from a bush
up the hill

A flinty chip!
and what-cheer!

a streak of
spark toward

birdseed spilled
in the herb garden

and crested
flame

skimming
the snow.

Norbert Krapf

Bob Schmitz

January 28

WINTER DAWN

Low tides at Sag:
dunlin & blackbellied plover
scouting the flats.
Snowy owl blinking
atop a duckblind.

Light comes on,
the sand retrieving hollows,
the land slipping underwater,
the horizon hastening to contour the earth
one bright pearl, one deadly winter day—

Things are not what they seem.
Neither are they otherwise.

Allen Planz

George DeCamp

January 29

COURTSHIP DANCE

The crane dips and bows,
turning, showing his best side
before his chosen mate, shifting
feet, stretching his long neck,
saying, See me? I'm the one—
handsome, tall, full-feathered,
at my best age and dress.
If she agrees, they cross bills
as emphasis, and hurry away.

You come to my door, hair shining,
wearing Sunday clothes, teeth
gleaming behind come-hither smiles,
teasing me with your ocean eyes.
I hear the sound of music. Drawn
together by an unseen force
we discover the same inland sea—
a private edge of sky.

Lynn Kozma

Christopher Corradino

NIGHTFALL

The evening nods with easy grace
Lower and lower from the western sky.
Velvety blues lie along the sidewalk
Lean against the walls of buildings
Touch the windows and slowly sink
Into the alleys to sleep in darkness . . .
A winter tree shadows the ground
And telephone wires stave the sky with unsung music.
The street lights in a slow crescendo
Ignite the evening.

David Napolin

Kathaleen Donnelly (Photoshop by Linda Russo)

FUTILITY

That wind knows how to walk on sand, leaving a dance of prints
To puzzle teams of cryptographers, that light colors water like a child,
That oceans shore up history even before its telling,
That logs ease up on a beach, ragged after years of adventure,
That a pale flank of sky steps gingerly on hard, cold sand bed,
That grains from the Indian coast wash up on Jones Beach,
A shock of maroon dots white rivers cascading from a fenced road,
That froth freezes into cream puffs, serving itself to gulls,
That an orchestra of dried weeds awakens fingers nesting in a lover's hand,
That waves find stillness in their movement,
That birds fall like messages, but rise again with the next easterly,
That wind and sun, sea and sand, weave into us their tales,
Makes this human telling the least spectacular of all.

Pramila Venkateswaran

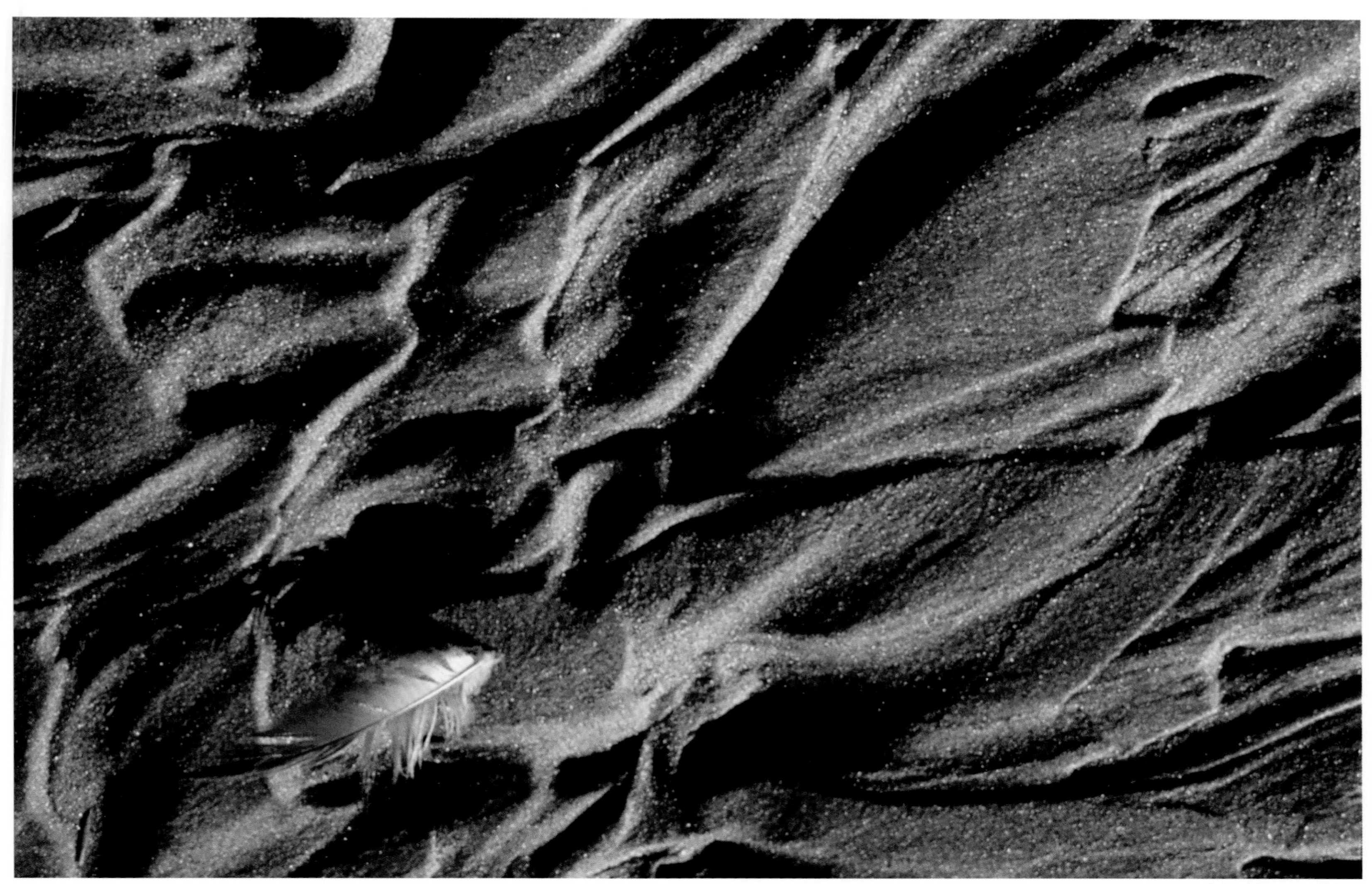

M. James Pion

IT IS NOT ONLY IN THE BOTANICAL GARDEN

of Brooklyn
that ice in new plates
stacks itself

end over jointed end
like a deck of oriental playing cards

on the carp-bottomed pool
of this Japanese garden
ice forms tonight

by the light
of a blue lantern

she leads you to the parking lot

the moon rises in a rice paper sky
it is shining through a wedding veil

there will be snow tonight
she smiles

you reach for her hand

George Wallace

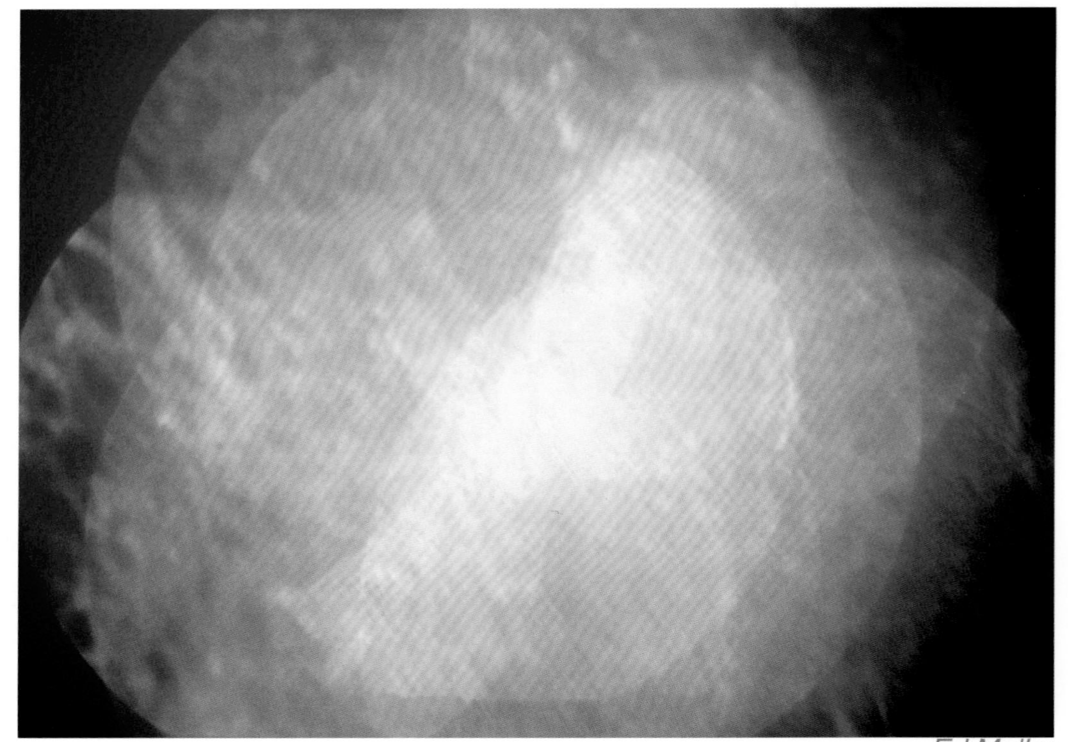

Ed Muller

February 2

STILLNESS

There is a little silence
in the night
that holds the world and me
in icy no sound stillness
and alone
the wall of night
closes quiet upon all its
seeing self
knowing the loss of light
as I know loss of you

Then your image
fills the full void
and flashes on
then is gone
and silent night
crescendos back
to stillness

Ray Makofske

William Duryea, Jr.

February 3

THE ICE STORM

Like bejeweled hands
that belie the burden
of beauty, the bent trees
groan and lust to stay positioned.

With a last lisp,
a silvered grip
that runs the glint
clear down to the taproots,
the thin brittle snap
of branches fling

ice hurdling high
just as we lunge sunward,
flashing splintered fragments
of mirrors and cry
to become forever fixed,
bright stars in the sky.

Judith Saccucci

Linda Russo

SYMPHONY

The world is made of ice.
Pines speak
in shattered whispers
to the willows
who toss their long glass hair
in the wind.

Lifeless leaves rustle
their dry grief.
With muted voices
gulls question the wind
wheeling through mist,
shadow against shadow.

The world is still,
holding its hoary breath.
Music sweeps the treetops
in a symphony of winter,
flinging crystal notes
against a milk-glass sky.

I dream of summer,
and one firefly.

Lynn Kozma

February 5

WINTER HAIKU

The sleeping berries:
Winds howling icy songs
through brittle branches.

Mia Barkan Clarke

February 6

Linda Russo

WINTER

Birds crowd feeders,
battle each other
for prime positions,
nudge the competition
off and away, chatter
ceaselessly, then rise
like a cloud of confetti
to the harbor of hemlocks,
wondering what became
of the benevolent sun,
warm blue air.

One day, as things change,
I shall learn the pecking
order, fly at lightning
speed, wear iridescent
clothes, sing rhapsodies.

How dull earthlings
will seem to me then,
plodding along, afraid
of the cold, living
in shadows, rooted
like trees.

Lynn Kozma

Bob Schmitz

NIGHT VISION
(for Sharmili and Laura)

It is our last time together before
we fly in three different directions,
our pilfered store of jokes,
our armor,

when the Northern Lights surprise us,
we pull off the road to follow
the long glowing tails, giant strokes
moving from maple to oak
to pine, a pale, pale green
washing into silver.

The unexpected detour:
Wet mud hiding a fox's paw
print, and above, a million stars.

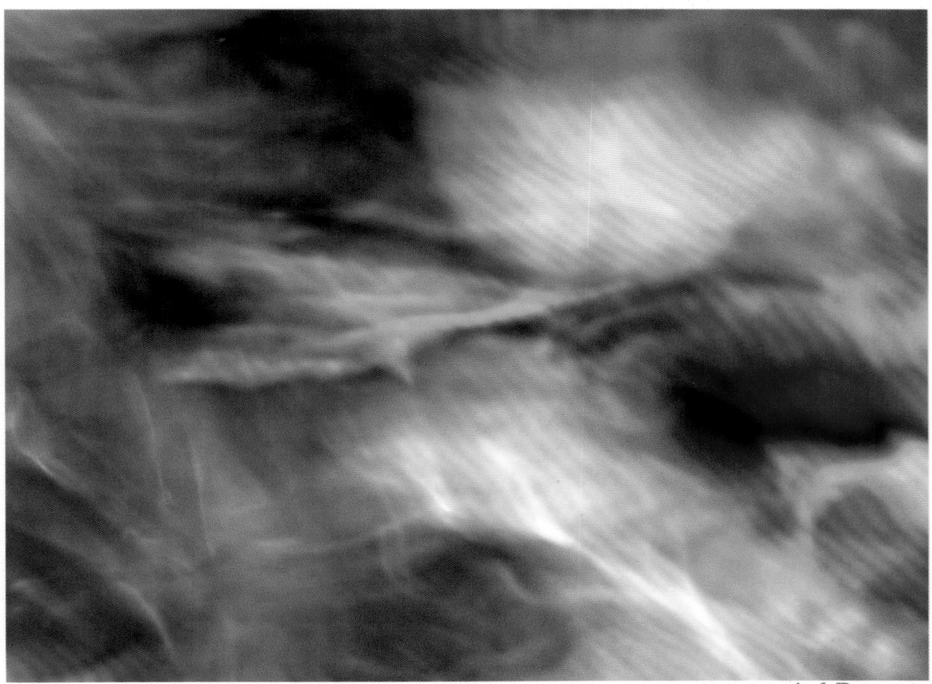
Jef Bravata

Pramila Venkateswaran

February 8

INCANDESCENCE

A few weeks after the light turned longer than the dark,
the luminous northern sky turned pale to deep blue
from horizon up. Much more than the cool northern light

in which dust motes dance, incandescent
through a large window in winter, much more than radiant
sunlight at the beach, burning haze away from waves,

this light was so thin it was not there,
so elusive you could try to hold it in both hands
and it would float away, like a just-filled balloon

without the balloon.

Adam D. Fisher

Ralph Pugliese, Jr.

February 9

THE LIGHT IN THE PRACTICE AREA

When air trembles with cold, and clouds
turn for land, for us banking our Cessna
down to the tug of Long Island—then a kindness
of rain has us cupping the fiction in our hands—
its gray threads tasting warm as tears

and without which we would fall into flames.
We perfect the learned hunch of body
before we are abandoned to last katydids,
to blades of frost on fingertips where
absences multiply among the cells.

But the light, it has no dimension,
this bottomless sea falling away without
wings, this bright country with no language.
The light comes to tell a sky full of truth
that we bear as long as we can upon our skin.

Elaine Preston

POEM FOR YOU

a moment of peace, palpable
draws me as a drop of living dew
into the morning   hawk-wild
an osprey nesting on steel
in the wind   among wires

visible   vast   the bloody heart of the world
quivers upon will
mechanical day   breaks up

I speak the air
attuned to affection
carefully uttering
the stones   the stars
the length of a true road
through a salt forest by an ocean
toward the snow mountain beyond which we are tending

D. H. Melhem

Gene Keyes

THE CRANE AT GIBBS POND
(for my mother)

The boy stood by the darkening pond
watching the other shore.
Against pines,
a ghostly crane floated
from side to side,
crooning. Maybe
its mate had drowned. Maybe
its song lamented
the failing sun. Maybe
its plaint was joy,
heart-stricken praise
for its place of perfect loneliness. Maybe,
hearing its own echoing,
taking its own phantom gliding
the sky mirror of the pond
for its lost mother in her other world,
it tried to reach her
in the only way it could. Maybe,
as night diminished
all but the pond's black radiance,
the boy standing there
knew he would some day sing
of the crane, the crane's song,
and the soulful water.

William Heyen

George DeCamp

February 12

TO MAKE A POEM

Sometimes a poem needs emptiness
to prepare for birth, a morning steeped
in sleep and newspapers, or stuck
between the pages of a book.
A poem may slide into life
on a wave of other people's words
as snow falls idly from a white sky,
sifting through a sieve of branches,
to make a light roof on your house.

You may feel the first stirrings
after lunch, while you're drinking tea,
as you watch three big windows,
side by side, fill with white on white
until the gaps between them disappear
and three make a panoramic one.

When the sky begins to turn an icy blue,
you'll feel the quickening, soft thrust
as from a growing flower.
Grab a piece of paper to catch
the words spilling from your pen.

They're never as beautiful
as you'd hoped and dreamed,
but don't let disappointment show.
Words too new to know their place
need to be cleaned up and tucked in.

Give them time to grow on you.

Orel Protopopescu

Jan La Roche

February 13

WHISPERING

Wanting to write a poem
is like wanting to talk
to a woman
I do not know
inviting as a campfire
on the other side
of the room.

But I don't
because I can't come up
with the first line—
my words like cheap candies,
nothing that satisfies.

Then later, not wanting—
a squirrel full of nuts in a tree,
she sits in the grass beside me
whispering her name.

Bill Graeser

Vidal Al Martinez

February 14

WINTER

Housekeeping done
by snow and ice,
the beds spread
with sharp embroideries
of bird's feet,
the sound of drip
a water metronome
on roofs from which
ice teeth containing
sunrays hang,

tree trunks defined
by dark discrepancy
and tangled webs of twigs,
the woodpecker's red head
knocking a hole
into this two-tone land.

At night, the dark is light,
the house invaded by
the bright outside
and all that space
invites a swelling.
Like a balloon
I need to rise
to the white magnet
        moon.

Claire Nicolas White

Richard Hunt

WINTER IN PORT JEFFERSON

Daily I dip into Port
lying in its furry nest.
Other towns spill out along
flat roads which here dive down
and come to rest, facing the sea.
Nowhere to go. The ferry on a leash
lies tamed. Dozens of Victorian turrets,
still haunted by sea captains' wives,
survey the peace.

Shamelessly, three smokestacks raise
a trail of silver plumes.
Cerulean blue, the hulls of skiffs
lie bottom up, and pleasure boats
stand buttoned into winter coats.
On Main Street, enigmatic junk,
stained glass, odd saucers, a captain's chair,
in bulging windows await an inventory.

Watchful, defiant, a stone lady stands
among funeral monuments
below a sign which reads, THE ROCK OF AGES.
She strides out of the sea on her stone feet
with pseudo-Roman nose and Grecian locks,
clutching an anchor. Do, lady, with your air
of pioneering virtue, plain yet sweet,
claim and protect this harbor
so singularly anchored in
a drifting land.

Claire Nicolas White

February 16

Frank Muller

MIDNIGHT
for Peter

my son wakes up and
will not be comforted for
he believes the bad Volkswagen
will eat him
he believes the moonlit water tower
will take five giant steps
toward him
he believes the man with the white beard
will ask him a question

on the other hand
I believe the Volkswagen
which is neither good nor bad
will indifferently run me over
I believe the water tower will run dry
I believe the man with the white beard
will ask me a question
thus proving he knows everything
and I know nothing

in our stillness now
waiting for the house to ignite
this is our faith
this is our kinship

Ron Overton

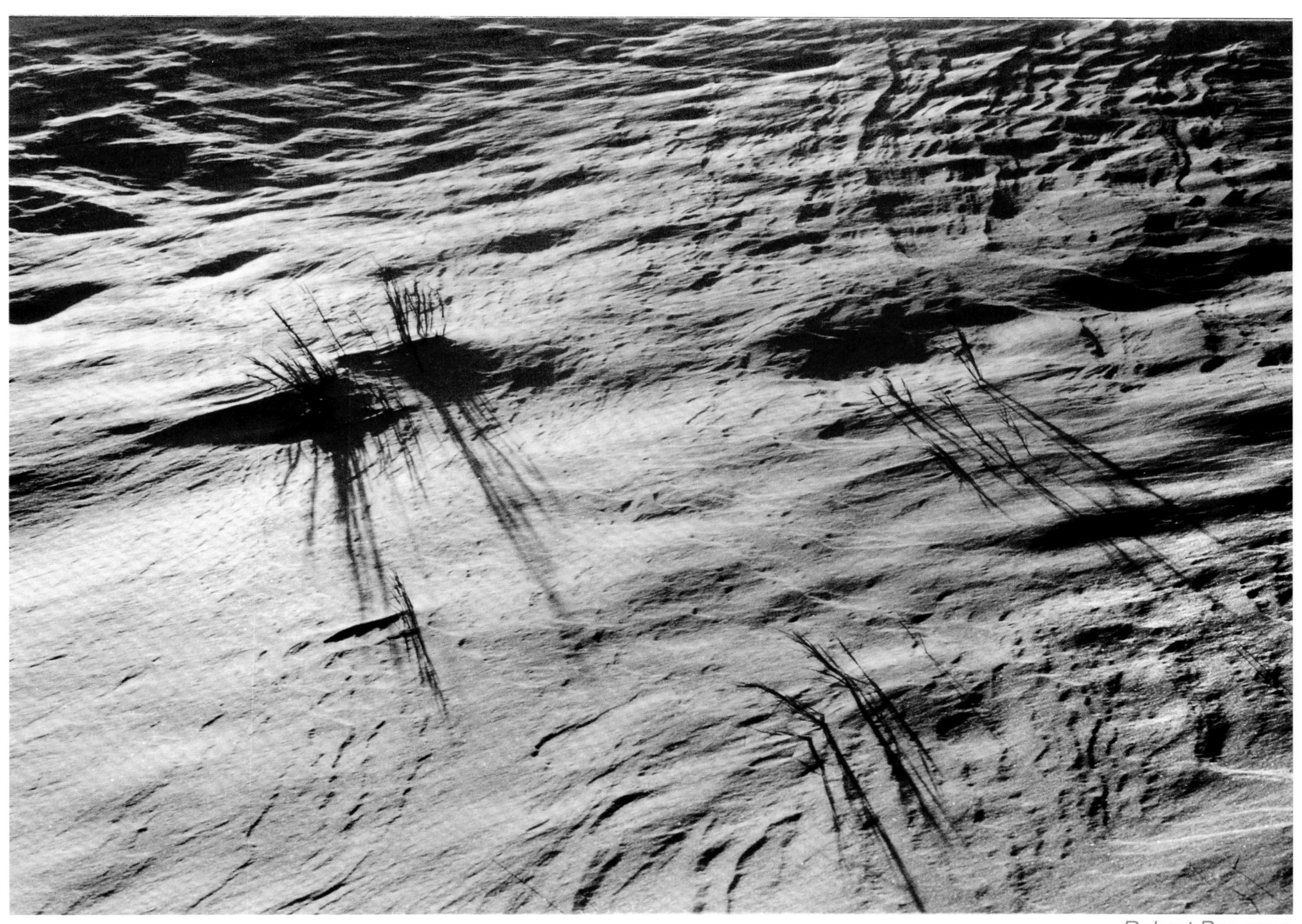

Robert Bonanno

OSPREY

Requiring heights for safety and command
he arrives through blue air silently
to clutch the jagged edge of a storm-killed
tree with his fish-trap claws. The wind's
fingers ruffle his snowy breast.

Imperious, ruby eyed, elegant,
the dark and light of him proclaims
pure majesty, dominion over inlet,
river, every small fish in the sea.

We rush for the camera, praying
he will stay—crawl to the opened door
to focus, fix the lens, freeze him
forever. He preens and poses.

Now, he lives within a frame, catches
the light from searching sun, flickering hearth.
I fill my eyes with his happiness.

Lynn Kozma

ALL COMES

All comes to sunlight.
A bird stirring its wings.
In the air it has the shape of a dream.
It too is perfect off the ground,
I follow its flight.

David Ignatow

Laura M. Eppig

February 20

THE NEIGHBORING SEA

At three in the morning the village is all in silence
But the silence is afloat on the roar of the sea
And all the streets are bathed in the roar of the sea
The waves are at their labors
Cresting and flooding all along the shore
Tumbling and spinning the kelp and the devil's-apron
Threshing to meal the morsels and crumbs of stone
And the light seashells with their storm-blue linings.

This is the time of day when I remember
That down at the end of the street there is an ocean
A Nation of fishes and whales
A sky-colored country stretching from here to Spain
A liquid kingdom dragged about by the moon.

Anne Porter

THE WIND OFF THE SEA

The wind off the sea says,
"Close your eyes, the present will disappear.
Let me surround you with my voice,
sway you with my strength,
bring you breath from foreign places.
I will stay with you forever."

Donna Demian

Frank Muller

February 22

THE SWAN AND THE POND

Like a swan
you are, a monarch
in your tiny pond,
your snowy down
unstained by the melancholy
rains which soak
the world in
woeful tears that
bead in deference
down from your
impervious shield.

While I am the pond,
insistent upon absorbing
the pluvious days
deep into my soul, offering
buoyancy, eternal reflection
and but the occasional
undulant murmur
of protest
in verse.

Daniel Thomas Moran

Richard Hunt

February 23

THIN ICE

Just at the brittle edge of love,
where life can snap off at a touch,
we glide along, testing
our toughness. It holds.
We circle back and try it again
and again, each time more daring
by the space of a thrill,
a sliding of fear and fever, knowing
that ice can melt as well as break.
So we take our chances,
holding our breath,
trying for something no one
has ever done.

Philip Appleman

Jef Bravata

February 24

THE GULL
for my sons, Michael and Jacob

Perching on the black buoy
White neck, throat
Gray feathers still at your sides.
Staring at the shore.

You try your wings for flight.
One lies limp.
The geese, the mallards pass by.
You peck at yourself.

Other gulls cry
Flapping about
Swooping down
Stabbing the surface.

Circling
Their images surround you on the lake.
Soaring upward
They disappear into the white ocean.

The wind blows its cool breath upon the lake.
You wrap yourself in your wings.

Arleen Ruth Cohen

Pauline Southard

THERE IS NO # ON THE ROAD IN SOUTHAMPTON

I couldn't tell
when the house on the bay
was abandoned.
I am inside walls
looking out windows.
I hear seagulls
and see herons, wading.
We are surrounded by mansions.

I couldn't tell
if this house ever had color—
the salt mist can be insidious.

I couldn't tell
if this house once had a garden.
There is wall-to-wall seagrass
and the high tide
floods the threshold.

I couldn't tell you
how I got here,
and I don't want to tell you
how I left.

There is no number on the road.

Jan La Roche

Frank Muller

February 26

FEBRUARY 27TH

Our dog whines, wants out in the night
to bark at prowling cats. One spouse
cleans the kitchen. The other writes
notes to friends. Dishes rattle. Pen
jumps and starts, and having writ moves on.
The dog goes out. The counter gets cleaned.

One spouse says, "I'm going up.
Don't forget to let the dog in."

The jet stream dips from the north.
Howling wind cold blasts kick up.
The boiler fires water to 180 degrees.
Heat circulates through baseboards.
The dog nestles, asleep.

Graham Everett

Ed Muller

February 27

GEESE

In the endless winter a man stands
at Miller's Pond covered with ice,
white with snow, the air a thick porous foam
through which reel shrieking birds.
The man brought plastic bags
filled with dry bread that he flings
while up above him soar
then land like bombers, wide-winged geese,
necks outstretched, gray, grotesquely long-legged.
"What are they doing here?" I ask the man.
"Once they went South. Now they hibernate."
Gulls and geese veer and squabble
over old crusts gathered at the baker's.
If still fresh he takes them to the soup kitchen.
"Better than the dumpster," he says.

He found a mission. I see him
in a cloud of wings, as if by flinging bread
into the air he liberates
this frenetic flapping, gawking flutter
        of life, emerging
            from his heart.

Claire Nicolas White

Richard Hunt

February 28

from

GOOD-BYE MY FANCY: UNSEEN BUDS

Unseen buds, infinite, hidden well,
Under the snow and ice, under the darkness, in every square or cubic inch,
Germinal, exquisite, indelicate lace, microscopic, unborn,
Like babes in wombs, latent, folded, compact, sleeping;
Billions of billions, and trillions of trillions of them waiting,
(On earth and in sea—the universe—the stars there in the heavens,)
Urging slowly, surely forward, forming endless,
And waiting ever more, forever more behind.

Walt Whitman

February 29

Adolfo Briceno

THE SWANS

All day I have thought of the swans
that flew skyward, bellowing,
maundering at first,
immense and web-footed,
fanning tousled wings,
parting the stream
then surging through air.
I know you will pass and return,
your body tense, then writhing,
undulant, coiled in sleep,
your silver eyes mirroring my eyes,
your hands raveled and free,
that somewhere the swans have alighted
on lucent water,
their spiral forms
utterly denying
turbulent flight.

Grace Schulman

Bob Schmitz

THE SPHINX

The sea crouches
  behind the houses
plying riddles
  at old children

Sighing, the sea
  insists
it is only being
  itself

It would like
  to be done
with pouring into
  its own throat

messages from
  rain, from light
done bringing the world
  around again

Like music, its tides
  consume themselves
Stars drown
  in its memory

What they think
  they've heard
what they try
  to fathom

what the children
  answer, answer
is in spume
  in spray

The sea, nevertheless,
  asks them:
If time is like water,
  how does your history stay?

Diana Chang

March 2

Aija Birzgalis

JONES BEACH

Wandering damp sand for unbroken shells
clams, mussels, other molluscs
foot impressions combed by incoming tide
March has just begun; no tourists yet.

Early morning mist fogs the boardwalk
a few joggers, moms with strollers
an elderly man in navy peacoat
carrying an aluminum cane.

Stomach grumbles remind me
I skipped breakfast
reflex look at my wrist tells me
I forgot my watch, but not my Nikon.

Look up to a crystal sky
where gulls swoop and dive
a blood orange beak breaks away
black and white body wings a landing

a few feet from me. Unperturbed, he tucks
black and white wings beside
a wide white chest; black hood, pale pink legs;
unmistakably, an American Oystercatcher.

Bright yellow eyes watch me
focus, click, click; shutter snapping
beak open, as if to chat, he turns
dips his head to feast on breakfast.

J R Turek

George DeCamp

A SIDE OF LIFE

watching this
snowy egret
racing its own
reflection
across a
still sky
blue bay

like a man

it senses
no matter
how hard
it flies
its best hope
is just
to keep up

with itself.

Daniel Thomas Moran

Bob Schmitz

March 4

LONG ISLAND CROW

He soars darkly above cars
crawling bumper to bumper

toward Manhattan, glides in a circle
above treetops in the village park,

climbs above apartment complexes
toward a grove of oaks

on the highest ridge in the county.
He perches, gazes back down

at the valley, and caws forth
from the shadows of his brain

a thick forest in which morning
campfire smoke rises like mist.

Norbert Krapf

March 5

M. James Pion (Photoshop by Linda Russo)

I'LL TAKE MY WINTERS COLD

I like to see the old men gathering dry sticks
in early March for firewood, along the highway;
the stubborn spray of small branches, miraculously
strapped to their backs, the pull and catch of wind

and sunlight streaking through their hair. There
are lessons for me in the gay air of defiance
which I detect, watching their jaunty movements
through woodlands thick with cherry stumps,

with ancient maples. And that's another thing. I like
the trees—how they show in winter the way
they have bounced back against the action of vines.
It is written in a kind of bold script, the supple,

patient survival machinations, which helped trees
get through summers of clinging vegetation.
I understand that in this world there are those
otherwise reasonable people who would choose,

given their preferences, Februaries that are filled
with sun and leafy growth. For sure, that sort
of action's well-suited to summer and youth. But
winter's when we learn to appreciate the survival

of the old against the odds. I'll take my winters cold.

George Wallace

Pauline Southard

HIDDEN POND

The pool lies asleep, undetected,
Behind its leafy fronds.
Ephemeral greens are reflected
As ghosts in the secretive pond.
Delicate winged ones gyrate,
Disrupting the satiny jewel.
Shadowy creatures await,
Beneath her emerald cool.

Barbara Reiher-Meyers

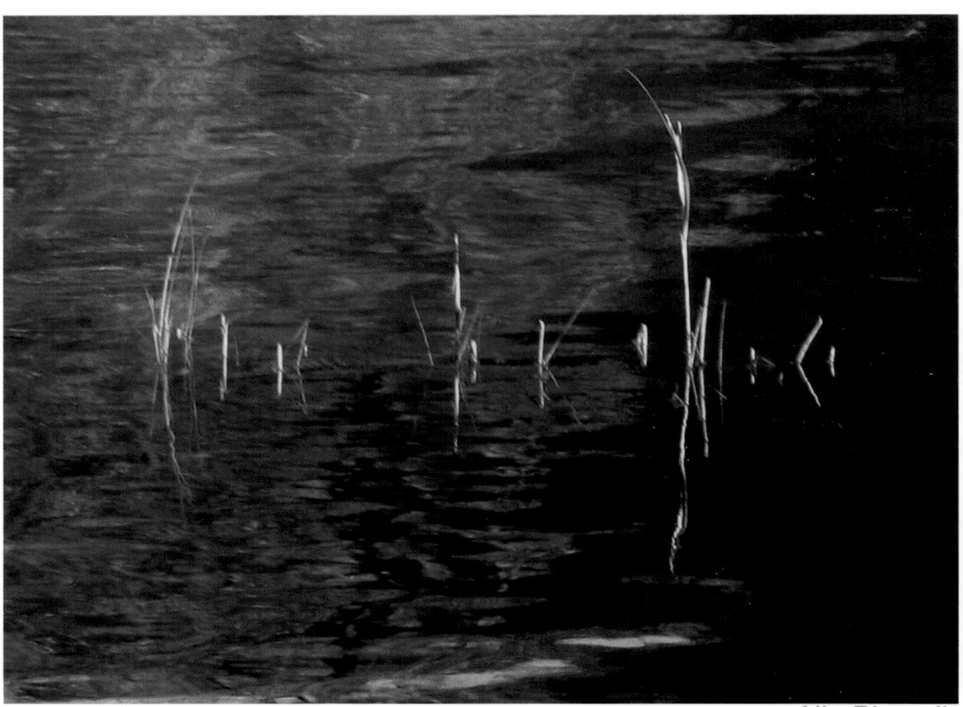

Aija Birzgalis

MONTAUK HAIKU SEQUENCE

whip of window wind—
vast sky above squat pines
lighthouse ahead

cold ocean wind
on warm day wet rocks shine
twelve-foot tall grasses!

water on three sides
rays of sun sing through clouds
what no words can

Arnold Brower

Mankh (Walter E. Harris III)

LANDLESS AND

tossed with thoughts
venturing the night, i walk in

the rose light of the last streetlamp
amid moths and a mind imagining soul

the crickets ask of hurricane

the ocean answering
the moon is my master

what i want to say is
i wouldn't be up this late

if i had a field to plow

Graham Everett

Tom Stock

March 9

WEST HILLS

Soil so rich you could plunge your hand
up to the wrist in it
like so much sea foam
tossed up from the stormy harbor.

With just one thumb
he could dig a furrow through it.

He gives a nod
toward the hills beyond,
and another
at the sun, banking down into the seas.

All good farmland, and a home
for carpenters, says he,
to the tune of the jug and fiddle.
Just like the artist showed it.

So Van Velsor says: *If the jug spills*
ignore it—
drink or no, this upland soil
don't snore.

Take heed of that, son.

George Wallace

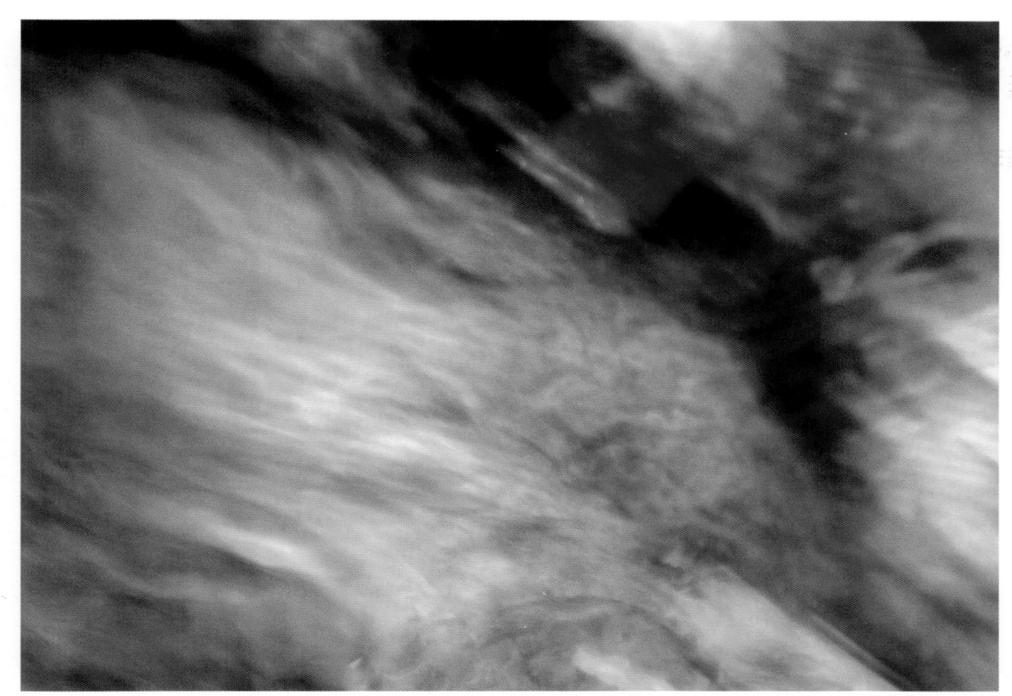

Jef Bravata

March 10

from

A SONG OF JOYS

O to go back to the place where I was born,
To hear the birds sing once more,
To ramble about the house and barn and over the fields once more,
And through the orchard and along the old lanes once more.

O to have been brought up on bays, lagoons, creeks, or along the coast,
To continue and be employ'd there all my life,
The briny and damp smell, the shore, the salt weeds exposed at low water,
The work of fishermen, the work of the eel-fisher and clam-fisher;
I come with my clam-rake and spade, I come with my eel-spear,
Is the tide out? I join the group of clam-diggers on the flats,
I laugh and work with them, I joke at my work like a mettlesome young man;
In winter I take my eel-basket and eel-spear and travel out on foot on the ice—
    I have a small axe to cut holes in the ice,
. . . .

Walt Whitman

Marlene Weinstein

March 11

THE FARMER

Watching, you carefully draw the worn oak
toward you—tines parting the loamy
soil, in neat furrows of precise depth.

As you hummed a tune you
uttered fifty years ago as light
as a feather, falling on the ears as downy frost.

Memories fool you—those days when you
liberated Europe and saw a new future
ahead live in your mind only.

Now all you see are the
nearly turned furrows parting to
the left and to the right of the wrought-iron spike.

And the only infantry you watch fly
v-shaped patterns
heading north for the winter.

David Martine

Ange Gualtieri

March 12

WILLOW POND ON A MORNING BEFORE SPRING

The wraith of
winter's final test,
having left
the impression of
its heavy steps,
rain-filled
on the side of
the softening hill,
has fled with
the wind which
played in the eaves,
and spun
wild and willful
eastward
to dapple the sea.

Left, a litter
of fractured branch
beneath a calm
which is blue
and weightless.
That snow, which we
cleared and piled,
while our fingers numbed,
and this world
we know
shimmered,
with chill and crystal,
has wilted and withdrawn
again into
the sodden earth.

Daniel Thomas Moran

William Duryea, Jr.

IN THE AFTERLIGHT . . .

In the afterlight
of March rain
a redwing blackbird
takes flight above the apple tree:
one flash of prescient red
to herald incipient green.

Weslea Sidon

Bob Schmitz

March 14

MIRACLE ON AVENUE D

This morning I saw a pheasant
alongside the road
in a middle class
neighborhood development,
its rainbow plumage
set against the mid-March snow.
It tried to hide underneath
a bare bush
in front of a wooden fence.
I took a few steps closer
to get a better look
at this scuttling rarity.
It crowed,
took two amazingly quick
six-foot hops,
and flew away
over the sleeping suburban
rooftops.

Paul Agostino

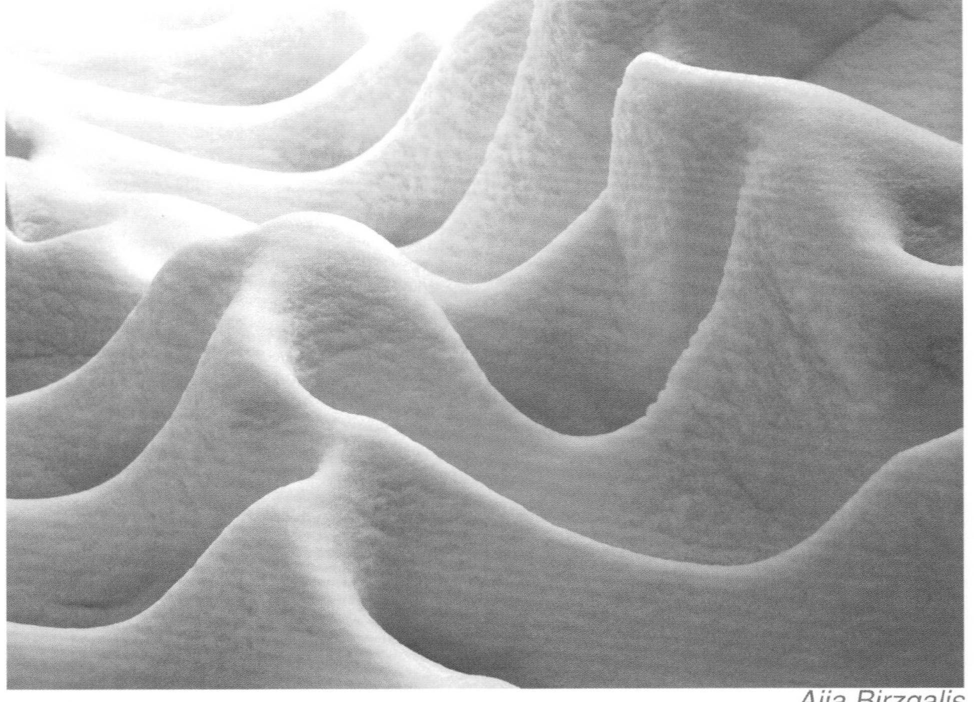

Aija Birzgalis

March 15

THE REPRIEVE

I first felt the brightness
shining against my lids.
Then I saw the snow.
I woke like a boy in a new room,
swelling toward excitement
as he puts aside the warm quilt.
Or as a lover wakes
to his love's white body—
love, overnight,
has turned the world strange
Or as the outlaw wakes, relieved,
knowing there are no tracks.
He'll hole up in this town all winter,
he'll joke with the townspeople,
buy them a round of drinks and
walk all over the merciful snow.
He'll go straight.

Ron Overton

MARCH

The stormy March is come at last,
With wind, and cloud, and changing skies;
I hear the rushing of the blast,
That through the snowy valley flies.

Ah, passing few are they who speak,
Wild, stormy month! in praise of thee;
Yet, though thy winds are loud and bleak,
Thou art a welcome month to me.

For thou, to northern lands, again
The glad and glorious sun dost bring,
And thou hast joined the gentle train
And wear'st the gentle name of Spring.

And, in thy reign of blast and storm,
Smiles many a long, bright, sunny day,
When the changed winds are soft and warm,
And heaven puts on the blue of May.

Then sing aloud the gushing rills
In joy that they again are free,
And, brightly leaping down the hills,
Renew their journey to the sea.

The year's departing beauty hides
Of wintry storms the sullen threat;
But in thy sternest frown abides
A look of kindly promise yet.

Thou bring'st the hope of those calm skies,
And that soft time of sunny showers,
When the wide bloom, on earth that lies,
Seems of a brighter world than ours.

William Cullen Bryant

Peter Rodriguez

SOUND EFFECTS

Listening, I hear the unexpected:
Ivy hisses, creeping up defenseless trunks.
New grass pipes through warmed soil.
Leaves whisper old secrets. Moss,
springing between red bricks, hums
long-lost tunes. Ceaseless chatter
of dandelions floods blue air.
Stones chant, hollow as drums.

I am dizzy with voices,
incessant clamor. Bracing myself
against the moving earth
I am powerless to stop
the surge and swell.

All of this happened
the day you said listen to the ocean roar,
and handed me a glistening, washed clean
pure white singing shell.

Lynn Kozma

John Brokos

PICTURES OF GREAT-GRANDFATHER HABITS

He rested in arms of nature's mother,
sailed a teal-sea mirror, on blade-shaft bow
through salt-grass and yellow leg. Gunmetal and shot,
matched his nature and habits.

Brow sweat and iced moustache
signatures to watch for; Veed honker
flocks intimate with him, as book and book-mark
pipe and smoke, v-gouge and caressed curled shaving
also signify his nature and habits.

Pine blackduck and mallard, Canadian geese and
snipe, sitting shoulder to shoulder glass
eyed, surveying incoming feathered cousins,
had their purpose realized after long winter months
as were their habit.

And dramatic arts—
"To be or not to be," and all that—whether
to expound it or just to breathe it in, rose in
him as sap sugaring time, as was his habit.

Final scene: down the old Parrish hall,
behind the old podium in Brooks Brothers
and flowered tie, he rallied constituents, friends for a cause,
which was also his habit.

David Martine

Gene Keyes

LONG ISLAND SOUND, THE FIRST DAY

of spring: Earth pulses
with the smell of old salt,
wing-whispers of blue heron over marsh,
just-birthed things too small to see,
and every molecule of now—

a huge heartful of moments
so even stars on the other side
of the sun ripple the waters
that inhale, exhale their musk
and shore lying shining and full, a coming
banquet for expectant gulls and crabs—

me sitting so still the bones
in my ears can hear skin growing
and the Atlantic beyond
making way for new countries
that will rise out of the sea,
breathing.

Elaine Preston

Mary Brennan

HAIKU

heron perched
    on a post, his beak
        points to his prey

Cliff Bleidner

March 21

Frank Muller

OPENING

Celery branchlings
curl around the rotted core
of last fall's strongest plants

Mint seedlings unfurl
under roots of garlic
whitened and stiffened

by winter: they rise
at the edges
of the herb bed

Strawberry leaflets flare
in the early dusk of March
New carrot tops expose

what leaf-mulch and snow
have hidden: the beginnings
of abundance

Wild onion, as always,
flourishes: nearly impossible
to lift intact from the cold soil

Chives send up green electric probes
Tiger lilies start the long voyage
skyward

Roots, in unrestrained billions,
push downward   Half-frozen tips
of peach branches open:

each small green leaf a flame
Like mute and rooted finches,
croci brave wind and rain

and spring's first cardinal beams
to the far reaches of the planet
the red voice of his feathers.

Charles Adés Fishman

Susan Tiffen

CHANGE

Rain
breaks the icy
crust of winter.

Drenched feathers
cling to the skin
of shivering chickens;
webbed duck-feet slosh
through sludge; leaves stew
in the ooze of earliest spring—

this fearsome, foundering time
before firm ground.

As moths dissolve inside cocoons
till bright, crisp wings emerge,
our visions blear

and are redrawn
through the clear,
kind rain of tears.

Marcia Slatkin

Marlene Weinstein

CROCUS

Through the loam of my dreams
I felt something push, take hold
after the long dark night
a purplish nudge into dawn
unfolding in small silken wings
twisting and untwisting, budding
up and open-mouthed,
stretched on tender stalks
breaking into sunlight,
lured by birdsong

Kathaleen Donnelly

Mindy Kronenberg

March 24

AT THE SHORE

A slow Atlantic spring
A lingering coolness
Trees quenched and stripped
As if for winter
The leafless bushes grey
Or brown as animals

But here and there
I see a field
That's newly plowed
Or one that's fresh and green

And under bramble thickets
The early daffodils
That have escaped from gardens
Are lighting their small fires.

Anne Porter

Ange Gualtieri

March 25

IT RAINED

and rain was chased
by the incessant wind,
its furious gusts
blown
into this clear bright day.

Tall grasses
whip themselves
along the bluff
like school boys
pretending to ride horses,

while below
water foams and rolls,
tossed onto mussel shell
and pebble,
well-holed whelk
thrust
onto a rise
of seaweed and sand,
this cacophony of odors
a magnet
to the nose
of my neighbor's dog
who knows this refuse
as no human can.

The sound
keens round corners.
I'm restless,
anxious.
When calm comes,
that inhalation of relief
is so brief,
the intervals of violence
each time longer
before the letting go—
or so it seems,
warning
against the notion
that we
are in control.

Joan Reilly DeRosa

March 26

EAST END ARCHIPELAGO

The sea in praise of women has sent
the daughters of fog,
a dark bank extending the island bluff,
a linen fraying over the saltmarsh,
arrayed on the spartina, poking into pine woods,
& come this morning
gold's gone from the hills, gods from the sea
but a taste of Bahamian flats
a thousand miles north
blooms aerial plankton

waves, wives
aves, huevos

& she bows wickering in the ten directions
& comes in the lilac inscape of a sigh

Allen Planz

John Gozelski

MARSH EVENING

On the Great South Bay
the spring tide floating the spartina meadow
where the old farmers pastured cattle for salt hay

Black-crowned Night Heron
sounds "Quok" from the orange moon
Black Skimmers in cloaks of night
furrow the water with long, lower orange mandibles

Apparitions of terns hover
over sperm-showered eggs of Horseshoe Crabs at tide's edge
Fowler's Toads inflate their throats in a Mesozoic Chorus

Maxwell Corydon Wheat, Jr.

Aija Birzgalis

FORSYTHIA

When did spring ever come
when it was supposed to? Set to start,
some interference of the gods
brings on an icy rain so numbing
the forsythia go into tailspin.

Other years, it's a matter of sun
coming on with such strength it incubates
the wet and broken remains
some seagull, or perhaps two terns,
left at tidepool's edge. There are those who learn

as it goes, to dress for the occasion,
follow the hesitant dance step
of March winds. They've got it measured
right, I suppose. For me, weather
is still a matter more of taking chances

than measurements. Like forsythia, which shoots
blossoms when its sap says "go,"
regardless of the seasonal passage of light
and moisture. Forsythia—which, guessing right,
erupts like ten thousand suns, in bright profusion.

Or guessing wrong, comprehends the truth
of the matter, and plays possum.

George Wallace

March 29

Pauline Southard

STILL LIFE II

You saw small, lost things:
Dimples over forehead veins,
Streams born to push
A millstone, vermilion growths
That gush to spring.

Fish and farm alive
On the island
Where a beach

Journey brought glass,
Turpentine, charcoal
Lit by the moon.

A forgotten harmony
Of another time:

Eggs by ferry to New London,
Dry goods by raft to Port Jefferson.
The past belonged to sand,

Shellfish,
A tripod on tarpaper.

Nature's quirks were God's character.

You waited for sunset.
When color faded
On the shacks

You saw the soul in the Sound.
When the shoreline died
Beside an acorn
In vainglorious bloom
On the aquifer

You drew out your Leica,
For one more try
On the coldest spring in years.

George L. Chieffet

Marlene Weinstein

March 30

MOON SHELL

Whatever sound the moon shell made
When I pulled it from the surf
And held it, native, to my ear
Is a wave I can no longer hear.

Cracked and stained with ink, it rests
Washed up upon my desk, a fact
I can follow by spiraling back
To a point on a beach on Long Island.

Aground too long to sing to me,
It is the shell of what used to be,
A keepsake for the sake of keeping
What, like the moon, is still around.

John Kaufman

Peter Brink

March 31

[I AM THE POET]

I am the poet of reality
I say the earth is not an echo
Nor man an apparition;
But that all the things seen are real,
The witness and albic dawn of things equally real
I have split the earth and the hard coal and rocks and the solid bed of the sea
And went down to reconnoitre there a long time,
And bring back a report,
And I understand that those are positive and dense every one
And that what they seem to the child they are
[And the world is no joke,
Nor any part of it a sham]

Walt Whitman

Kathaleen Donnelly

HORSE ON THE LOOSE

It is dawn. I hear
at the seam of my dream
the talkative hooves of the horse
on the road going West.
Now that the drought
has reduced the paddock to dust
the large beast on a quest
for green, for grain, for equine romance
roams through yards where neighbors
wake to this oversized pet.
In alarm they alert
police and firemen. The phone
rings. Day has its strings reattached.
Brief outburst. Soon
the leash on its neck
leads it home, head bowed,
to its fenced-in yard
where its nose nudges
the dull, exhausted ground.

Claire Nicolas White

Craig D. Robins

MOLA MOLA

The fish that eats the moonjelly
this moonless night
floats sideways a few fathoms down
in the deep Gulf Stream water of Block Canyon,
mola, mola, the ocean sunfish, turning its span
enormous to the sky,
a luminescent fog around the eyes and gills.

*

Ocean sunfish, ocean sunfish, no fish like this fish,
not even in dreams, the size of trawl door
with a wobbling gait, two big fins & no tail on a shape
like a rudder out of whack, careening hingeless,
whose whim is warp, whose swim's a cam, whose fins flop,
a stalker of medusae, eating what nothing else eats,
eating little more than water but when grown close to ton
it swallows the Lionsmane neat.

I have seen it turn away the mako's best bite
from a hide scarred by propellers, and turn and turn
till the shark went off snapping its spite.

*

What is it about the depths offshore
that the seal sleeps there safe in its blubber
and the sperm whale knocks about for squid?
At night water gets clearer
and creatures never seen alive rise to the sky
and some never seen at all.
A spark shot from the abyss
strikes a palp of jellyfish.
And the mola breaches in the dark of the moon.

Allen Planz

Aija Birzgalis

AT THE SEAM OF EVERYTHING WE ARE

Spring's everywhere out there,
stitching itself in hot and early and unexpected
a hundred miles, a thousand, from the fettered tongue,
a universe away from our first valedictions.

Flies zigzag skylights, a blue buzzing
as if no world will ever be large enough.
Wet things slit their shells, pink or ocher
or an odd oval blue
as we might have once been ourselves,
feet slicked with the brown translucence
of soft, uncertain bottomland.

Fern-feet, silver-fish disappear
when we cut through the dark we see
only wisps of them slipping around
the notch of bark, rim of green. Old dreams
unravel in starlight, overturned from winter logs.
Spiders whisper over porchwood,
slip under the door, navigate the arm in sleep.
The crumbs dropped on yesterday's floor—
now a trembling froth of ants pinned to windfall.

Below thicket and grove, in spartina
thickening with the sudden season,
so many bodies bear the news—
jellyfish, horseshoe crab,
last November's fleeing wings,
yesterday's history in the channeled whelk.

Though all of these may be melodies
of the undone, we still remain,
our hungers poised at the intersection
of every place we are,
syllables of ribbons and rags,
lucky legs dancing down the road.

Elaine Preston

Aija Birzgalis

April 4

TABULA RASA

Tiny crystals fall
glistening through air.
All is silent save for
hushed wings of wind
whispering peace.

Carolyn Emerson

Jyoti Ganguly

April 5

APRIL SNOWSTORM

A raging sudden storm
Piling the ground with white
This pinkish April night
Is quite beyond the norm.
It really is poor form
To treat us with such spite,
When days were turning bright
And just a little warm.
The storm seems not to care.
And look!—each budding twig
Holds clumps of crystal flakes.
This must be magic, where
A force so vast, so big,
Such delicacy makes.

John A. Williams

Kate Kelly

April 6

APRIL

Winter's pen-and-ink world,
blurs before my eyes—
it's stark light and shadow infused,
pale green air,
pleats of leaves.

Dragon's teeth
thrust from bare brown earth,
soften, unfurl overnight into hosta,
Solomon's seal.
A lacy haze of henna
floats inches high where the astilbe grow.

Such an intimate joy,
too urgent to last—
all tree and plant,
shrub and vine,
here we are,
as if they'd never left.

Joan Reilly DeRosa

Kate Kelly

SPRING CLEANING

Winter
is soaped
by the suds
of a blustering squall.

Sear leaves
are crushed
by sudden flakes,
black boughs
are rinsed
in foaming bleach,

and spinning dryers
green the world,

as light
flicks dusk
from naked trees.

Marcia Slatkin

PALM SUNDAY HYMNS

Bent knees of salt wheat reflect as golden ribbons
on the smooth inlet, when the wind blows,
they break away and return.

I am alone except for a green-capped fisherman
who struggles his way over the dunes
towards the bay where fish are abundant.

Palm Sunday and I am not in church
with Father and Uncles clothed
in our black-and-white choir gowns
singing “All glory laud and honor.”

I am here sitting in my car watching
hallowed reflections bend across the cove,
the smell of new grass and salt mist
coming through the open window.

A satin rippled inlet wraps around the beach
as beautiful as any faire linen, and the gulls
sing their Hosannas above me.

I leave the car and walk to the edges of salt wheat,
in my hand a long reed, golden as a young sun.

I wave it across the morning.

Gladys Henderson

Kate Kelly

JUST BEFORE A BIRTHDAY

Floating
downwind
from the bluff
above my
Long Island
littoral. Warm
April air,
chill water,
a fresh light
spring gale
in my face.

Richard Elman

Barbara Keenan

April 10

APRIL MORNING AT THE LILY POND (MILLER PLACE)

All morning
I watched the willows swelling
cracking their sleep-caked skins
as if they couldn't wait
to begin it all again—
the ritual   this miracle
of squeezing out buds
soft and golden
flowing
like angel hair
above the green eye
of the lily pond
where only swans moved
white as the summer lilies
their great wings blossoming
in the waking
of spring air.

Florence M. Hughes

Christopher Corradino

HOWEVER TODAY

I see slips of crocus
tipping the snow
with green
and the stream
near my house
once bursting
with ice
is released
and running,
its black water
the blood flow
of spring,
swimming
the brook bed.
coaxing awake
those that slumber.

My life tied
so tightly
to the sureness
of everything
gone gray and dead,
feels for the flowing.

Gladys Henderson

April 12

PARTING GIFTS

An April snowfall set off
Gene Hamlet's blooming
crocus-covered lawns
embroidered gold and purple
petals luminous in young sonne
on new laid blue-white ground
a lavish evanescent masterpiece
planted in September in hope
she'd live till sp

Toby Lieberman

Barbara Keenan

CALEB SMITH PARK

"The woods are lovely, dark and deep . . . "
—Frost

1. Sounds

Snow falls,
from over-hanging cedars,
sifts through gnarled branches
casts quick shadows
like a silent bird
darting among the trees.
Listen! A woodpecker;
wind through dead leaves—
a waterfall.

Cardinals call celebration red.
A crow flaps—
a great black hand
grasping and kneading the air.
Sun through dense clouds draws
each beige branch, conifer
into clear luminescence.

2. Trees

Larch buds—tiny cabbages
on arabesque branches
of rich umber.

Red cedar's straight trunk
wisps of bark
color of rust.

3. Fields

Stop! A spray of deep-blue ilex berries
on branches tangled like string;
field of straight stems,
large, sharp thorns.
On the trail, cut oak-logs,
orange faces bright against white.

Snow in the tongs
of queen anne's lace—
small white eggs
in a filigree cup
of wild carrot.

Skunk cabbage—
tubes of rolled green-paper
unfurl through snow,
open floppy leaves,
at the edge of the stream.

Fox tracks along a low ridge
edge of the field
peppergrass, meadowsweet,
graceful arches of motherwort's
tiny dried flower-heads
bend over snow,
a double arch of wild roses
hips still hang,
a single, ethereal stem of tansy,
its dried flowers barely there,
a last chance for us
to revel in spring snow.

Adam D. Fisher

George DeCamp

PECONIC

Two terns and a loon and I fish an inlet
catching nothing:
Then the wind about to put on flesh
carries away the birds.

This early spring
fog carries me everywhere
veering over the ovarian trill & tea
of peconic underwaters.

And there's the sea coming on or going
after
and the hedgewich. Listen
she whistles

bobwhite!

Allen Planz

April 15

Drew A. Pantino

Richard Hunt

April 17

AN EASTER LILY

Tonight the sky received
A paschal moon
It came on time
And through half-open shutters
Its ceremonial radiance
Enters our houses

I for my part received
An Easter lily
Whose whiteness
Is past belief

Its blossoms
The shape of trumpets
Are mute as swans

But deep and strong as sweat
Is their feral perfume.

Anne Porter

EASTER

I clear away dry leaves,
the irises' gray beards,
hollow stalks of last year's
chrysanthemums, plume poppies,
uncover the earth's skin,
pubescent tips of lilies,
fat budding hyacinths,
tight-lipped primroses,
bare naked buds
unfolding in air.
Under the blanket of the dead
the living brood,
the living rise
crowding towards the light.

Claire Nicolas White

Laura M. Eppig

April 18

APRIL WIND

From my Manorville Home

A leaf tumbles across the deck
Like a scampering mouse.
My eyes follow it to a resting place in a shadow.
April wind lifts fallen leaves to dancing.
These drying breezes sway bare branches,
Move clouds eastward over the meadow in a parade of motion.

In the hoop house, tropical warmth, deep stillness,
And hope in basil seeds spreads on damp starter mix.

I am that tossing and turning leaf
Allowing outside forces to move me.
Let me fly across the lawn, find a lee spot to rest,
Catch my breath;
Move on . . . move on

Marlene Weinstein

Tom Stock

from
INSCRIPTIONS: SONG OF MYSELF #46

I know I have the best of time and space, and was never measured and
never will be measured.

I tramp a perpetual journey, (come listen all!)
My signs are a rain-proof coat, good shoes, and a staff cut from the woods,
No friend of mine takes his ease in my chair,
I have no chair, no church, no philosophy,
I lead no man to a dinner-table, library, exchange,
But each man and each woman of you I lead upon a knoll,
My left hand hooking you round the waist,
My right hand pointing to landscapes of continents and the public road.

Not I, not anyone else can travel that road for you,
You must travel it for yourself.

It is not far, it is within reach,
Perhaps you have been on it since you were born and did not know,
Perhaps it is everywhere on water and on land.
. . . .

Walt Whitman

April 20

Christopher Corradino

SPRING OUTING

From the L.I.E, Exit 59-60

Just the beginnings,
Shrubs are green-misted globes.
With blackened branchlets from a steady rain
Catkins look like swarming caterpillars.
Bursting buds
Hint the fullness yet to come.
Delicate dabs
Of green offer a haze
That lets one see through the tangle.
Little pieces of dangling green.
Green, green, green.

Tom Stock

Ange Gualtieri

April 21

WARM RAIN
for Earth Day

My skin is afire
in the earth's flow
as drizzle falls
traveling through its circle
round, round
from the depths
to the heavens and back
safely landing
for me to feel
a part of the earth.

Kathaleen Donnelly

Frank Muller

April 22

DAWN FOG

Mornings like this are cut with silver paper:
negatives of the sun that the dawn imprints
eventually when scrubby cedars daub horizon
across the flat water sheened by sandbars,
like phantom limbs, the whole new day
stretching from our windows and retreating
as though the brightening of every wave with air
like silver leaf may just go black as jet.

Such April fogs won't always lead to rain.
Sometimes these new days, seeming fuzzy and misshapen,
later are clarified like melted butter and
sometimes the afternoon returns the day
to intimations of such vaguely original beginnings
we're only heading backward by going forward,
as though our boat has loosed its mooring
in the tides of weathering so much time
and come around again upon the darkness.

Days and nights are tentative and indeterminate:
like losses we endure in fog, just as soon as pleasure
holds out the prospect of another dawn to come
the morning rubs the smudge off tawdry afternoons
and sparkles in the Sound one wave at a time.

Richard Elman

Ed Muller

SERIOUS SPRING

When flowers first give over to leaves
the serious, interior work of trees,

the adding on of girth to pulpy rings,
begins. This is also the season when,

on their knees, gardeners normally begin
to dig their way down sunny furrows—asking

nothing else of earth but fertility
within the boundary of their individual fences.

How alone and proud they stand in each garden,
rolling up white-buttoned blouses by both sleeves!

Meanwhile in town, Main Street toughs also heed
(surreptitiously, at least) the promise of spring—

I know this is true, don't ask me how—and quietly
each notes with pleasure the budding of trees.

I suppose each of us somehow must believe
that our own miraculous response to spring

is beyond the comprehension of skeptics. But see
how so many and various thrive in nature's moment

as if in a dream beyond the swaggering beauty
of first blossom. This is a thing of mystery! This

is serious spring.

George Wallace

Bob Schmitz

APRIL 25TH

Spring! Finally its flowery face
aglow 'neath blue, aflow
in whips, wind wisping
from all directions adance
blessing, saying earth again
blooms its secrets, still
colors rich loam
weaving worm and decay
into life in such
intricate variations
we can but laugh
and step light

Graham Everett

April 25

Susan Tiffen

RETURN

The world is half forgetful of the snow,
  And all unheeding of the Winter's way
With wind and sleet across the hills of gray.
Lo! he has gone, and April does not know,
Coming her path with glimmering feet and free,
  To what dark under-land of dreams and night
  His steps have passed, heedless of that new light
Which floods the earth from happy sea to sea.
Singing she comes; and Hope is one with her—
Hope of new joy in tender leaves that stir
All tender thoughts. And Love is swift to bring
To these fair days fair promise of her spring.

Pan is not dead. Within the fir wood's shade,
  By heron-haunted lakes, when days are fair,
  Blithe rustic notes, far filling all the air,
On magic woodland pipes again are played.
And mingling music of a thousand lives
  Within her lengthening train, fair April brings
  Up the south wind the birds on swiftening wings,
As thick as summer bees from murmurous hives—
The clear triumphant song of mounting larks,
Soft twittering of the swallow in the dark
Before the dawn creep over sea and plain
And the low note of thrush through quiet rain.

Juliet Isham

William Duryea, Jr.

MY NATIVE ISLE

My native isle! my native isle!
For ever round thy sunny steep
The low waves curl, with sparkling foam,
And solemn murmurs deep;
While o'er the surging waters blue
The ceaseless breezes throng,
And in the grand old woods awake
An everlasting song.

The sordid strife and petty cares
That crowd the city's street,
The rush, the race, the storm of Life,
Upon thee never meet;
But quiet and contented hearts
Their daily tasks fulfil,
And meet with simple hope and trust
The coming good or ill.

The spireless church stands, plain and brown,
The winding road beside;
The green graves rise in silence near,
With moss-grown tablets wide;
And early on the Sabbath morn,
Along the flowery sod,
Unfettered souls, with humble prayer,
Go up to worship God.

And dearer far than sculptured fane
Is that gray church to me,
For in its shade my mother sleeps,
Beneath the willow-tree;
And often, when my heart is raised
By sermon and by song,
Her friendly smile appears to me
From the seraphic throng.

The sunset glow, the moonlit stream,
Part of my being are;
The fairy flowers that bloom and die,
The skies so clear and far:
The stars that circle Night's dark brow,
The winds and waters free,
Each with a lesson all its own,
Are monitors to me.

The systems in their endless march
Eternal truth proclaim;
The flowers God's love from day to day
In gentlest accents name;
The skies for burdened hearts and faint
A code of Faith prepare;
What tempest ever left the Heaven
Without a blue spot there?

My native isle! my native isle!
In sunnier climes I've strayed,
But better love thy pebbled beach
And lonely forest glade,
Where low winds stir with fragrant breath
The purple violet's head,
And the star-grass in the early Spring
Peeps from the sear leaf's bed.

I would no more of strife and tears
Might on thee ever meet,
But when against the tide of years
This heart has ceased to beat,
Where the green weeping-willows bend
I fain would go to rest,
Where waters chant, and winds may sweep
Above my peaceful breast.

Mary Gardiner L'Hommedieu Horsford

April 27

ROMANCE

    Late April.
I go down to the spring
where a spigot spits
its clear water out
from under the hill, at the harbor.
And yes, it is there again
A field of watercress
hiding behind skunk cabbage
under low branches
growing in thick brown mulch.
My boots squelch wet
as I cut spicy green leaves
careful not to uproot
their hairy white feet.

Who, while my back was bent
deposited on the stone
by the water spout
perfect, like a heart,
one red strawberry?
An angel? God? Clearly a gift
from some benevolent
silent passerby.
Rich with water and cress
I bless the donor of
this wealth, and eat.

Further down the road, I pass,
a white-haired, sprightly man
walking a cocker spaniel
through a cloud of forsythia.
  Hey, I think it's him!
    A love affair!

Claire Nicolas White

Victoria Twomey

APRIL 30TH

Yard-work, the one activity where the mind stops
bugging me with its unsolved problems,
calls me to put on my sweat-stained cap.
Its brim salt-residued, a hieroglyph.

Planting Carpet-Bugle, I repeat
the steps throughout the backyard's border
wherever bare ground could use cover
glove-less fingers scratch and
dig the soil worked by decomposure
and its worm. Watering the fresh transplants,
I realize no quarrel with the world
not even with the reluctant garbage pick-up
or the out-of-town driver passing through lost
on a lark or some family pilgrimage.

Spring breezes a sudden wave
through the rising ocean of trees.
Highway noises drown in birdsong.

Graham Everett

Victoria Twomey

THE FIRST OF MAY

Now the smallest creatures, who do not know they have names,
In fields of pure sunshine open themselves and sing.
All over the marshes and in the wet meadows,
Wherever there is water, the companies of peepers
Who cannot count their numbers, gather with sweet shouting.
And the flowers of the woods who cannot see each other
Appear in perfect likeness of one another
Among the weak new shadows on the mossy places.

Now the smallest creatures, who know themselves by heart,
With all their tender might and roundness of delight
Spending their colors, their myriads and their voices
Praise the moist ground and every winking leaf,
And the new sun that smells of the new streams.

Anne Porter

Frank Muller

from

INSCRIPTIONS: SONG OF MYSELF #33

Space and Time! now I see it is true, what I guess'd at,
What I guess'd when I loaf'd on the grass,
What I guess'd while I lay alone in my bed,
And again as I walk'd the beach under the paling stars
    of the morning.

My ties and ballasts leave me, my elbows rest in sea gaps,
I skirt sierras, my palms cover continents,
I am afoot with my vision.
. . . .

Walt Whitman

Robert Bonanno

May 2

SWEET MAY RHYME

White
tulips pink
azaleas, lush
above in billowing
dogwood flushed
a cardinal
whistles
to the
glittering
dusk

Weslea Sidon

Linda Russo

May 3

GRANDMA'S PRAYER FOR AVIVA

When you awaken, may light zephyr breezes
through newgreening willow wands
whisper peace,
like the peace that is on your eased brow,

May the yellow butter daffodils
thicken in the fields
beneath a slow churning sun,
like the mellow warmth you wrap
around a proffered finger
with your whole hand,

May the chorus of twittering voices
encircling your rocking carriage,
threading through your dreams,
be colorful birds calling their mates
to nestling renewal,
and not the twittering of human terror,

When you awaken, Aviva,
oh little wondrous child
of Spring,
may you never forget,
and may we all remember,
what you somehow already know.

Gayl Teller

THIS DAY IN MAY

A cry of gulls signals
the joys of a mussel bed
early morning, low tide.

A glimpse of black and white,
a warbler perches on the dying limb
of a still bare oak

then is gone. A late blooming daffodil
whose name I lost long ago,
blooms within the lances of its leaves,

its gold cup filled with drops
from last night's rain,
the scent of spice.

I sieve the blackness
of compost through my fingers.

Joan Reilly DeRosa

Richard Hunt

May 5

FOR THE HEMPSTEAD PLAINS

The Hempstead Plains—
To me, it always seemed a Puritan name—
Evoking only grass and simplicity—
Conjuring images of stiff, white weeds
Standing straight in pews of prairie,
Bending only occasionally, in unison
To worship a dry-soiled god.
But to visit the fields with the unadorned name—
To come to them in spring,
See the wheat and wine-colored grasses,
Corn-colored wildflowers thrashed by wind
Until they beat their bodies in Shaker dances—
Well, the name connotes in me now
Fervor of natural grace.
East of the Allegheny there was only ever one prairie
Island-born in the outwash of a glacier.
Before European tongues named it
It stretched smooth and level
With Little and Big Blue Stem,
With Broom Sedge tall grasses,
And in May, a mantle of Bird's-foot Violets.
Before European tongues named it
It was peopled with heath hens,
Upland sandpipers,
Grasshopper sparrows.
And now even after it has been named,
On the Hempstead Plains,
The bushy rock rose,
The handmaid moth.
The Sandplain Gerardia.
On the Hempstead Plains,
Beauty . . . flat and persistent.

Annabelle Moseley

BIRD'S-FOOT VIOLETS

In May
before the coliseum and mall sprawl
Long Island's prairie was celestial
with lavender petals of Bird's-foot Violets

Today
in a lot, I kneel
smell the fragrance my mother knew
the days I ran home with bouquets
she snuggled her face into
and taking me on her lap
tell the story of why the leaves
are shaped like plover's feet

Maxwell Corydon Wheat, Jr.

Bob Schmitz

Susan Tiffen

May 8

from

SANDS AT SEVENTY: SOON SHALL THE WINTER'S FOIL BE HERE

Thine eyes, ears—all thy best attributes—all that takes cognizance of natural beauty,
Shall wake and fill. Thou shalt perceive the simple shows, the delicate miracles of earth,
Dandelions, clover, the emerald grass, the early scents and flowers,
The arbutus under foot, the willow's yellow-green, the blossoming plum and cherry;
With these the robin, lark and thrush, singing their songs—the flitting bluebird;
For such the scenes the annual play brings on.

Walt Whitman

MAY EVENING

The breath of Spring-time at this twilight hour
Comes through the gathering glooms,
And bears the stolen sweets of many a flower
Into my silent rooms.

Where hast thou wandered, gentle gale, to find
The perfumes thou dost bring?
By brooks, that through the wakening meadows wind,
Of brink of rushy spring?

Of woodside, where, in little companies,
The early wild-flowers rise,
Or sheltered lawn, where, mid encircling trees,
May's warmest sunshine lies?

Now sleeps the humming-bird, that, in the sun,
Wandered from bloom to bloom;
Now, too, the weary bee, his day's work done,
Rests in his waxen room.

Now every hovering insect to his place
Beneath the leaves hath flown;
And, through the long night hours, the flowery race
Are left to thee alone.

O'er the pale blossoms of the sassafras
And o'er the spice-bush spray,
Among the opening buds, thy breathings pass,
And come embalmed away.

Yet there is sadness in thy soft caress,
Wind of the blooming year!
The gentle presence, that was wont to bless
Thy coming, is not here.

Go, then; and yet I bid thee not repair.
Thy gathered sweets to shed,
Where pine and willow, in the evening air,
Sigh o'er the buried dead.

Pass on to homes where cheerful voices sound,
And cheerful looks are cast,
And where thou wakest, in thine airy round.
No sorrow of the past.

Refresh the languid student pausing o'er
The learned page apart,
And he shall turn to con his task once more
With an encouraged heart.

Bear thou a promise, from the fragrant sward,
To him who fills the land,
Of springing harvests that shall yet reward
The labors of his hand.

And whisper, everywhere, that Earth renews
Her beautiful array,
Amid the darkness and the gathering dews,
For the return of day.

William Cullen Bryant

Richard Hunt

AT THE DEATH OF WINTER

We watch from windows
wet with warming tears
see the cease of gales
scourged on bitter land
witness bare limbs hang
with humility, have faith
savior rains will fall, carry away
agony of frozen gardens
quench roots of bone-dry beds
birth worms and bees to duty
heal hands of scarred stems
hold hope in a passionate embrace
encourage bulbs, bushes, trees
to burst forth in choruses of
Alleluia
rejoice, arise in resurrection
behold a miracle
five pink blossoms
on an azalea branch
    at the birth of spring.

J R Turek

Marlene Weinstein

May 10

SUMMER CULTIVATION

The first step defines all others.

Which is why I visit garden centers in Spring.
I like to speculate
on the red and white possibilities
that sticks of rose bushes, or azalea
rooted in bags of soil, may bring
to the dark spot I like to call my garden. Of late
the rage is all impatiens, I observe. Like
the scrubby weeds that already inhabit
my garden, they tend to please when blossoming.

This fine flower, I reflect, began as a weed.
As have all, I suppose. And left in my garden
to fend for itself, would soon return to the wild
or die, no doubt. Still, I cannot be too concerned
with death, when summer returns. This is
shovel time, when cultivation attends my days,

early and late. This, I say, is no time
for pondering fate. Let the digging begin!

George Wallace

Sheldon Pollack

May 11

from

SEA-DRIFT: OUT OF THE CRADLE ENDLESSLY ROCKING

Once Paumanok,
When the lilac-scent was in the air and Fifth-month grass was growing,
Up this seashore in some briers,
Two feather'd guests from Alabama, two together,
And their nest, and four light-green eggs spotted with brown,
And every day the he-bird to and fro near at hand,
And every day the she-bird crouch'd on her nest, silent, with bright eyes,
And every day I, a curious boy, never too close, never disturbing them,
Cautiously peering, absorbing, translating.
. . . .

Till of a sudden,
May-be kill'd, unknown to her mate,
One forenoon the she-bird crouch'd not on the nest,
Nor return'd that afternoon, nor the next,
Nor ever appear'd again.

And thenceforward all summer in the sound of the sea,
And at night under the full of the moon in calmer weather,
Over the hoarse surging of the sea,
Or flitting from brier to brier by day,
I saw, I heard at intervals the remaining one, the he-bird,
The solitary guest from Alabama.

Blow! blow! blow!
Blow up sea-winds along Paumanok's shore;
I wait and I wait till you blow my mate to me.
. . . .

Walt Whitman

George DeCamp

May 12

MY LATEST GODDESS

Today I will be Phragmites, the many-bodied,
pale reeds lifting skyward
from the scalp of Tiana Bay.

I will be the beach wheat
un-harvested in the morning,
long hair eager for the comb.

It will be good to be Phragmites,
life that springs where water pauses,
in the glare of afternoon
when water swells against my strands.
I will be the oracle slipping snakelike in the breeze
as sand-scribes take my lines.

An acropolis of ants attends my offerings:
dead horseshoe crabs,
headless fish,
stones left for interpretation.

Subjects crave my many gifts.
In my stems:
arrow-shafts,
rope fiber,
aphid-sugar.

They do not know what waits inside my fence
how much I want to bow to the sand.

Yes. Today I will be Phragmites,
Rush-goddess, until evenings falls
and minnows press beneath my power.
Then I will rustle like a flourish of notes
in an untuned wind
and call flatly to be enfleshed.

Annabelle Moseley

Vincent Noto

May 13

THE CASE AGAINST WEEDING

First the weeds take charge
of the ornamental borders
obscuring even the gladiolus
until a perfect, green
grasshopper, two inches
long, emerges to sun.
Then, a praying mantis
pauses with a headless hopper
to remind me how wildly
beautiful nature can be.

David B. Axelrod

Stuart McCallum

MAY 15TH

Spending the afternoon doing what I set out
to do months ago: whacking weeds and sowing
lawn seed that may yet grow solid root.

Sunshine soft and cool on this day off.
Winter seems far off, ages to go.

Graham Everett

Kate Kelly

THE POLITICS OF WEEDS

I vote for weeds

blue chicory and white Queen Anne's lace
sharing the waste of the roadside
taking over territory nobody claims
regenerating and proliferating

yes and straggly ragweed and gaudy
goldenrod
because they never waver
from their teary mission
of propagation and dissemination

and I am of the party
of the wild onion
that will not discriminate
between the homeowner's greening turf
and the farmer's fenced-in pasture

and even though I confess
to the urge to pull and spray
I admire the dandelion's pushy takeover
of the cultivated green that stretches
almost from coast to coast
leaving the lewd sign of sunburst flowers
and the naughty legacy of floating fuzz

and I applaud the spunky cockle
whose seed intermingles with
the farmer's precious grains
and clings to the wool socks of hunters
and the shanks of their hounds

and I silently support purple loosestrife
as it flares along the creek bank
streaking toward closed caucuses at dusk

and I even forgive my nemesis poison ivy
its platform of itchy rash
that has crept up my arms
and down my crotch

for mine is the politics of weeds

they depend upon the favors
of sun, wind and rain alone
in their uncompromising devotion
to survival and rebirth

they indeed shall inherit the earth.

Norbert Krapf

MID MAY

Jagged white and pink
full blossoms extolling
all the squeaky clean glass
contours of the morning.
Amid lilac plumes, and
dogwood peelings, the very
green grass displays azalea
swatches, red, pink, lavender,
white, like shirt fronts. The eye,
so abashed by so much spring
beauty, wanders towards the
heavens where greens are
again interlaced with sway-
ing boughs, and branches. This
day seemed so bright it was
brittle, at first, and now
it softens, nuzzling summer.

Richard Elman

Bob Schmitz

BEYOND WORDS
for Mark Egan

Yes
there are some things
that elude words &
simply must be sung:
how the rimshots of rain
& the bass line of wind
make more than a rhythm section
how the laughter of musicians
before the set is also a music
how the pretty girl suddenly
a beautiful woman makes
concentration tough all day
how the color green defies definition
is simply what it is
cannot be described
beyond the naming
beyond the singing
of green things

Ron Overton

Donald Case

May 18

GREEN

What vibrant flavor coats the tongue,
seeps into the skin, is vaporized
into breath by the air?

Trees pollinate and burst
onto the lawn, stalks poke out
and dig their verdant feet
deep into the earth.

The curtains sway,
emerald shadows mingle
and ripple up the stairs
and suddenly—the taste

of something green, a thirst
echoing from a well,
the throated tone of a bird
who digs into the grass

because he senses
the lush bounty of the rain.

Mindy Kronenberg

May 19

THE DOGWOOD

There's only a hint it was ever there,
a shallow dimple in the green blanket
of the broad back lawn. But I tell you,
it was something.

It stood at the edge of the woods,
one side always deep in shade, the other
soaked in sunlight. In bloom, it was
a lustrous white curtain, flowers
weighing down delicate branches
like snow, until they brushed the ground.

Each time I walked barefoot
on the fallen blossoms, I had an urge
to lie down, stretch my body full length,
feel the silky flowers on my skin,
maybe sleep for a while.
I never did.

An April ice storm took it in its prime.
I remember waking in our bedroom,
seeing my husband silhouetted
against the morning half-light,
looking down into the garden.
He said, without turning to face me,
"This will break your heart."

The trunk had broken off
low to the ground. It was hollow,
consumed by something unseen.
Losses. The worst are the ones
you don't see coming.

Arlene Eager

Linda Russo

A DOGWOOD SAPLING MADE CLEAR

of the twisted battle for sunlight
on the edge of the thicket
will right itself in as little as one season.
Not at first, mind you—
but before your average gardener
has time to start cursing,
the green tips of new leaf will pop out,
promising riches in a direction

formerly occupied by honeysuckle vines,
silverlace, and the like. Imagine for yourself
a new window opened to the sun! Wouldn't you

tend towards it? In a few months, tendency
has grown into intention; your young,
tenderleafed stems are climbing skyward
against a grain which now exists
only in sapling memory.

As it happens, I know all this to be true—
because on this land, I have been the one
to set a dogwood sapling free. Skinny, perhaps,
but no longer overcome. And by this, I have learned
that nature, in the form of a dogwood tree, at least,

in adversity may seek only survival—
but given its freedom, it will strive for something
higher: balance. Which is to say that Philosophy,
it now appears to me, sometimes requires

the intercession of an outside hand. Especially
in modest grounds such as these,
so badly in need of clearing.

George Wallace

May 21

DUCK WALK

At the crack of dawn
as the sun nudges through
a nest of branches
the garrulous yawp of ducks
ripples the sky.

I am roused from slumber
into daylight, find trees feathered
to greet the spring.
Earth softens beneath my shoes;
the ducks' webbed slippers

flap from pond to grass
and we meet on firm ground,
their wooden profiles
spreading wings to the bread
that floats like small clouds from my hand.

Frank Muller

Mindy Kronenberg

May 22

"CEDARMERE"
(Home of William Cullen Bryant)

I walk the pond
the old poet rowed
taking his ill wife
among the glories of water lilies
white as fair weather cumulus
golden as the high noon star

POND LILIES

large round leaves
landing platforms
for odenta helicopters
damselflies—dragonflies

HAIKU

Seven after dawn
sun's reflection awakens
water lily yawns

Maxwell Corydon Wheat, Jr.

HAIKU

neither the water lily
nor blue sky cheer me today,
but the bird's song . . .

Mankh (Walter E. Harris III)

Laura M. Eppig

May 23

MORNING

A first escape will be the plunge
outside to taste the day, to be
awash with air clean on my skin
to feel it slide as smooth as rain

into my eyes, to smell the light,
the wet, the sweet, the new delight
that weighs inside my nostrils with
a prick, an effervescent sting.

This quality of atmosphere,
this garment that I slip inside,
that fills me in and out is all
I need to be a part of mind

and matter. Chill hangs in the mist.
I swim through it and touch the wind,
fold it about my shoulders, lift
the veil of sun to strike me blind

and then return and close the door.
Dressed to begin the dailiness,
accepting its restraint once more
I strap the time around my wrist.

Claire Nicolas White

Vidal Al Martinez

May 24

from

MEMORIES OF PRESIDENT LINCOLN:
WHEN LILACS LAST IN THE DOORYARD BLOOM'D #3

In the dooryard fronting an old farm-house near the white-wash'd palings,
Stands the lilac-bush tall-growing with heart-shaped leaves of rich green,
With many a pointed blossom rising delicate, with the perfume strong I love,
With every leaf a miracle—and from this bush in the dooryard,
With delicate-color'd blossoms and heart-shaped leaves of rich green,
A sprig with its flower I break.

Walt Whitman

Pauline Southard

May 25

SUNDAY MORNING MOMENT

The blue flower of day
Widens over these vacant shores
And sea-lands, over the blue vacancy
And bloom of ocean. Now, where the beaches run,
Curving and fading, east and west,
Their tawny road between
The dunes with their tufted green
Pale against a blue sky
And the white line of foam that fringes
The sea-blue sea along a less blue sky,
The mounting sun pours down
His blessing; and on the inland ways,
On Whooping Boys' Hollow and Toilsome Lane
And on the road to Georgica,
His benediction falls. I sit here, musing,
An open book upon my knees.
Great trees bend over me. It is Sunday morning.
From Montauk Highway no murmur. A jet
Gargles its way across heaven, and fades
Seaward. The silence is so great,
Almost I fancy I hear
The wing-beat of the butterfly
Cavorting with happy aimless flight
Over the garden, over the thicket,
In the still light.
I take up my book and read.
At the head of the page,
"O heart be at peace."

John Hall Wheelock

Bob Schmitz

LITTLE DEEP

When light first penetrates the tidal basin
I swim underwater, looking at tracks
scooped by blind worms on the prowl,
weeds feeling out nuances
of countercurrents, rocks tumbling in their wash
whatever passes over them,

& farther down,
into the dark cowl where the tide furls into itself,
stripping the light

& beyond, thru dimness,
to boulders grown great with holdfasts,
to striped bass grazing on shrimp
that flick sideways, to ancient
horseshoe crabs moving tails-up,
a brightness flitting from under their shells,

& still farther, beneath layers of sand
to fossil shell & coral packed under pressure
into this molten earth, molding
the torso of this sea on me.

& I know it's not dark that draws me down,
but the floating of things in it
that deepens the vision
before the tide ebbs & turns,
& what had not been eaten or lodged somewhere
once more begins passing by.

Allen Planz

Sheldon Pollack

SLEEPING LATE

Dawn comes
to find
these robins
already
at their
tasks.
While
we work
to pay
the early
no mind,
we sacrifice
those worms
the early birds
find.

Daniel Thomas Moran

Bob Schmitz

May 28

UNDERSTANDING HEAVEN

Savor sun,
the sound of a lover sleeping,
mist rising on a secluded pond,
the delight of sight.

Relish a robin's call,
fish feeding on a green-skinned lake,
the flight of barn swallows
and how they work to remain in flight,
brief bodies almost too short to fly.

Praise imperfection,
the gesture towards flight,
we each make in the morning's
measured light.

Gladys Henderson

FRAGMENTED WINGS

Walking hard and breathing in labored gasps,
Thinking about too much,
resolving
nothing—
Allowing my feet a kinder rhythm, choosing with purpose
not to have any, briefly,
—for just a moment . . .
stopping.
It was the dance that caught me—enticing me,
NO—
taking me to be even more than merely
a distant spectator.
So crouching down, joining through wonderful
senses
the world thriving beneath our feet
despite
the oils, grime, toxins and odious refuse of the roadside.

The ever so present Long Island breezes were playing
roughly with the stained puddle.
ripples and swirls
two-stepping all over it!
A speckled feather and the right wing of a butterfly
—both caught
mercilessly—
Were being tickled to death!

Their Divine craftsmanship intricate symmetry and
delicate beauty.
Once riding the winds, masterfully
playing in the air's breath.
I imagine their purpose—carrying one across the sky . . .
I want to drink a toast to them
"To wings!"
Laughing, I rise,
Coming down from sensational dances of the winds,
wondering if I am the only one
seeing things this way . . .
Even so, troubles fade away briefly . .
Chilly; evening approaching,
pulling my jacket closed,
bracing
as the wind tries to tickle me further,
thinking; June-opening shop—Bring a little more warmth, pleas

Walking hard again—must try to keep step with this Island.

Linda Sack

May 30

Kate Kelly

THIS HARBOR

The whole Sound melts at sunset,
cools with afterglow to cobalt,
a twilight upside down.

This island, long and intricate,
crabbed with fingers in and out
by estuaries, lifts a dark smudge
here, some clumps of cedar there.

It's a Dutch painting,
a Hobbema, where nightfall
tilts the still
pond waters oily with refracted lights,
so frayed, first red, then
startled yellows.

The old oaks brush in sky
as snails, and barges, motor
launches propel a churn
through streaming marshes
against this island's welcoming
gesture.

Richard Elman

May 31

Ann Glazebrook

SASSAFRAS

Along railroad tracks
and service roads
you flex a waxy
awkward mitten
on one hand
and with another
offer egg-smooth
ovals of green
to the sun.

Rub your leaves
or bark between
fingers and inhale
the fragrance
concealed behind
the ear of
an empress.

Dry your leaves,
mash into powder,
sprinkle as filé
in a bowl of gumbo
and stay young
like the Cajuns.

I have sipped
the juice of
the bark of
your roots
boiled in water
on a drizzly
winter day and
felt summer sun
burn in my veins.

Norbert Krapf

June 1

Linda Russo

BEACH AFTER RAIN

After a week of heavy rain
the beach was an archipelago

I would explore each captured
islet   Cast adrift, I would be shipwreck
and mariner   and waded in deep
my feet trolling the bottom

A flat green stone   like a dropped arrowhead
pointed the way   The sky was white sun—
so bright the trapped bayous glittered

Here was the place I had looked for
the way one relearns life's sweetness
In this space, the smallest act would taste
of ritual: to breathe   the first gift after drowning

I would learn each dune and lake
I would dream the world new again
as it was in the wake of the glacier.

Charles Adés Fishman

June 2

Tom Lindtvit

WHEN THE CALL CAME

When the call came
I was about to cut the grass
for the first time. Wild
onion and dandelion were
sprouting across the lawn.
Sheaths of lily of the valley
bearing round green bells
were surrounding the lilac.

When the call came
the yellow marsh marigolds
were rising like the sun
against a boulder in
the flower bed. Bees
buzzed around bunches
of purple grape hyacinth.
The operator said, *I have*
a collect call from Columbia.
Do you accept the charges?
I replied, *Yes, I accept.*

When the call came
the leathery leaves
of bloodroot along the ledge
of the stone wall were
wrapped around stalks
like green sheets on which
white petals lay. Beside
the fishpond the fronds
of maidenhair fern were
unfurling in the sun.

A voice with a Spanish
accent spoke in my ear,
This is a social worker. We
have a baby girl born eight
days ago. Will you accept her?

When the call came
the white blossoms
of the wild cherry at the edge
of the woods were fluttering
on black boughs. The tips
of Japanese irises were
pushing through the soil.
Specks of Bibb lettuce
lay like green confetti
on the upper level of
the rock garden. *Yes, we*
accept her, I said. *Yes.*

Norpert Krapf

Frank Muller

NOON GARDEN TOUR WITH MY GRANDDAUGHTER

(For Liana)

Look there, under the maple,
Light filtering through leaves,
A pas de deux of sun
And dappled shadows.
Green and white
Hostas thrive there on light
Filtered through maple's thin
Branches—even those ferns
Like a bit of sun.
But there in beds facing south,
Black-eyed Susans love to bake,
Turn a scorched single eye toward the torch,
Their bright, yellow petals
Mirror the sky's fire;
Day lilies stretch out their necks,
Like women holding reflectors
To gather sun to their faces;
Phlox, dazzling white, in shimmering
Noon sun, their heads cool
In seersucker white. Listen, cicadas
Sing in harmony with katydids as if
To revel in noon heat.
A lesson: See these geraniums?
A cut branch placed in soil
Will root, send out velvet leaves,
And bouquets—new ones will bloom.
Quick over there! That yellow-and-black butterfly,
Flops and dances like a puppy
Whose feet are too big for his body,
Then glides in perfect control of huge wings.

Liana, did you see it all?

Adam D. Fisher

June 4

CLEOMES

It’s not about the flowers
but who we are as we tend
to their spidery pinkish wisps
to seed-pouched splendor

It’s because we bend
before them with meal offerings
as we wonder if
beauty like God

didn’t really exist
would we will-o’-the wisp
petal by petal by petal
have to invent

with our fists full
of white powdered animal bones
as we stoke what we know
of earthen fireworks

so as they release their
small starbursts they feed us
on air- loomed
essences . . . . . .

Gayl Teller

June 5

Linda Russo

AT THE NASSAU COUNTY MUSEUM OF ART'S FOUR WOMEN SHOW

Birdsongs pierce the silent fog.
Trees rise out of the unlit earth.
Leaves scatter the paths of poets
padding over the brickways.

Bronze Boteros startle squirrels
leaping overhanging branches.
Orange needles cover the shaded benches
where ghosts of artists ruminate.

Mary Cassatt's little ladies
paint and pastel between ukiyo-e.
Georgia O'Keeffe's photographic
florals open ecstatic deserts.

Helen Frankenthaler actuates
Pollock's drips and dreams.
Louise Nevelson collects
black foundlings on floors.

Four women drawn together
by the nature of their sex,
their new vision of reality,
and what could and should be.

Stanley H. Barkan

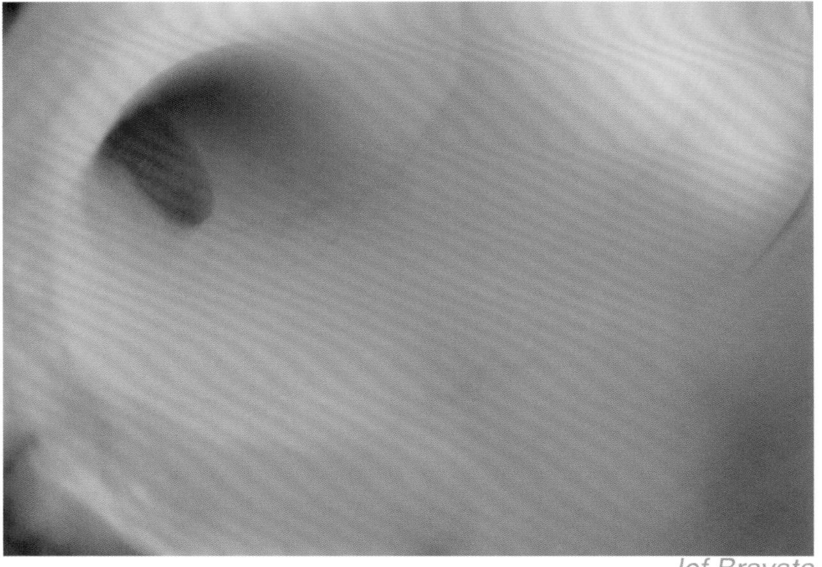

Jef Bravata

JUNE 7TH

Clear sky, but it's tough
what with the trees all fully leafed
to get a good look at Venus,
Jupiter, and Mars, the red star,
lining up from some point
out there where we matter none.

Nights like this when the humidity lifts
and the fireflies proliferate, all summers return
our childhoods as real as we lived them.

Graham Everett

Larry Landolfi

June 7

THE NEST

It was on the ground, propped on a tree root,
cocked like a thrown bowl
emptied of its contents.

I bent with the fear
of finding shattered eggs,
but the nest was empty

as if gently blown, chaste,
down from the branches.
It was an artful basket

in my hands, impossibly light,
prickly as a crown of thorns

and touching as a child's gift.
It was scented with peat, and
within its weave, ribbons

of grass and reeds twirled
in unbridled design.
It was about to rain—

I carried it to my porch
gently placing it out of harm's way,
not knowing exactly why.

(Could it be used again, should
I nestle it in the crook
of a tree?)

All I can do now is look at it
and wonder when small speckled eggs
might appear,

wait for the bright thread of song
to weave the air.

Mindy Kronenberg

June 8

Vidal Al Martinez

JUNE

In green shadows, leaning
ferns are brothering
leaf & unfathered moss.

A shock of upright yellow,
profusion of blameless daisies,
one is my daughter.
Abundance.
In its quickness,
the fidgety dispatch of crickets.

Over the blue bay,
flecks of pepper
trail down the twilight sky:

a community of gulls,
beaks open like tongs,
banks around the sedge
on utter tongues of wings
& lands a family
of squatters on the water.

Just before dark,
the astonishing chime of stars.

Dan Murray

Vidal Al Martinez

LATE SPRING QUICKENS

After a month of rain,
I ride my bike to the beach
and give myself to the wind

blowing in from the Atlantic.
It's late in the day, too cool
to sit and read. Swings

in the make-shift playground
hang empty yet drift to right
and left, as if ghost children

sit in them, waiting for a push,
for that first swift launch
out of *ordinariness*

into the ocean of new life.

I walk the tidal sift at the edge
of this sunless bay, listening
for the quick trilled notes

of the blackbird's song
the whispered epic of the reeds
the deft music the buffeting wind makes.

It's good to be silent and alone
where fate's hammer may not strike.
Someone else walked this way today

and saw the luminous spill of the waves
the combed hair of the rocks   moss-green
in late spring sunlight   tide-wrack

of smashed lobster pots on the eroded beach.

Here is the sill of the world
where each cold shimmer comforts
and rebukes.

Charles Adés Fishman

Ed Muller

CITY VISITS

Cities
continue to owe me a debt.
I expect to be paid
with some kind of vista:
distant horizon,
lights that blink at sunset.
Masked in glass,
geometry textbook skyscrapers
reflect rivers.
Cement and granite
cleverly shaped and piled
arching towards evening
leave no doubt
that all roads
lead to home.

Arlene Greenwald Cohen

from

CROSSING BROOLYN FERRY #9

Flow on, river! flow with the flood-tide, and ebb with the ebb-tide!
Frolic on, crested and scallop-edg'd waves!
Gorgeous clouds of the sunset! drench with your splendor me, or
    the men and women generations after me!
Cross from shore to shore, countless crowds of passengers!
Stand up, tall masts of Mannahatta! stand up, beautiful hills of Brooklyn!
Throb, baffled and curious brain! throw out questions and answers!
Suspend here and everywhere, eternal float of solution!
. . . .

Walt Whitman

Ralph Pugliese, Jr.

June 12

THE ROSES OF QUEENS

Among the topless dancers,
warehouses, factories,
disorderly patches of weeds
and rubbish on traffic islands,
behind the endearingly dated
façades of Steinway Street,
bloom in the pocket-sized gardens
the astonishing roses of Queens.

The brick row houses with
their awnings and stoops, as neat
as paintings by Pieter de Hoogh,
line up their rival heavens
with Dutch precision, no doubt
echoing earlier settlers
who could not have foretold
the astonishing roses of Queens.

Yet here they are, as lush
as those of Ispahan,
on ramblers or on bowers,
on shrubs or trees or hedges,
as full as cabbage heads,
crimson and gold, their scent
a heady wave on the wind,
the astonishing roses of Queens.

Tied to the difficult land,
the port of immigration,
by the iron umbilical cord
of the borough's rattling bridge,
this modest array of lives
with the Babel of Europe behind,
invested its capital in
the astonishing roses of Queens.

A place to grow old in the end
when transplanting has borne its fruit,
where bread has as many shapes
as the languages grandfathers speak,
sitting on stoops in the sun
among all this blossoming wealth . . .
their hopes have come to rest
in the radiant roses of Queens.

Claire Nicolas White

Christopher Corradino

DAISIES GROW ON MY WINDOWSILL

I'm too young to join the kids who garden
at the neighborhood park, Mom says.

so I'm gonna grow little daisies on my windowsill.

Grandma calls me a windowbox Gardener,
and I like that.

The colors of my daisies are as winter as snowflakes
and as summer as lemons.
I planted some snips of hanging ivy at the edges of the box,
hoping some leaves would reach down to
Mrs. Sander's window (I hear she's lonely).

My window box is made of cedar.
Uncle Emil built it. And I think I'm a leader
of windowboxing . . .

People have been watching my daisies grow
in this city
and whattya know—
they've got window gardens of their own.

Linda Carnevale

Susan Tiffen

UPHILL

i am sitting in a car
in the parking lot
behind the european-
american bank.
it's nighttime.
across the peconic
looms the white hulk
court building. i wonder
how much concrete it takes
to sink an island

later, driving east on 58
past the shopping centers
car dealers, and a lessening
of farms and woods

i think of the old houses

Graham Everett

Ann Glazebrook

June 15

THE OLD COUPLE

He lies sleeping
head on her lap,
not less than eighty.
She, too, is old
and could not care
but she does,
caressing his hair
as he shifts, sighs.
The sun warms
his eyes. He smiles.
Sixty years
if a day, together.
Somewhere in
the next world
a house of love
is being built.

David B. Axelrod

TWO BOYS AT THE SEASHORE

They live in a desert of strangeness,
step lively on a strung wire of dreams
that sways dangerously above the seabrine.
Like firewalkers, they cross where only faith
can navigate. Ignorant of lethal winds,
tsunamis; gawky, white-blond, and nearly
hairless; their boxer swim trunks
are all that distinguish them from figures
drawn in sand.
                                        A sudden gust
off the wave crests is reason to run:
*quick quick quick quick quic*k—sandpipers.
A shadow at the shoreline is where-to-dig:
dark, wet, gritty, yielding, without
bottom. Sand is to scatter, not to protect,
and energy is what grows luminous
on their bodies: sheen over burned skin,
aura over pallor.
                                        They mine the beach
for treasure, move in a haze of friendship
and unknowing. Green trunks and red,
they disappear slowly, dissolve into purple
blackness, into seagrape air, at the horizon.
What is left are hieroglyphs: tracks
of sea ducks, sanderlings, oyster catchers,
plovers, phalaropes, turnstones—

Shadows caught in flight, let them be gathered
like shore birds wading tidepools of sun.

Charles Adés Fishman

Sheldon Pollack

IN THE TIME OF IRISES

Beyond the line
where shadows
from the woods
expire into sunlight
on spring grass

these battalions
of blue flame
blaze in June sun
flanked by rows
of green spears
raised to the sky.

I surrender to
their powers
of color and shape

become captive
and convert,
renounce all ties.

Without even
leaving a note

I march away
hands behind my back
perfectly in step

and descend deep
into their realm
of smoke and haze.

Norbert Krapf

Linda Russo

June 18

SATURDAY SPRING PORTRAIT – SELDEN, NY

There is a sudden comfort
of fresh magnolia blossoms
and young leaves arched
toward suburban side-streets,

a pale rain sprays
the pavement and lawns, quietly
the town awakens

a dog barks
with a deeper resonance
than the crow's announcement
of day!

both sharper than
my first coffee.

With sun's forecast—
by afternoon
the ice cream truck bells will tinkle,
clear as ice cubes

and children will sidle
up to the colorful display
of creamy confections.

Late afternoon will linger
about as long
as an orange creamsicle,

the sun paling
behind a row of houses,
with clouds spilling over
the sparkle of rooftops.

Mankh (Walter E. Harris III)

Craig D. Robins

STRUTTING IN PECONIC

Out of her coupe
she struts past us,
amid the rams and goats,
and becomes a silent filmstar.
Dressed for the ball
in white ruffles
our eyes pop like flash bulbs,
illuminating the rubies
at her neck. And blue eyes,
so clear and pale.
Her tiny feet step
from rose petal to rose petal,
exempted from the wet ground,
leaving us soaked in a downpour
and limelight in our eyes.

Jan La Roche

June 20

Linda Russo

GREEN KNOWS

Green knows
when to stretch out her fingers
when to stroke the trees
when to coax into bloom
their bright hopeful leaves.

Green knows
how to slide her spine
along the land
how to spread her hands
on the horizon.

And green knows
when to cradle a forest
in her arms
when to play her flute
for the grass.

Ginger Williams

June 21

Ralph Pugliese, Jr.

from

INSCRIPTIONS: SONG OF MYSELF #6

A child said *What is the grass?* fetching it to me with full hands;
How could I answer the child? I do not know what it is any more than he.

I guess it must be the flag of my disposition, out of hopeful green stuff woven.

Or I guess it is the handkerchief of the Lord,
A scented gift and remembrancer designedly dropt,
Bearing the owner's name someway in the corners, that we may
see and remark, and say Whose?
Or I guess the grass is itself a child, the produced babe of the vegetation.

Or I guess it is a uniform hieroglyphic,
And it means, Sprouting alike in broad zones and narrow zones,
Growing among black folks as among white,
Kanuck, Tuckahoe, Congressman, Cuff, I give them the same, I receive them the same.
. . . .

Walt Whitman

Ange Gualtieri

HEMPSTEAD HARBOR

Delightful spot! glory of all the earth,
  Bright miniature of Eden's blissful bowers;
Beauteous, as when in thy primitive birth,
  Thou stood'st array'd in shrubs and blooming flowers.
Before the blight of sin faded thy bloom,
  Unbounded nature knew no fairer spot;
And when creation felt her withering doom,
  Amid her works thou surely wert forgot.

Thy hills and streams, and each pellucid pool,
  Reflecting soft the silvery orbs of even;
Thy purling brooks and limpid waters cool,
  Sweetly resemble faith's bright views of heaven.
Hill after hill meets the enraptur'd eye,
  In one unbroken, undulating reef;
Stretching along beneath the blue-arch'd sky,
  'Till all appear in striking, bold relief!

From Moulton's heights, how beautiful the scene,
  Varied and bold, magnificent and grand;
Lakes, vales and streams, mingle the hills between,
  And the blue Sound laving the solid land.
I stand delighted 'mid the tangled wood,
  I gaze enraptur'd from his lofty dome;
I look around, and wish my pencil could
  Portray the beauties of his pleasant home.

Oh, I could gaze upon this heavenly spot,
  And feast my soul upon its magic charms;
'Till time itself, amid the scene forgot,
  Should steal like friendship from my folded arms.
Not only trees, and shrubs, and wooded hill,
  Lakes, ponds—the bay, and the blue rippling sound
Attracts and please, but manners soft distill,
  And show a genial influence all around.

Mary L. Gardiner

Adolfo Briceno

June 24

THIS ISLAND

Low tides, early mornings,
I'd walk the mud flats for nothing,
saying, as reeds bowed, straightened,
and bowed again in the brine wind,
or an eel or flounder startled
a cloudy trail through low water,
know you have forever, now,
know you have forever.

The Sound fallen back, this Island
risen, I kneel, touch my head
like a reed to the mud home of the crab,
wash my face in a gull's shadow,
knowing I have forever, now,
knowing I have forever.

Stuart McCallum

William Heyen

June 25

BIRD WADING

not an ibis—but there is something in the muscular bend
of his prayerful neck
that recalls in crooked letters the still banks of egypt

he works the leaping channel
for his supper

a low tide so full with mud, sun & mussel shells
the world is become
all blue shimmering luminosity

it is a wonder he can keep himself
so white

across the harbor a churchbell rings
our lady queen of martyrs
calling someone to prayer or celebration

three bells & two old men
seated by the railing

their necks bent in rare devotion to bait buckets
fishhooks & brown bottles of beer
they are just waiting for the tide to roll in

soon it will be them
fishing

George Wallace

George DeCamp

June 26

OASIS (FRIENDSHIP)

Red sunrise,
After gray daydawn:
Shade-trees, limpid pools,
Apart from burning noon-tide:
God and carmine, blending
Into purple twilight:
Moonlight,
Caressing silent stars.

You, heart's-ease,
Urging me forward,
Leading me onward
To the hopeful distances,
While the mist clears,
On the far horizon.

Olivia Ward Bush-Banks

Frank Muller

June 27

TRANSFIGURATION

After seeing a field of Firewheel (Gaillardia)

In the soft folds of mid-summer
below a dirt road that runs
along its ragged edge
I found a forgotten prairie
ablaze with crimson flowers.
Arrowed petals with tongues of flame,
wheels of fire spinning in the wind,
whirling into an inland sea.
There no time or space existed.
I stood spellbound and speechless,
adrift between two worlds
and offer this psalm,
in reverence for its briefness.

Gladys Henderson

Gil Weiner

June 28

ONE MORNING IN JUNE

Let me tell you about miracles—
how one by one, perfect, thin
as threads the newborn mantises

emerged from their crisp womb
on a bayberry bush wavered
against hard branches,

descending warily
onto rich grasses, measuring
the vastness of earth.

No one could count them all.
At once their pale green bodies
blended with the colors of summer.

What voice did they hear
saying *"Now"?* How many survived
in the blinding light?

When the last one disappeared
I turned away with a feeling of grace
that lasted for days.

Lynn Kozma

Laura M. Eppig

AS SKY COMES UNDONE

Day is beached
on a purple

tumbling

Overhead
reefs and shoals

appear

We ride out
an aquatic hour

Swallowing,

the horizon takes in
the blazing wafer

Brooding,

warm hedges
sequester the swift

and small

A wilderness of air
roves about,

seeking

Then the world surrenders
Then the land

walks away

Diana Chang

Pauline Southard

GOING BAREFOOT

On that first warm day
when the air was eiderdown
and sunlight
beckoned, we would
kick off our Buster Browns
and ankle socks
to race across the lawn,
green velvet underfoot,
until we reached
the gravel drive
where our pace slowed,
feet pierced
by sharp-edged stones
and toes burned
by sidewalk. We winced
but would not retreat.
Feet must be toughened
for days of summer stretched
in an endless cloverchain
beneath a turquoise sky.

Lynn Buck

July 1

Elinor Schoenfeld

LONG ISLAND MAGIC

Down our narrow lane at night
we ride under the
crescent moon.
Flashes of daisies shine
among tall phragmites, then beyond,
in the shadow,
something moves—a pale shape,
small patches of white, graceful head, and
antlers.
It does not turn to look
at our intruding lights.
The car stopped, we
watch, blink.
Gone.

Left behind, we're softened, and
content.

Next day on the beach,
we walk under the
hazy sun.
"Remember last night," I say, "the deer?"
On that word
it appears
between surf and rise of sand,
bounds up the slope to the top,
and stands,
ruler of the mountain dune,
then slips into tall grass.
Gone again.

"It was conjured," you marvel.
"When you said 'deer,' there it was, like magic."
"Coincidence—conjuring's out of style. But . . . "
I squint into the mist, "What a magical
coincidence."
Now every day I search
the fields from my window, then
give in to superstition,
whisper, and wait.
But the deer does not appear,
has left our open meadow
to stride among sheltering trees,
away from conjuring,
done with coincidence.

Left behind, I still feel its
magic.

Marjorie Appleman

Vidal Al Martinez

HAIKU

silence grows
Louder
as the mind clears

Stuart McCallum

Stuart McCallum

JULY

Your neighbor's telephone
rings & the morning glories
bloom riper than carnival lanterns.

Piano song from a pavilion,
full-blown, drowns
in afternoon ocean breezes,
drifts to another ear.
Strangers stop on the beach
to pet your unleashed dog.

Fireworks burst in the night:
golden spidery chandeliers,
showers of copper filigree,
tan the faces in a crowd;
fountains of lime spray
& wiggle like sperm.

A boom echoes along the surf
& lingers in the spirals of shells.

Dan Murray

Bob Schmitz

July 4

FIRST BEACH DAY
(For Carole's, East Quogue)

1.

Tiana Beach tide wanes with the moon,
sea slips out, leaving flat sand
where tardy water washes in overlapping sheets,
glazes sand molten steel under glinting sun.
Foam at the edge of high water,
a graceful undulation—
the curve of a back or breast.
Here in the damp sea air, under the sun's heat,
spindrift flows off rollers like hair in a breeze.

2.

The teenager in bulging tank suit,
holding his gold bikinied girl friend.
The grandma, zinc-white nose, dozing in her chair.
The lifeguard whistle-warning swimmers.
Black-suited surfers ride just under the curl.
A heavy-set walker
wiggles his toes in the soft sand,
wondering how he lived all year
without this.

Adam D. Fisher

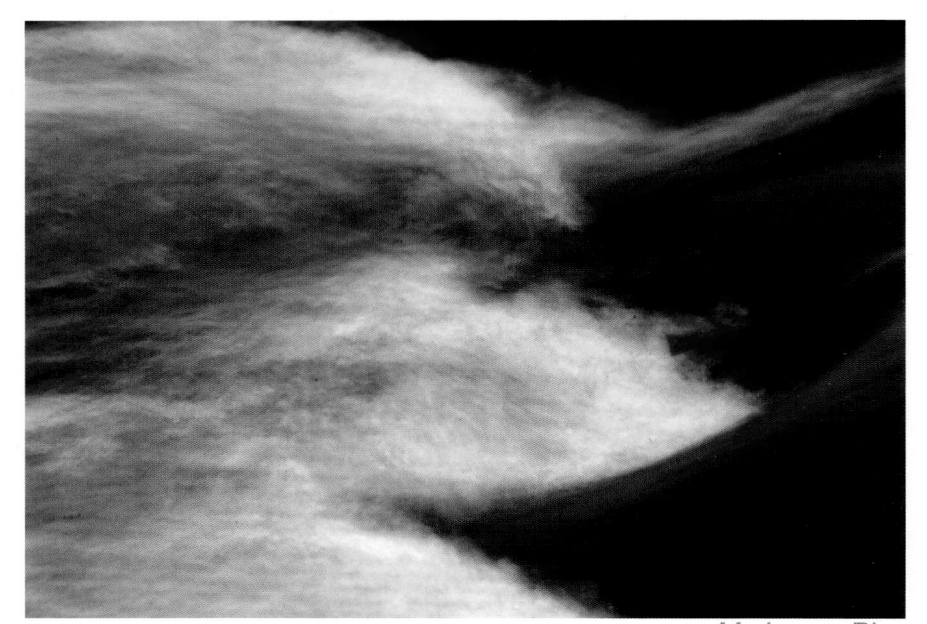

M. James Pion

July 5

from

SEA-DRIFT: THE WORLD BELOW THE BRINE

The world below the brine,
Forests at the bottom of the sea, the branches and leaves,
Sea-lettuce, vast lichens, strange flowers and seeds, the thick tangle,
openings, and pink turf,
Different colors, pale gray and green, purple, white, and gold, the play
of light through the water,
Dumb swimmers there among the rocks, coral, gluten, grass, rushes,
and the aliment of the swimmers,
Sluggish existences grazing there suspended, or slowly crawling
close to the bottom,
The sperm-whale at the surface blowing air and spray, or disporting
with his flukes,
The leaden-eyed shark, the walrus, the turtle, the hairy sea-leopard,
and the sting-ray,
Passions there, wars, pursuits, tribes, sight in those ocean-depths,
breathing that thick-breathing air, as so many do,
The change thence to the sight here, and to the subtle air breathed
by beings like us who walk this sphere,
The change onward from ours to that of beings who walk other spheres.

Peter Brink

Walt Whitman

HOUSE GUESTS

"All of us are coming"
No they are not coming
They may be coming
They may not be coming.

Four of them are coming,
That is, if they are coming!
Five will come on Friday
Three will leave on Sunday
Two will come back Tuesday,
That is, if they are coming.

If they were coming
Two of them would be coming
But they are not coming . . .

Six of them are coming!

Anne Porter

Jan La Roche

July 7

HAIKU

on the back
of the ladybug
the sun rises

Cliff Bleidner

Richard Hunt

July 8

LONG ISLAND

Oft have I wandered
O'er sea, and pondered
Upon the blooming
And unassuming
Beauty and quiet
(As I sail'd by it)
Of sweet Long Island—
Its low and high land.

In orchards planted,
And groves enchanted,
I heard the murmur
Of playful summer;
Birds were caroling,
And lovers strolling
O'er fair Long Island—
Its groves and high land.

The peaceful hamlet
Stood by a streamlet,
And by its waters
Its beauteous daughters,
Sweetly reclining,
Were flowers combining,
To grace Long Island—
Its vale and high land.

Its twilight shaded
Was serenaded
By happy farmers,
Wooing their charmers.
Fair is the maiden,
With milk-pail laden,
Of sweet Long Island,
On low or high land.

I thought if ever
My roving fever
Should cease its motion,
I'd leave the ocean,
And, with some creature
Of Heavenly feature,
Dwell on Long Island—
Its low or high land.

A land so peaceful,
So green and graceful,
I said, would render
A life of splendor
Despised and hated,
If I were mated
On sweet Long Island—
Its low or high land.

Tis there the graces
Adore the faces,
And sweet compassion
Is all in fashion;
E'en want reposes
On beds of roses,
On soft Long Island—
Its low and high land.

Blest and contented,
And unacquainted
With folly's glitter,
No thoughts embitter
The happy quiet
Of them who diet
On green Long Island—
Its low or high land.

'Twas thus, pursuing
My thoughts, and viewing
The landscape glowing
And overflowing
With milk and honey,
And "lasses bonny,"
I passed Long Island—
Its low and high land.

John Orville Terry

July 9

Bob Schmitz

WEB

Its silky softness like a wisp of hair
can greet you unexpectedly
whenever you approach the snare
where she creates a filigree
from which she swings

her spinneret's extruding strands
of delicate but tensile strength
that float in pliant lustrous bands
allow the breeze to strum their length
like gentle fingers over strings.

Vidal Al Martinez

Joan Higuchi

SPIDER LIES

the tiny white ones
hanging by their slender threads
almost invisible
almost impossible to catch
they could be anywhere

the bulbous clumsy ones, gray-black
that try to hide in cracks
too narrow to contain them
or dangle in midair
obscene and undeniable

the quick thick ones that scuttle
and the stilted ones that pose
those that are lethal

the ones so intricate in their design
that they intrigue
the ones so beautiful
so perfectly strange
they cannot be believed

Susan Astor

Sheldon Pollack

GARDEN

Alone in a cloud of green
the butterfly blinks its frantic
punctuation when I descend from sleep
to drown in what I own,
leaves on twisting branches
raising fountains of leaves
like spume! Existence is enough
considering the alternative.

My garden, my colored wardrobe,
my lilies, my roses, my dreams
of difficult beauty, in rows
I order you, processions
of tall plume poppies, the columns
of this vegetal church, wrapping me
in a self-made ecstasy
of air, song, and plants,
a refuge high as heaven.

Like a virgin of old,
I'm cloistered in your keep.

Claire Nicolas White

M. James Pion

SALVATION

Describing a perfect circle
the lone mallard dips her yellow bill
into blue-gray water over and over,
facing the end of the world.

Starving she edges closer
to the shore. Sun strikes sparks
from a lure hanging loosely
out of a tight mouth. Softly,
quietly, I lower a dip-net,
raise her, exhausted, from the inlet,
gentle her to the weathered wood.

She lies still as morning,
onyx eyes imploring, as I snip
the pronged hook in two, restore
her to sweet freedom, then slide
easily into her joy of deliverance.

I don't want to remember
the clamped mouth, the hopelessness—
only how it feels to love the world
one small life at a time.

Lynn Kozma

Robert Harrison

AFTERNOON IN THE PARK

Grist Mill, Stony Brook, NY

Here where umbrellas of trees
push up against the sun
where pebbles of white light
slip through strong-ribbed
branches through tight nets
of green beech leaves
then flutters like blown
spangles over pale grass
and shadow-painted earth
light settles
like stepping stones
across emerald-stained
pond water peers through islands
of water lilies glazes
the floating backs of swans
etches the iridescent heads
and necks of mallards
pinpoints the eyes of geese.
Here light and air meet and move
in a delicate balance
carefully snipping edges of shadows
tirelessly measuring the breadth
of the dark.

Florence M. Hughes

Frank Muller

ONE SWAT

On the deck where I sit,
a paper wasp hums next to me.
She's claimed a spot on a wall high over my head
and purposefully mixes chewed fiber bits and saliva.
She's attached a small stem.
Cubicles form. It grows. She's quite the builder,
but wants more than a place
to rest her weary wings.

I try to let her be,
knowing she and her progeny
could help me in my garden.
They're as fond of tasty caterpillars
as I am of their riddance.

I empathize with this single female;
her brood cells worry me.
They will hatch, become a busy hub
and before long be agitated
by my lone presence.

Numbers rule, they'll outgrow the nest,
start chewing and building anew.
They'll find spots ever closer to my chair.
Soon even that will be claimed.
Try as I might to coexist
there'll come that moment
when they will decide I'm the intruder.
One swat now, or many later.

Geraldine Morrison

Ange Gualtieri

FAIRWAY

Beautiful, birds! that you have learned
to hear no more the traffic sounds
and care to congregate on what's available
and warm—the signs across
the six- and eight-lane highways
cut through what had been your land.

In rural sites you rise like clouds
from shrubs and trees beside the road
when cars pass, settling back
before they're even out of sight.

But here, where housing dominates
you've lost your fears—or manners—
and just keep your place, regardless
of your betters, as unseeing of our
cares and contemplations, and our rights
as we have been yours.

Charlene Babb Knadle

Laura M. Eppig

July 16

THE ISLAND

So slender
is the island
that I can see sun ignite the bay
and strike the ocean
at the same time.
Larks sweep the sky
soon to be scarlet;
beyond shadblow trees
presumptuous catbrier climbs
a pine tree, and tall stalks
sway like metronomes,
displacing patens,
claiming the marshland.

Here I find it strange
to find peace strange.
The island
is no more real
than the moon's singularity;
it will change
as a cloud's shape
alters in wind,
as storms move dunes
and sea-spray chops
their heather.

Surely as the ocean batters
the sand's composure
prodding the shoreline inland,
this land will change
just as the boat develops out of fog
and courses through water
to carry me
from my house
on stilts in sand.

Grace Schulman

Terry Amburgey

July 17

LITTLE BUG MAN

He plucks Japanese beetles
like fruit from raspberry
bushes and drops them abuzz
into a warm broth
in the sprinkling can.

From the distance of a few
feet he watches the green
praying mantis prepare its
ritual of entrapment at an odd
angle on the basil plant
beside the back door.

He kneels on the patio
to observe ants stream
from a hole in white sand
between red bricks.

He stands up and stares
for minutes at a stretch
at the magic a spider weaves
between branches of the yew
tree below the cedars.

He comes around the corner
of the house bearing
the shell of a silent
cicada like a Host
in the palm of his hand.

Before falling asleep
he turns the pages
of colorful books
illustrated with webs
and trackways and calls
for me to come see
what will crawl
and creep and flutter
across the dark loam
of his dreams.

Norbert Krapf

Ed Muller

July 18

FOX

The fox that runs
its twenty miles a night
stopped at my house
stood nervously,
shrilled its electric note
to the open air—
a challenge? A mating call?
I thrilled at its quivering stalks,
wondered that it survives
beside the expressway
somewhere in suburbia.
Our patch of woods behind the house
can't be enough.

Charlene Babb Knadle

Jyoti Ganguly

FOREST

Green is a code, saying itself, unable to stop—
blissfully in love with its secret.
A bird whirs by me, wrapping up the air.
I gather courage
and say
the bird deep inside myself.
I say her movement, her eyes, the body
and the little feet.
As I move past the word suspicion disappears
and she answers
landing closer.
I say things over and over, not knowing
where else to start:
branch, eye, feather, moving toward each meaning
so the forest may begin to recognize me
as someone who knows
without the word.

Yaedi Ignatow

VIVARIUM

You & your kids slip
in one at a time, zip
the fly behind you,
push through the screen
that circumscribes this Eden.

You pause in a mesh-
draped vestibule
to keep a single jewel
from drifting free,
then move in, carefully

where a novice lepidopterist
pins pupae evolution paints
like hot rods to a makeshift
cardboard nursery. She spouts
pleasantries & canned facts

but the paper fires
Nabokov desired
dizzy you with bright,
off-kilter flight,
pilots learning to fly.

They'll scribble arcs
from bloom to bloom
a fortnight here, doodle
from milkweed to rue,
drill bee balm for nectar.

A swallowtail boutonniere,
proboscis rolled
like a garden hose,
lights on your shirt.
You & your brood peer

through cheese-cloth
where a luna moth
calm as a philosopher
waits to mate
starvation. Eyes

on its wings beg
for the silence haunting the hour
you wait for. You've never
been so sure. Your offspring
romp like flames among the flowers.

Dan Giancola

Arnold Brower

AWAKENING

Crane-slim he glides
across the lawn
on blades of sun

his long arms
arch the late noon
agile fingers strum the air

hovering in gray mist
his resonance
bathes my skin

in the falling light
trees cloak him
an oblong shape

drawing me beneath
his spreading wings
folding me inward

my counterpart of him
breathing here in me
awakens

growing new
each passing through the other
we breach the half-light

Janice Bishop

Christopher Corradino

July 22

SEVEN SWANS

All five cygnets reappeared today
two together
two together
one
one parent in the lead
another at the rear
assessing risk
hissing at the geese

With human notions I had worried
their absence
signaled
the juveniles
had wearied of
their parents'
overbearing vigilance

Now puffed with confidence
and ready for
their flight
the young are
proof
that caution
is to parenting
what pictures are to poems

Carol Schmidt

Eddie Mooney

July 23

CIRCA JULY

Such decisive heat: the day wavers.
Moths fluctuate between the lilies and the Queen Anne's lace.
I am not sure of anything.
Haze raises questions
As your leg moves
Just that much away.
Cicadas nag.
The dog considers barking.
High away a siren cries out and dies.
Dark comes between us.
All through the garden
Fireflies light up like small, untenable ideas.

Susan Astor

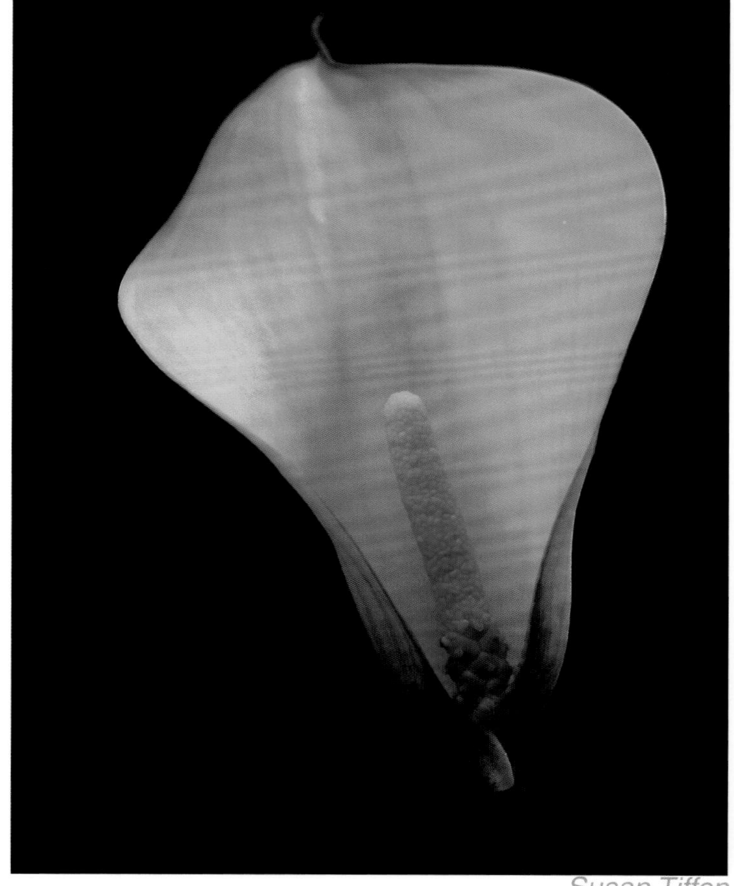

Susan Tiffen

July 24

DAYLILY

morning . . .

the first bud unfolds
a kaleidoscope of colors
tangerine   baby pink   oyster white

mid day . . .

petals flare like outstretched arms
accepting the rippling golden
strip of sun

late afternoon . . .

loss of tone   a turning inward
throat shrivels and shrinks

evening . . .

a limp remnant hangs on the stalk
the next bud stretches
peels open

Beverly Pion

Bob Schmitz

SMALL CRAFT

We moored our ark on wheels
next to the garage, a sixteen-foot
Penn Yan, a vessel of wood,
forty horses worth of Evinrude.

Warm weekends we'd haul her to
the shore, slide her ceremoniously
off the trailer into the salty river.
Knee-deep, I held the bow

until my father fish-flopped in
and the oily engine snorted life.
Then I pushed and leaped
onto the varnished deck, over the

bow light half-red, half-green
which was the way it seemed as we
thumped into the Sound keen
for fishing, afraid to drown

in all that wilderness without a tree
or sidewalk or lawn, fleeing
from job and school and church
to try our luck with God.

John Kaufman

William Duryea, Jr.

WITHOUT GIVING NOTICE

The sun has moved,
abandoned the red vase
it tried to ignite,
snitched its dazzling circlet

I find it now at four
inflaming the goldenrod,
torching a barn

I pursue it past lawn mowers grinding
their teeth, across fields
beginning to harvest shadows

I run, reaching
the next town and county,
expanses of states,
and continent

Everywhere, I almost
grasp its four o'clock
I nearly have it!

Tearing, I reach the rocky edge
and dive into ocean
Through channels of blindness,
swim a gasping course

The sun has moved
and leaves no wake
When surfacing to shake
its mane, throwing gold,
it remembers never to promise
itself to anyone

Diana Chang

Robert Bonanno

July 27

SPELLBOUND

Azure sea;
shimmering strand;
high-riding sky

Pines black as shadows;
gnats swarming like consciousness;
and lawns inflamed

White curls peak and dissolve
Dunes shrug as they dream
Air rollicks over the field

Leaves glance like nervous eyes
The mind says: See, perfection, too,
is reality

People—under a cloud
—nevertheless laugh,
charmed

Diana Chang

Ralph Pugliese, Jr.

July 28

WALKING TO THE SEA

we are walking to the sea
we have no compass
we have no map

we circle round
pick up clues
attend to small details

a shoe in the brambles
mushrooms
a paring knife

on the way to the sea
we listen for waves
look for osprey

tell stories about
high blue skies
and sudden storms

knowing there
are wrong turns
we follow the light

when talk
is difficult
we pile up stones

we are walking to the sea
composing letters
for our children

who will want
to know
of our journey

when a hairline crack
opens
we peer in for

what is found there
try to make room
in our hearts

we know the sea is near
when we find feathers
blown in by some sweet wind

colored glass is a sure sign
Bottle green
foam green
jade

walking to the sea
we listen
to each other

try to describe
the lump
in our throats

when we arrive at the sea
we will throw off
our coats and shoes

swim underwater
learn
how to fish

Ginger Williams

July 29

SUBURBAN STREET

A kite string hangs from a telephone wire,
chalk marks the foul line for hoops,
a bike, its blue paint chipped, lies
in a driveway, a lawnmower
drones, cicadas throb,
a retiree edges his
lawn for the third
time this week.

Adam D. Fisher

Kate Kelly

SUMMER, SUNDAY NIGHT

We go upstairs to read bedtime stories.
A ghost flashes across the dark front yard.
The phone rings and quits ringing,
a hard knock hesitates on the door.

The stories are about animals and good deeds rewarded.
Our ghost comes in by a separate entrance.
The phone rings once.
A downy woodpecker flies by the window

and a car passes, a neighbor coming home. Headlights
bewilder the thick July head of hair on the trees
and the child sneezes, giggling toward sleep.

The door closes. The house lights lower.
The moon gains height, fills out, pulling water's weight
along the shore—the tide times an early dream

Graham Everett

Bill Kreisberg

July 31

GETTING TO KNOW YOUR HOUSE

Sitting

Have you sat in every chair in your house?
Have you sat in the dark in every chair of your house?

Fidelity

Do you glance at other houses out of the corner of your eye?

Hats

As a courtesy, do you take your bowler off in your house?

Sleeping

Have you slept in every room of your house?
Have you had the falling dream in every room of your house?

Plumbing

Do you understand plumbing?

History

Climbing the stairs, do you ever meet a younger you coming down?
In this dark way, have you also slipped past previous owners?

The House in Space

When the oil burner goes, does the house seem to be motoring through space?
When it stops, does the house come to rest?

At Sea

When you wake in the night, does the house seem to have pulled up anchor, to be adrift?

Smoking

When you smoke your pipe, does the house fall asleep?

Death

Have you considered your house living on, after you?

Ron Overton

August 1

SENRYŪ

Clothes on an old stick
where blackbirds dig up breakfast . . .
Stalks of corn staring.

Hornets in their nests,
ants in hills, and bees in hives . . .
Can it be Sunday?

Stanley H. Barkan

SUMMER

It is an orgy that makes me nervous.
The weather goes on and on
to be loved with continuous ecstasy.
But things interrupt, like calling the dentist.

The memory of summers intervenes with the present:
a picnic by the roadside in Pennsylvania,
driving a car full of sleeping children through moonlight,
water, its cucumber smell,
its blue window to shatter, its cool embrace
to gather around me.

But the desire exceeds the consummation,
the memory more vivid than the present.
Summer, rushing by uncaptured
restlessly burns away like grass.

Then comes the rain.
I sink into it with blessed torpor,
my bones heavy, my blood turning to mud.
The wind on its great wings erases sound,
wipes out all desire, all preconceived notion
of pleasure with the music on the panes
and the leafy branches sweeping out there,
shaking their green hair.
Even the garden chairs forgotten
in the bower seem more blissfully fulfilled
with only rain sitting on them.

I lean out the window, wishing I were
a chair.

Claire Nicolas White

Jyoti Ganguly

FISH-SHAPED PAUMANOK

I ride my horse
on soft dirt surfaces
hugged by fields of corn

these roads I know
are the roots that clutch
trees bent toward each other
a canopy hovers over the path

showers of leaves
winding asymmetrical stone walls
meadows dotted with farm stalls
brimming with mosaic of fruits   vegetables   flowers

stands of shrub oak and pine
make pockets of dark woods
where deer   rabbits   raccoons watch me

I ride to the everlasting beach
sweet with the scent of salt water
seaweed and what the breeze carries

this is the East End I know
the land speaks for itself . . .

Beverly Pion

George DeCamp

PERHAPS I'M SEVEN

exploring
in the eel grass by the water's
edge. My blue suit's a dot down
the beach to Grandma wearing pearls
and white wading shoes.
I imagine she's been berrying
with my mother who's probably
gathering up our towels.

I'm busy following the flow
of some scuttling crabs called
periwinkles, I think, and pretending
I don't notice my relatives' voices.
I am not going back even as
their cries become more distant.
I want to chase waves,
poke seaweed into bubble holes
and I will not eat corn on the cob
or blueberry cobbler. Tilting my face
to the sun, I stick out my tongue
for its yellow shine.

And suddenly I'm running
on the sand, leaving
squishy footprints, running
for my feet, running
for how we come
into this life by falling
away.

Ginger Williams

Vidal Al Martinez

CONSIDER THE LILIES OF THE SEA

Their salt wet life erased, eroded, only
The shells of snails lie on the sand,
Their color darkens toward the whorl's conclusion,
The center is nearly black. Even the fragments
Faithfully observe their tribal custom
Of involution; the motionless whirlpool
Is clearly written on the broken shield.

The two joined petals of a small
Tooth-white clamshell stand ajar, and mimic
The opening of wings or of a songbook;
Leaves that a minute and obscure
Death sprung open in a depth of sea;
Held in one's hand, they still present
The light obedient gesture that let go of time.

And close to these frail, scattered, and abandoned
Carvings which were the armor and the art
Of dark blind jellies that the fish have eaten,
The big Atlantic cumulates and pours,
Flashes, is felled, and streaks among the pebbles
With wildfire foam.

Anne Porter

Russell Cameron Perry

August 7

from
INSCRIPTIONS: SONG OF MYSELF #21

. . . .
I am he that walks with the tender and growing night,
I call to the earth and sea half-held by the night.

Press close bare-bosomed night! Press close magnetic
nourishing night!
Night of south winds! Night of the large few stars!
Still nodding night! Mad naked summer night!

Smile O voluptuous cool-breathed earth!
Earth of the slumbering and liquid trees!
Earth of departed sunset! Earth of the mountains misty-topt!
Earth of the vitreous pour of the full moon just tinged with blue!
Earth of shine and dark mottling the tide of the river!
Earth of the limpid gray of clouds brighter and clearer for my sake!
Far-swooping elbowed earth! Rich apple-blossomed earth!
Smile, for your lover comes!
. . . .

Walt Whitman

Ed Muller

August 8

SEWING MACHINE IN THE PINES

A warbler flits
From branch to branch, tree to tree,
A summer voice in the Pine Barrens.
I stop to look to these twittering notes high in the canopy,
Only catching brief glimpses of a tiny, olive-yellow bird
Who is all business,
A pine Warbler hiding in heavy cover
Of bushy pine needles without knowing it.
With no binoculars, it teases me with a voice
Whose trill, fine as silken thread,
Running off a bobbin of an old sewing machine,
Has stitched me to this forest tapestry.

Tom Stock

Arnold Brower

RIDING THE DORY

She pulls against the tide,
trembles from the movement of sea
flowing outward and the wakes of boats
that parade with us into the channel.

We surrender to the currents
and steer our way towards
the green and red buoys that mark the way.

This is my brother's first boat,
dressed in new paint, spotlessly clean.
It is cobalt and white, has new fish wells
sanded so smoothly, they bright like the sides
of blue fish when they school and return in unison.

We pass a small island,
homes inches away from the tide line,
a bait station suspended above the waves on pilings.
Open water lies ahead, turning turquoise
as it breaks against the beaches off Democrat Point.

A gull sees us, changes direction and follows.

He cries behind our boat
for the favors of old bait, and the bellies
of cleaned fish to be thrown to him.

After an hours, we are alone.

The sound of the diesel and the chimes
of the anchor line become a mantra for our work.
White sun arcs across the Great South Bay,
stenciling shadows on the bottom of the boat,
my brother's shoulders and capped head,
wrists bound to the rake, my hands separating the harvest.

Blue sky and clouds race across the fish wells.

Gladys Henderson

Sheldon Pollack

LONG ISLAND SOUND
Nissequogue

When you live in a place
a long time
you learn its secrets.

At supper time
all along the Sound,
no one is swimming
in the sun's reflection
as it sets
on green salty water
that envelops your body,
heals all your wounds;
where the sky meets
the edge of earth's curve
and becomes one.

Kathaleen Donnelly

Sheldon Pollack

August 11

NATURAL, AS WASTE . . .

In high summer
plants cluster
together. The growth
so many different flowers
makes on soil
never plowed con-
fuses yellows and pinks.
Green still predominates
of course. Everywhere
there's a flower there
also is much green
surrounding, or
encircling it, or
intersticed between
it and another.   Brocade
we call a cloth
so textured. This
is natural, as waste;
a world is breathing
upward through this
earth. High summer
growth headies us
with perfumes: grass
mashed beneath a foot,
the high rancid
sweet smell of sap

Richard Elman

Bob Schmitz

I SIT VERY STILL

If you sit very still, they said,
with a bit of food in the palm of your hand.
If you sit long enough, day after day . . .

One green summer morning
I will myself to be utterly still,
perfectly quiet.

I hear my breath. They hear it too.
They hear me swallow,
they hear my eyes blink.

I am noisy, enormous, the wrong color.
A restless misfit in this cool still life,
they see that too.

Then one lights on the heel of my hand,
takes a crumb, flits away, returns
at least a dozen times, brings others.

I am patient, they are hungry.
We are partners on the threshold
of a small future.

I will tell them that each time
one ate from my hand,
it felt like a kiss.

Arlene Eager

Bob Schmitz

August 13

FEELING FLIERS

I sit in my suburban garden
listen to sparrows' gentle peep,
doves' soft coos, imagine
a sparrow landing in my palm,
feel its twig-feet grasp
my fingers, gently
close my hand to feel
its soft feathers flutter
against my skin, then open
to watch it fly,
the feel of its body
still in my hand.

Later, damsel flies
electric blue, flit by.
One, then another rests
on my arm, my knee. I'm glad
to give them a place to stop.

Adam D. Fisher

Bob Schmitz

August 14

NEAR VIEW

The ant
does not measure
the circumference
of the earth,
the
distance of the sky.
Its territory
is not allotted
in miles, kilometers
acres, or plots.
It
climbs the tree
surmounts the rock
invades the cave
letting each exist
in its enormity
making no effort to
reduce to something
comprehensible. In
the Zen moment of
its focus, it
is able to
act.

Charlene Babb Knadle

Vidal Al Martinez

CONVERSATION WITH A GRASSHOPER

That ratchet, ratchet, click-click-click,
was difficult to ignore,
his song to lure a lady.
I wanted him to stop,
offered watermelon rinds, lettuce,
to bring him nearer, make a pitch for quiet.
But he just ate, lifted a leg and grated some more.

I wasn't attracted to his tune.
He told me it didn't matter,
claimed I took him for a locust,
said I wouldn't know a cricket if I stepped on one.

I was close to it; he was near my shoe,
one quick stomp, silence.
But his sad melody softened me,
even if it wasn't my kind of love song.

Geraldine Morrison

Laura M. Eppig

from

INSCRIPTIONS: SONG OF MYSELF #52

The spotted hawk swoops by and accuses me—he complains of my gab and my loitering.

I too am not a bit tamed—I too am untranslatable,
I sound my barbaric yawp over the roofs of the world.

The last scud of day holds back for me,
It flings my likeness after the rest and true as any on the shadowed wilds,
It coaxes me to the vapor and the dust.

I depart as air—I shake my white locks at the runaway sun,
I effuse my flesh in eddies and drift it in lacy jags.

I bequeath myself to the dirt to grow from the grass I love,
If you want me again look for me under your boot-soles.

You will hardly know who I am or what I mean,
But I shall be good health to you nevertheless,
And filter and fibre your blood.

Failing to fetch me at first keep encouraged,
Missing me one place search another,
I stop some where waiting for you.

Walt Whitman

Gene Keyes

PEBBLES

scud the beach creating
counter-waves to driftwood
ringing in the tide like warning bells
on buoys saving ships from ruin.

The pebble is harbinger of peace.
No land mines here as the sun
rather indulgently splays across the surging
whitecaps
frothing toward the sand
tossed ever so insolently back to sea
knowing, as every child does,
that this was a wasted voyage.
The room unkempt was actually okay.
The lounge chair jutting sneakers
attached to a leggy body was home.
The cell phone a mere evolutionary attachment.
So grain by granulated grain and sand comes home
mistress to neither sun nor surf.
It has its own resiliency.
Footprints marked forever there
are removed like a half-finished sentence in a
gust of wind.
And young writers carved here are like
a first novel frozen
in a pre-celluloid state.
Testimonies written by day,
sand castles, moats, gray out around
the furrowed brow.

We gather up toys at night,
a lone soda can, a hapless straw,
a burnished tree stump never captured in a
captain's log—these remain.

James P. Friel

It is half-past life on the beach.
We are measured kindly but firmly.
There is not the show of the office,
there are no press releases washed ashore.
Only the seashell cocked to ear captures a
symphony
that at age three Mozart used to hear,
and the tide rises within us,
with the mere thumping of the heart,
all that blood skin-encased . . .
so, only the cruelty of sand remains:
When all is said and done
we will tear.

Aija Birzgalis

August 18

TIMELESS MOMENT

From Fire Island National Seashore

Cloudless day.
Lazy, empty beach.
I sit against a piece of driftwood
Resting, waiting.
I let a handful of sand drop,
Forming a granular column
Like an old-fashioned hourglass.
Minutes and seconds drop away.
Dark particles fall straight down,
Light particles fly away . . .

Like this moment.

Tom Stock

Aija Birzgalis

August 19

AUGUST 20TH

The drive home in pre-weekend traffic goes fairly well.
No one makes any stupid moves and that's good
because I'm driving my thirteen-year-old son
back from camp. He sits quiet for a while
watching out the passenger-side window.

As we turn off the expressway
and head cross island, he notes that the place
looks like he's never been away.

We're both another summer older.

Graham Everett

Heather Cirincione

EDWARD HOPPER'S *ROAD AND TREES*

The trees form a line of dark green beside
the gray roadway. The sun's
lowering light breaks ocher and aquamarine

against the two trees that face the decline
of the afternoon.
The road shoulder closest to us, catches more

of the bright, showing grass-green with patches
of brown. A pale-blue band
of sky is creamed over with cloud in one corner.

We never see the road this way. We are always
only on it, headed somewhere
or at an end and getting off. We never

keep in mind the ordinary sight
and what having it
has meant to us alive to our passages.

Everywhere here light dances
with its absence,
the shadows that have so much to offer.

Joseph Stanton

RHODODENDRON

I found a rhododendron blooming in
the spring and took one blossom
into my room where it spread in
a gown of bubbles, budding bells,

pink petals, mouths closed tight at first
then opening in layers. Bodies burst
and tongues like adder clusters curl and thrust
their pollen at me with their golden dust.

The road into their hearts are dreams I dare
not follow. How they draw me in
to where they branch off from a pale green stem
embraced by darker leaves, their diadem.

Claire Nicolas White

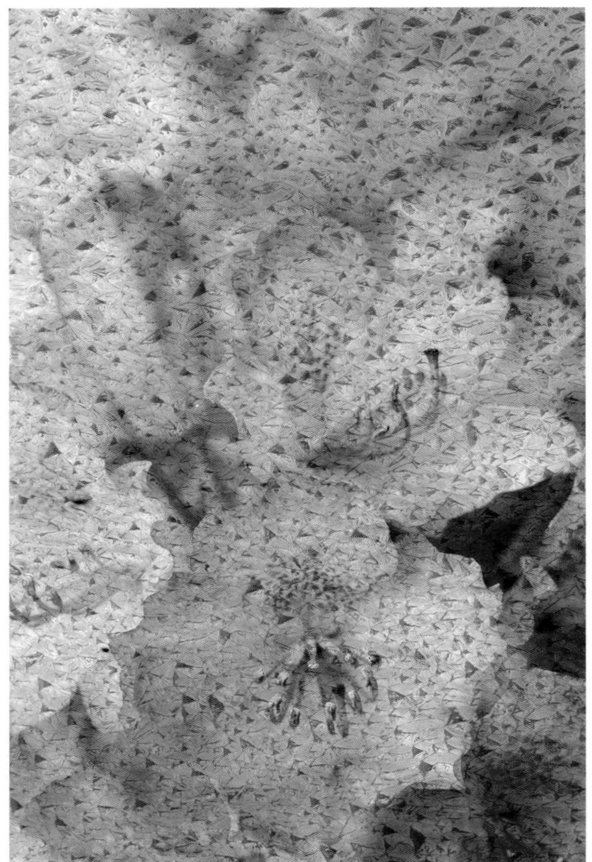

Linda Russo

August 22

TURTLE FOR GRAVES' POND

She owned everything,
shadows of water lilies,
flashing sides of minnows,
the clouds of August racing
across the skin of an old
farm pond. Her feet
were planted firmly
in the callow silt
and if she chose to move,
a froth of mud lifted
with each gesture.
She was the Thoreau
of the world, judging the quality
of spring and the price of living.
All creatures remained enclosed
by her choice, delicate bud,
earthworm, duckweed and cress.
At night, when the moon
glazed the surface and stars grasped
the edge of ripples, she would rise.
Her body illuminated,
she would float motionless,
while the night offered anthems to her.
Once satisfied, she would slip back
into the blackness, a blade of moonlight
under the scales of the pond.

Gladys Henderson

Marc Oliveri

THE GLADNESS OF NATURE

Is this a time to be cloudy and sad,
  When our mother Nature laughs around;
When even the deep blue heavens look glad,
  And gladness breathes from the blossoming ground?

There are notes of joy from the hang-bird and wren,
  And the gossip of swallows through all the sky;
The ground-squirrel gayly chirps by his den,
  And the wilding bee hums merrily by.

The clouds are at play in the azure space
  And their shadows at play on the bright-green vale,
And here they stretch to the frolic chase,
  And there they roll on the easy gale.

There's a dance of leaves in that aspen bower,
  There's a titter of winds in that beechen tree,
There's a smile on the fruit, and a smile on the flower,
  And a laugh from the brook that runs to the sea.

And look at the broad-faced sun, how he smiles
  On the dewey earth that smiles in his ray,
On the leaping waters and gay young isles;
  Ay, look, and he'll smile thy gloom away.

William Cullen Bryant

Vidal Al Martinez

STUMP POND

1.

A stage road and a watermill,
a river plugged, a hollow flooded.
Here we drank our fill
of pastoral and bass, rented
Sundays of serenity in flat-bottomed
boats, rowing, father and sons
above the trees, between
the turnpike and the highway innocent
of history, afloat, adrift . . .

2.

Once by the pond
a turtle tumbled like
a hubcap down
into the water.

I felt crosscut,
a man stumped
and teetering between
flight and gravity.

3.

I heard it first. Rhymed vowels
of dusk across Stump Pond.
Response wicked up to *owl*.

I followed the clear margin,
homing on the sound
until I stopped and cocked

my ears and raised my sight
above the ground. I saw
arched ears and ponded eyes,

ancient Roman face
of the great horned owl—
imperious, incredulous gaze

on what stood below,
hunter or prey
it could not say until

I shifted a foot
to hold my ground
and it lifted its wings to claim

thickening air, all
the nights my island wakes
to comforting sounds.

4.

Blunted by bone,
weather or error,
it held its sharpened
shape, the uttering

line, flawed harmony
of art. I hold it
now in Oregon, fondling
an arrowhead like a rosary

bead, like Paumanok
crystallized and lost
as the river of a tribe
called Nissequogue.

John Kaufman

WHISTLE OR HOOT

The bird that sings to itself
is never a lonely or frightened bird;
though if before it were silent,
darting its head for worms
or worrisome matters,
now that it sings to itself
it triumphs, whistle or hoot.

David Ignatow

Kathleen Hervey

August 26

AN ENCOUNTER

In the early shade
of my yard,
I sit alone
in the company
of flowers.
A bumblebee
appears.
His black body
seems to be
armored in leather.
The hum
of his wings,
taken as warning.
He is the size
of a fat thumb.
He never moves
in straight lines.
For an instant,
it is I
who is anxious,
anticipating
the pain
of his wrath.
To him,
I am the invisible,
prepared to strike.
As he leaves,
I remember, he
is only a bee,
Like me,
out early
in search of nectar,
hoping
to add a little
sweetness
to this world.

Daniel Thomas Moran

HAIKU

They're only flowers,
golden petals and pollen—
but look at the stars!

Stanley H. Barkan

Richard Hunt

August 28

RED SUNFLOWERS

Black as rusty suns
shine these high overhead.
I take them in my room
and watch their pistils shed

a rain of gold. Inside
the pools of their dark hearts
squirm myriad furry signs
of vegetable sperm.

The velvet petals turn
a red dark as wine.
A sudden orange flash
highlights them at the tips.

Then, fading, one by one
they shyly fold upon
themselves to hide the burst
of seeds, and winking, close

their monstrance in eclipse.

Claire Nicolas White

Richard Hunt

THE ISLAND

At night I can hear the Island
counting her losses
like an old gypsy poking
at loose change
in the palm of her wrinkled hand
pretending that her bright
fish-eye did not see the slow
wasting of her wild beauty—
the bird singing woods of pine
and oak, the wide-eyed flowers,
winding paths of berry bushes,
owls, the soft-footed fox, farmlands
and cornfields with stalks
straight as flagpoles, reaching
for the sky
and she did not see the loss
of clam-filled bay waters
clear as a polished mirror
threatened by careless hands
casting poisoned sludge
over gentle tide waters…
Still I can hear the Island singing
when the moon rises above her
like a faithful lover strumming
the sea
while the salty air settles
around her to listen.

Florence M. Hughes

Bob Schmitz

August 30

THE GREAT BLUE HERON . . .

skims over mirrors
of watery places
flashes up like flames
dips down to court
the green reeds.

In our canoe
we float close
to her hunched form
draw in a breath
fold forward
to listen
to her coarse wild song
song in the wind
song to fly with
song to curl up in

a stillness
down
to the ground.

Ginger Williams

Frank Muller

from

SEA-DRIFT: OUT OF THE CRADLE ENDLESSLY ROCKING

Out of the cradle endlessly rocking,
Out of the mocking-bird's throat, the musical shuttle,
Out of the Ninth-month midnight,
Over the sterile sands and the fields beyond, where the child
leaving his bed wander'd alone, bareheaded, barefoot,
Down from the shower'd halo,
Up from the mystic play of shadows twining and twisting as if they were alive,
Out from the patches of briers and blackberries,
From the memories of the bird that chanted to me,
From your memories sad brother, from the fitful risings and fallings I heard,
From under that yellow half-moon late-risen and swollen as if with tears.
From those beginning notes of yearning and love there in the mist,
From the thousand responses of my heart never to cease,
From the myriad thence-arous'd words,
From the word stronger and more delicious than any,
From such as now they start the scene revisiting,
As a flock, twittering, rising, or overhead passing,
Borne hither, ere all eludes me, hurriedly,
A man, yet by these tears a little boy again,
Throwing myself on the sand, confronting the waves,
I, chanter of pains and joys, uniter of here and hereafter,
Taking all hints to use them, but swiftly leaping beyond them,
A reminiscence sing.
. . . .

Walt Whitman

Kathaleen Donnelly

NORTH SHORE

A land made tall by its trees.

Hidden in rooftops
the crow recalls a cruel punishment
which the sea endured on rock-heavy shores
to the west.

Summer cries
like a teakettle in the neighbor's kitchen.

Hoping to capture the sound of crows,
I step outside into wet morning grass—
and discover, instead, the pawprints
of a neighborhood cat.

This bird sang until it was bidden.

George Wallace

Kathaleen Donnelly

TRAVELING
for Glenn Cuyjet

Sometimes
I take the
long way
home.
To see
what
I have not
been missing.
To be
nearer
those things
I can
do without.
I fulfill
that need
for distance
and
misspent time.
Semi-circles
in exchange for
straight lines.

Daniel Thomas Moran

Stuart McCallum

September 3

THINGS ARE FOR GOOD

The ocean is practicing white writing on its liquid tablet
never done finding out what it needs to say
Day after day the afternoon develops itself in arias
  lofted across the earth

Each summer walls of wheat recur,
trees change and prevail

On any side of the world
beyond friends and ties

what happens
happens

miraculously now
and again now

The moon, too, has no visible means of support
It wills its way across the night

Robert Bonanno

Diana Chang

September 4

NAUTICA

It was the ocean and then
the bay that beckoned—
a liquid ballroom of delight
summoning me to enter.
There I would romp and dance
as Thetis smiled taking her ease
among the placid dunes.

Relying on the current's flow
which never fails to soothe,
I ventured, always returning,
compelled to celebrate the minnows
roaming by the horseshoe crabs,
motley, polygamous attendants
boldly courting along the shore—
a wedding feast triumphant
while daisies crowned the sand
and swayed beside the piquant herbs.

In conjoint acquiescence
they all remained
determined to collaborate
and grant me perpetuity.

Clementine C. Rabassa

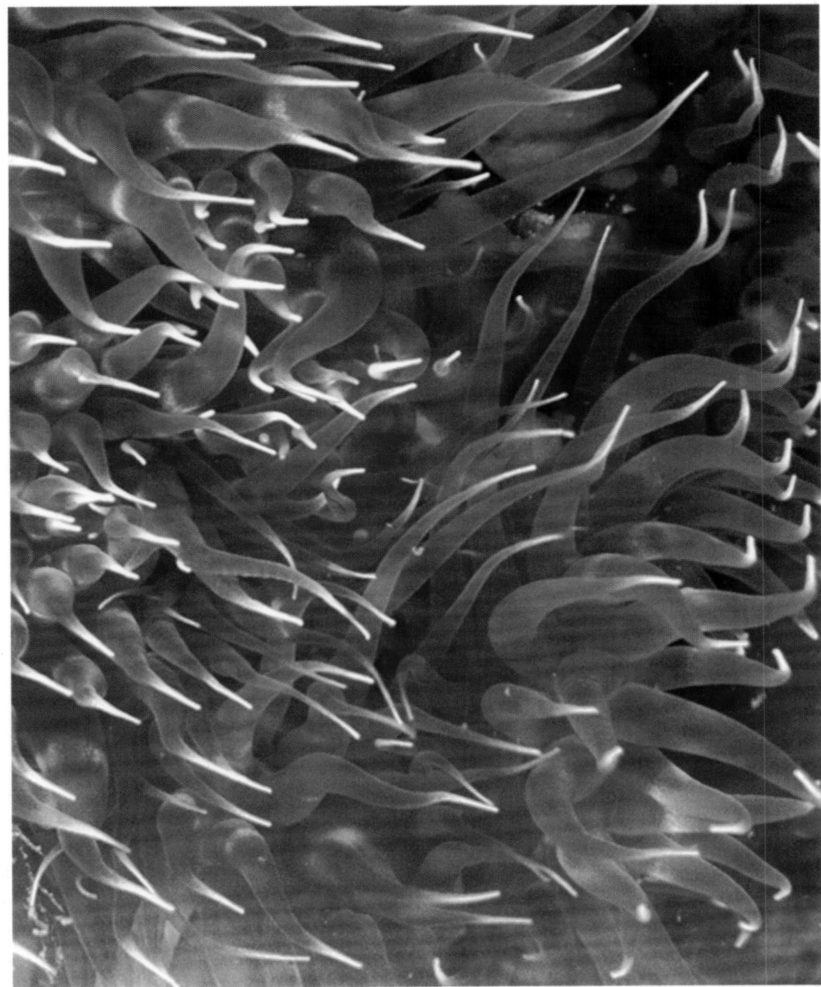

Peter Brink

September 5

NOTES FROM PORPOISE COVE

September 12, 2001

After the fall, I wade along
the tide, lie down in the dunes
to rest in a nest of sea and sky.

After the fall, I sift and pile
what is left: filigreed shells
in shades of rose and ecru

hollow bones from a gull
the empty carapace
of a horseshoe crab.

Ginger Williams

Aija Birzgalis

SEDUCTION

The skin of the pool
taut as a veil
tears as I slip in
then weaves about me
a web of light.
Ravished
I'm trapped
in sun.

The beach, a perfect arc
of pebbles embraces
water in which float
viscous corollas
of medusas.
No matter where I go
water, my lover,
prepares its sting.

Claire Nicolas White

Aija Birzgalis

September 7

from

INSCRIPTIONS: SONG OF MYSELF #22

You sea! I resign myself to you also—I guess what you mean,
O behold from the beach your crooked inviting fingers,
I believe you refuse to go back without feeling of me,
We must have a turn together, I undress, hurry me out of sight of the land,
Cushion me soft, rock me in billowy drowse,
Dash me with amorous wet, I can repay you.

Sea of stretch'd ground-swells,
Sea breathing broad and convulsive breaths,
Sea of the brine of life and of unshovell'd yet always-ready graves,
Howler and scooper of storms, capricious and dainty sea,
I am integral with you, I too am of one phase and of all phases.
. . . .

Walt Whitman

Marlene Weinstein

September 8

SEPTEMBER 9TH

What a wonderful full moon in the last month
of a way too hot summer! All about the house
crickets' stridulated song rises
with the incoming humidity and its
flimsy blindfolding of the moon.

My own habits lie not under the microscope
of this looking. They're not even mine.
Centuries of breeding shape their actions.

Like the wolf feeding itself through winter
with vicious endorphins, I am more animal
than something complex as personality
blessed by cricket and star-filled sky.

Graham Everett

Kate Kelly

FOG

This morning
I cannot see
the garden from the porch
I try to remember the rows
    squash, beans, carrots, dill
I am not sure

I am not sure
I can remember your face
What I see is a picture
    you, standing in the roadway
    waving
    looking elsewhere

If I walk
I can push back the fog
    porch to fence
    fence to woodpile
    wood to garden

Is there a path to your face
    fingers to forearm
    forearms to shoulder
    shoulder to neck
I am not sure

I am not sure
I can find what is knowable
by way of what is known

This morning I cannot see
the porch from the garden

Weslea Sidon

Frank Muller

ABSOLUTES

absolutes
run aground
where the tern
speaks
the gull
is real
at his red-spotted bill
like blood of a fish
swimming too high
to the dip of hunger
in the eye

senses brim
and beach birds fly to beach plum
with rugosa rose

have been seasoned
by these
in a disc of sand
where the arc of a stone is carrying
a star to the sea

D. H. Melhem

Bob Schmitz

"THE ANGLER"
Georges Seurat, 1884

By the river's grassy edge
the dark brown form
in bowler hat holds
the yellow pole with his right hand
He rests the other in his pocket
His coat covers the
knees of his creased trousers
He's dressed for a poem

Maxwell Corydon Wheat, Jr.

Stuart McCallum

September 13

FROM THE PORCH IN SUMMER

That peace we seek, is
that peace we find.

The peace we make.

In the exhalations of sky
upon leaf and limb.

In the ripest berry on the tree,
and the most bitter.

In the journeys which lead nowhere,
and the ones which find us home.

In the reassurance of muted sun
through a thin gauze of cloud.

In the perfect and
uncountable nuances of green.

In the silence beyond speaking and
our surrender to mystery.

In knowing what we must,
what we can, and what

We can not.

Daniel Thomas Moran

M. James Pion

SOME SEPTEMBERS

It feels like summer
will go on forever.

This one for example
well into the middle of the month
and you can tell it's going to be a hot one.

It is not exactly the stillness of the morning air

I guess it is the way
all across the neighborhood
locusts are buzzing like defective
electrical appliances, and one crow

starts barking over by Ezra's Pond
the way they did centuries ago, when Matinecock
told time by the crows. Oh, and off
in the distance, it is in the way

a lone motorboat scuds across the harbor.

Somehow you know the summer heat
is going to be oppressive on mornings like these
even though it is mid-September.

There! In the eave beyond your line of vision
a dove moans. You moan once, too—
if the air would only just move!

This is about the time that,
chucking the window up one last notch
trying to draw a broader breath

you finally discover exactly how it is
those hornets have been getting into the house.

George Wallace

September 15

Eric Lohse

A POEM TO DOORS UNLOCKED

I seldom lock my doors

thieves will certainly choose one of my two
neighbors' well-kept blacktop driveways
  neatly lined with Belgian block
  and scoured clean by leaf blowers

instead of my dirt one
  full of stones and rutted by so many winters
  and so much mud in spring.

In summer I do latch the kitchen screen door after dark
  when nimble-fingered raccoons
  come down to the river for mussels.

I seldom lock my front door,
although in my house
there are valuable things everywhere,
  but nothing worth stealing.

Some compact discs,

The Canterbury Tales read in Middle English
Fantastique by Berlioz
the *Goldberg Variations*
the *Vivaldi Glorias*

Some birds' nests found on woodland trails
  dropped by furious winter winds

and a Christmas angel
well-fashioned of paper,
holding a tiny songbook

in September, still poised atop
her Christmas pedestal,

a green painted wooden bucket
that once carried milk from barn to kitchen.

In the living room
a beloved table saw

idle now, but still holding memories of cupboards
made with raised-panel doors,

its rustic surface
yearning for the touch of Northern White Pine.

Russell Cameron Perry

Russell Cameron Perry

September 16

LOCAL TOMATOES

None of this namby-pamby
vine-ripened California cardboard
that's green in Orange County,
stripped and shipped to us,

while being coaxed to ripen
through six color stages
by blasts of ethylene.

Nah, just feel the weight.
There is no mistaking
that solid, stolid love apple,
that reliable red, eat-me-tonight
Long Island beefsteak tomato.

Barbara Reiher-Meyers

Stuart McCallum

September 17

THE VISITOR

Almost within reach
of the breakfast table

a sudden whir of black
and white fastens onto

the dying lilac. Elizabeth
climbs onto the Quaker bench,

presses her nose flat against
cold glass, and chortles,

Birt! A hairy woodpecker,
the first we have seen,

flutters onto a log
of the dead ash I felled

along Main Street. Its beak
drills wider the holes beetles

bored through its trunk.
Ash dust sprays the patio

like holy water. Traffic
sounds fade like bad memories.

We breathe in rhythm around
this beat of beak on wood.

Norbert Krapf

Vidal Al Martinez

SEPTEMBER

September is a month of déjà vu.
We look for a classroom in the past,
For someone who calls back somebody else.
Summer hovers in the clean gone sky
In dappled richly leaning greens.
The huge lit sea is heaving full.
It's cool before the apricot of dawn,
A giant orange moon hanging on the sky.
We head toward the core of winter
And stirrings of the summer still to be.

Kay Kidde

Frank Muller (Montage with Larry Landolfi)

MOON-DAWN

Along the somber east the flower of night, full-blown,
  A sad and sacred perfume breathes, and the heavy Vast
The huge odor of the sea fills with a sense unknown,
  Of mystery and sleep. Dim twilight hangs aghast—
Save for one trembling star, unlit from zone to zone.

Bitter and sharp and sweet, stern as all things that are,
  The odor of life is here—wet sand and rank seaweed.
The waters, clear and cold, make music from afar—
  Along the low, flat sky recede, recede, recede
The unwinged wastes of wave beyond the evening-star.

But lo, from out the darkness—now, from the clouds unfurled,
  A sudden sword of moonlight strikes on sea and lands:
Odor and sound and light mingle, a breath is whirled
  Ecstatic through all things, that feel the vibrant hand,
Holy, harmonious God, upon the strings of the world.

John Hall Wheelock

IN STORM-WATCH SEASON

The foaming clematis
Has finished blooming
The autumn
Equinox is here
The air is very still
But day and night
Storms in the Caribbean
Keep the Atlantic roaring

The ocean
Is pouring fog
Into the trees
And with it the fresh smells
Of eelgrass and of kelp
Float inland from the torn
And churning beaches

In the storm-haunted evening
A cricket
Has begun to sing
A streetlamp shines
Deep in the fog
A burr
Of golden light

In three months' time
We will have snow
In three months' time
The savior will be born.

Anne Porter

Ann Glazebrook

AUTUMN EQUINOX

Decaying leaves crunching
underfoot
running from the wind.
Tones of burnt orange
ochre and rust
paint the timber
a canvas
that only God could paint.

Mia Barkan Clarke

Bob Schmitz

September 22

REFLECTIONS ON A SWAMP MAPLE IN EARLY AUTUMN

Could it be I never noticed
how her early blush is rose
shot through with ochre
then flames of tangerine, vermillion, scarlet
and how each serrated leaf
trembles before the winds of September
how that tight August connection
suddenly slackens
letting go in a flurry of color?

Is it possible that I never
sat at this window gazing
across porch and lawn, ferns and ivy
to observe the twist and spin, the float and flutter
of each leaf setting sail into a blue sky?

Did I never pray at this altar
where summer's curtains close
where autumn's slant light pleats
inward as if folding a fan?

Now I wonder if our every move
towards darkness is as if
for the first time,
driven by the need to blaze.
Each motion quick
and fleeting as any gesture
made by desire.

Ginger Williams

John Brokos

NEXT DOOR
Westbury

Our neighbor plants the earth
As if this were Iowa.
Her husband for nearly fifty years
Grumbles about his receding lawn
Being gobbled by tomatoes and autumn flowers.
They eat food that tastes of soil,
Look at each other with dimming eyes,
And their hands warm for they are fire
And they are music and their house overflows
Like an apple tree in autumn.

Arthur Dobrin

September 24

MONTAUK CHIAROSCURO

for Jean

A rock, hump big as a sea turtle,
rides the tide by Montauk Point,
lower half blacked by wet, upper whitewashed
with guano.

A great black-backed gull struts
on the rock, head and breast white.
A double-crested cormorant, black as
ebony,

lands besides him. They compose the black
chop of sea, the azure sky with cotton
cumulus on the horizon, the gray North Fork,
the bleached beach.

Along the strand six towheads, teens
in black spandex shorts and white t's,
stroll, spy, not the vista, but a target
for their stones . . .

The birds, the boys have flown. The clack
of stone on rock yields its echo
to the low hum of a distant
fishing boat.

George Held

Eric Lohse

September 26

CLAMMING AT ST. JAMES HARBOR

I

As I dragged the bullrake belted at my waist,
backed away, my weight against the chain,
my arms hauling at the crossbars,
and brought the basket up

filled with waterlogged driftwood, starfish,
stones, spidercrabs, snails, shells,
and sorted out the few clams
big enough to keep,

flounders scribbled ahead of their mud wakes,
schools of transparent minnows dotted
and dashed codes against my legs,
young eels kissed my sneakers

with words: this you shall always remember.
This water is the true blood, this
shore is the true body, this
sky the incarnate light.

II

Now, years later, perhaps walking, or reading,
or talking to someone I've long loved,
I leave my self to kneel
at my own grave.

I kneel in a flat of the harbor at low tide, beside
a trench I've raked, facing the mill's oars
that now whirl down a lattice
of sun and shadow.

I hold relics in my arms: the jeweled claws of crabs,
strands of seaweed shining like saints' hair,
skates' eggs like black scarabs,
clamshells white as time's

waters could wash them. Each time now I kneel longer,
until the tide shall turn, the sun's red blade
drop, gulls fall from the night's tree
to my eyes like dark leaves.

William Heyen

SCALLOP

Robust, yet finely chiseled,
You exude confidence;
The channels of your experience
Make you wise, lend strength
To your character;
Hidden in the crenellations,
Are the many facets
Of your self.

Carolyn Emerson

Peter Brink

September 28

BLACK-FACED LAMB

In your arms you clutch
the zinnia harvest
the farmchild cut
in a field
high above the Sound,
petal-tips already seared
with autumn: mauve
night-blue, russet-brown.

The night upon us, Annie,
we'd better go.
It comes like a black-faced lamb
that finds us in shadows
just below the timberline,
then runs its mouth along the thighs—
but look: the longing,
oh, such longing, there
in its eyes.

Vince Clemente

Linda Russo

PASSAMAQUODDY SUNRISE

Not awake yet, the sun begins
through fog, a still life:
a radiant melon on a quilt.

Eight minutes late,
I rise, try to meditate,
to choose with love, not need,
to weed illusions:
the magnetism of money,
the lustered petals of lips.

Webs of mist vanish from the valley,
an arrowhead glitters on the lake.
Pure spring water waits under pine,
but wild lupine & lilac distract me.

Ah, Lord, weave
surplices of Queen Anne's lace,
propagate the daisy in purple clover.
Expand the rings the feeding bass
break on the gold of peaceful water.

This is what all night the rain
on the cold roof was praising,
this is the promise of sunset kept.

Dan Murray

Ann Glazebrook

from

SEA-DRIFT: AS I EBB'D WITH THE OCEAN OF LIFE #1

As I ebbed with the ocean of life,
As I wended the shores I know,
As I walked where the sea-ripples continually wash you Paumanok,
Where they rustle up, hoarse and sibilant,
Where the fierce old mother endlessly cries for her castaways,
I musing late in the autumn day, gazing off southward,
Held by this electric self out of the pride of which I utter poems,
Was seiz'd by the spirit that trails in the lines underfoot,
The rim, the sediment that stands for all the water and all the land of the globe.

Fascinated, my eyes reverting from the south, dropt, to follow those slender windrows,
Chaff, straw, splinters of wood, weeds, and the sea-gluten,
Scum, scales from shining rocks, leaves of salt-lettuce, left by the tide,
Miles walking, the sound of breaking waves the other side of me,
Paumanok there and then, as I thought the old thought of likenesses,
These you presented to me, you fish-shaped island,
As I wended the shores I know,
As I walked with that electric self seeking types.

Walt Whitman

Ann Glazebrook

CENTERPORT CONCERT

A scarlet moon spotlighted sable brown water.
White-hot waves rippled fire flames.
Geese glided in pencil lines
shadow-brushing the ebony night.

Silence broke from the church,
bell- like voices ringing sea echoes.
Geese wings, angel wings
soothing new wounds.

As the geese settled in,
for a moment
there was peace.

Frank Muller

Jeanette Klimszewski

October 2

GRAY DAY IN AUTUMN

A ragged line of geese
skeined the sky, left
conversation floating
behind, dissolving in low
clouds. Changing leads,
flying in the wake
of each other's wings,
they spoke of homing
and myriad things known
only to their kind: marshes,
sweet grass heavy with seed,
a surge of life so strong
it stilled spirits in the air.

How did they know the sky's roads
without markers or names—
which lanes went north or south
since no stars shone to guide?
What commandments led them
into unknown salvation, tunneling
into the mouth of chance?

After their voices died
I felt the loneliness
of an abandoned child,
a yearning to surrender
all my years—to stand before
a secret wilderness
where I would comprehend
the incantations of birds—
where I could easily fly.

Lynn Kozma

AUTUMN

Autumn, a season that I love very much.
I whisper in its ear, it whispers in mine.
I wait for it impatiently.

Fall is a short season, I wish it would stay for a while.
I prefer things the way they are.
It comes at a certain time—
not before, not after, not more, not less.
I watch the leaves of the trees falling down.
One day, I will be that leaf that falls down.

Branches are naked, the way I was born.
It is funny how things start, then come to an end.
Life is short, my life is short.
I just cannot have enough—life goes through everything.

The birds are singing while they fly by.
Day by day, they leave their nests hungry,
then go back full and satisfied.
Our Lord blesses our food and gives us the day.
The mountains stand still, to me they walk by like clouds.

The earth moves around itself and around the sun—
that is what Science says.
I wonder what it feels like to walk day and night
and never stop.

It is amazing.
The circle of life is in creation and within us.
All these are signs for us to consider, we must think.
A man without thoughts is like a stone.
I beg your pardon, I should say:
A stone without thoughts is like a man.

Fuad Attal

Donald Case

ON THIS PARTICULAR MORNING

the man of the woodland wakes up
and it is autumn, and he is amazed
at how fast his feet and leggings become soaked
in the tall grass

when not so long ago it was all a wild clinging on
of seed and insects in the dry summer sun

But now it is morning and he wakes up
and the leaves and branches
he chopped from the walnut in August
smell like cider along the trail. The man

of the woodlands breathes it in, and deeply,
expecting the usual intoxication. Instead
his breath returns, in a clean and quiet
exhalation of clouds,

into the general decay of the forest.
There is more dignity in the heavy going
of the red maple, with its wet, rusty leaves
that nearly touch the ground, now ready

for another brush with death, he reflects,
there is more dignity in that, than
in the raucous combat of God knows
how many crows on Kettleback Hill,

in the linden trees—so the man of the woodlands
decides he will not take a swing at the red maple

on this particular morning. No! on this
autumn morning he will head for Kettleback Hill.

George Wallace

Barbara Hoffman

AGRITAINMENT

Potatoes, Cauliflower,
now North Fork farmers produce a new commodity.
The bureau calls it "agritainment."

Manhattan families drive out Autumn weekends
to be agritained
with maize mazes
pumpkin picking
hay rides
scarecrow clowns.

Farmers figure, "Agritain the city folk,
sell a bushel, make a buck, send them back."
Locals don't find traffic all that agritaining.

Sunday afternoon, as audience departs
buicks bearing bales of hay for condo lobbies
kids arguing which pumpkin
will be jack's best lantern
and Indian corn destined for office doors,
agritainers return to harvest chores.

William Batcher

Craig D. Robins

October 7

FALL LIGHT

Spartina in October along the beach
are glazed with residues of summer daylight,
their long green leaves are almost gold
or silver in the watery sun. Here and there
I wade these mirrored puddle roots
as warm as August was, watching the white
surf thickening on West Meadow beach.

A few dry stalks are victims of this Fall.
When the wind blows they rattle a little
while the live spears bend like metal foil.
Some egrets haven't fled the season yet.
They still enjoy these warmish afternoons
and people swim now without even noticing
the rush of birds and cloud shapes overhead.

Suppose I die before another summer.
This Sound will be the same without my sound,
Those same spartina shoots so green once more
will overlook the same dry clumps of lavender;
And plumy afternoons turn soft with heat.

Richard Elman

Frank Muller

EDIBLE LANDSCAPE

The descant of willows is hazy,
a wraparound, a covering up,
not so much weeping but laziness
as if their world could be transformed
ash green and undulant
in down sprawls. Maples
are uppermost posturers—
through every leaf and branch
there is display and a vain
self-regard inviting you
to come in and under and among
and be all the more dappled
a deep dark green. In sugary
light the sky has been powdered over
and the elms are missing
like giant broccoli stalks clipped
from a garden, but at night
there's the sudden smudging of the dusky
evergreens, soaring
of new sweet ears of corn
buttered with late
smears of sunlight.

Richard Elman

Linda Russo

AN APPLE IS A POEM

pome—a fleshy fruit consisting of an outer thickened fleshy layer and a central core with usually five seeds enclosed in a capsule

an apple is a poem
sweet, nutritious
growing without care
on a random branch
one may pluck it innocently
peel away its glossy skin
admire its improbable purity
slice it, serve your poem to friends
or give it ornate preparations
as sauce with cinnamon
or baked in pies and pastries
one may analyze its contents
its tart pectins and astringent flesh
some apples, some poems,
are rotten to the core
some fall unripened
some come pummeled by angry hail
or pocked by larval worms
some are pecked by witless birds
a good poem fits well to the hand
it is a gift to jugglers
easily digested
extract its mysterious juices
dehydrate for preservation
or let it stand till autumn
till it drops in its time and rots
either way, the best part
the miracle
is the seed

Red Diamond

Barbara Imperiale

REVISITING THE ORCHARD

Fresh news
in the apple press—
the cold liquors of autumn.

The orchard is bursting
with luscious, wide-hipped pears,
plump Buddha-plums
chilled and beaded blue,
apples heavy on the trees,
ruddy and swollen
on their pendulous boughs.

Ladders carry us
up the chakras
to the sweet summit,
rungs poking
into red delicious sunrise.
The good Eden is back,
and every fruit wholesome.

The shed blood of Eve
and a million years of toil
across the furrowed brow
of earth
revivify the garden
of royal pear,
sacred olive and ritual grape.

Angels leave the trees unguarded,
the trellises run purple,
the grass is deep in apples
and the cidery smell of redemption.

Pride shed
like an outgrown skin,
we take sabbatical in Paradise,
naked as green, untasted fruit.

Michael C. Walsh

Linda Russo

October 11

LEVITTOWN

The small apple tree bears that first year.
The fruit is imperfect but plentiful.
And there's a pear in the far corner
of the yard, where the stern geometry
of Cyclone fencing keeps us
and the neighbors apart.

The trees at the streethomely
adolescent things, we own them, too.
"Believe in your potential,"
I would tell them, if I spoke to trees.
"There's nothing to do here but grow,"
they would tell me. "We're all young."

I own so many things now.
My front-loading Bendix went on fire
the first time I used it, but it's working.
Baby clothes and nursing bras toss
and slosh on its sudsy ocean.
Some mornings, when I'm really tired,

I stare at the porthole, watching
my laundry at sea, sipping coffee,
waiting for the baby to cry.
This is a safe place to be
while we become something else.
But like the trees, I don't know that yet.

Arlene Eager

TRAVELER

The butterfly emerges
like a bit of blown taffeta,
clings to her chrysalis

sways in warm sun,
amazed at form and color,
spreads her pleated wings.

At once her life depends
on the beckoning face of flowers,
a carrying breeze in autumn.

This miracle occurs outside
our usual vision—tantalizing
segment of summer.

In my life's bondage
I shall never own her grace
or know her secrets.

Rooted to the ground, I am
colorless, insecure,
afraid to try my wings,

while she, complete, incomparable,
sips nectar, enchants us,
a drifter on the wind.

Lynn Kozma

Richard Hunt

AFTERNOON AT SHORT BEACH

The river's mouth widens here
strewn with salt marsh islands,
reeds burnished a dull gold
in autumn at low tide
waving lean limbs, or flattened
to the sand like wet hair.

This broad expanse of emptiness,
its water rippling silver in pale sun,
extends to darker, wooded coasts.
Distant sounds of life, a barking dog,
A pounding hammer, a motor's dull
drone, and the sea-torn cry
of a gull, reverberate in silence,
even the wind's voice stilled.

A few men stand, alone,
with bucket and pole to catch
something, or nothing.
They ignore each other
having found their peace
while somewhere, inland,
women congregate
to talk, like birds
that twitter in the trees.

Claire Nicolas White

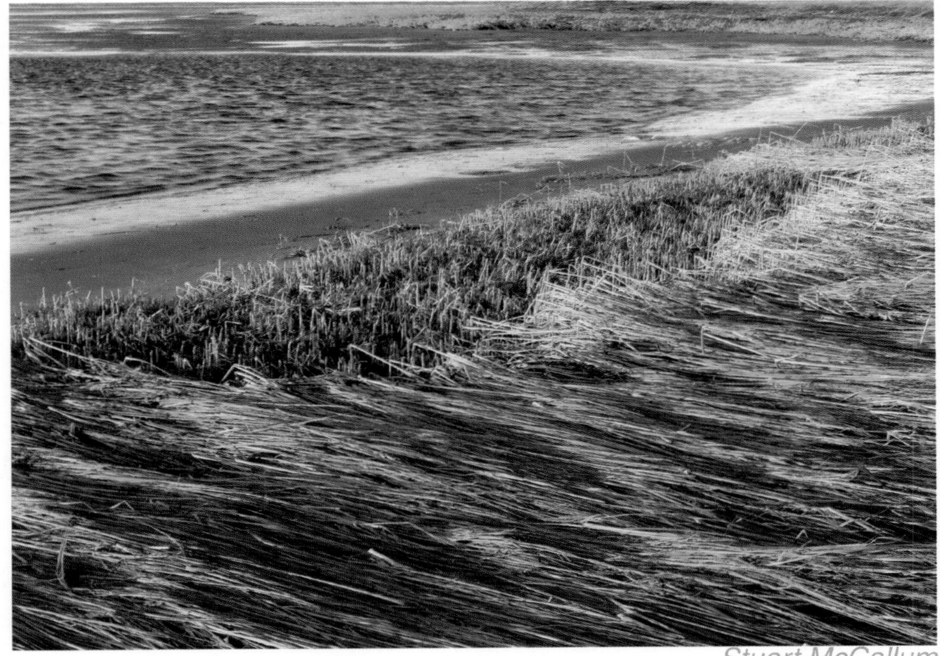

Stuart McCallum

October 14

AN OLD FISHING VILLAGE AT DAWN

There is a time of day
in the earth's remembered stillness
when the sun breaks hazy over the left shoulder
of the oversized remains of an industrial building
and geese hold steady to their pre-flight positions,

forming up in memory of previous migrations
out across the flat gray harbor.
A time of day when fish by the dozens,
you can hardly believe it, come flipping
out of the meager, almost expressionless,

face of what many in these parts
consider to be dead water. Guess again!
Between the semi-yachts and the last true
fishing boats, before the swirl of oil
and suburban commotion can soil

the morning, a whole school of fishes,
predators themselves at the moment,
and some of them quite full-bodied
for harbor dwellers, break water
and in such numbers that a seagull,

which has been floating peacefully
somewhere mid-harbor, is suddenly
compelled to take shelter on a pylon
close to shore. It is at times like these
that I walk home with the Sunday paper

and warm rolls tucked under one arm,
encouraged by the continued presence
of two pigeons pecking their way
down Main Street, and this unexpected
communication of life from the harbor.

And am content, by God, to ignore
the sun's weak performance in the October sky.

George Wallace

October 15

William Duryea, Jr.

OCTOBER

Summer still winks
through the changing leaves—
kaleidoscopic motion.
Winds rush about
the high tops of trees
whispering, "It's over!
It's over!"
Pumpkin & squash
reflect the red and orange
of Autumn moon,
larger than any sunburst—
brightening even the blackest nights.
Cornstalks
dry with the waiting,
ears pricked,
pop out
of their kerneled rows.
The spirit of harvest,
celebration, festivity
fills the afternoons
heavy with fermenting apples.
All days end with equinoctial night,
crossroads of calendric time.
The eve of fruits transforms
to cider charms.

Stanley H. Barkan

Vidal Al Martinez

October 16

RAKING LEAVES

I want to be the colors of flames
that seem to lick at tree branches
as leaves ready themselves for flight

to be made pure
thoughts released

to be carried away
in darkened skies
mingled with smells of wood fires
burning in homey hearths

to dance
spiral earthward
become part of the forest bed
for animals to rest on

to be brilliant sunlight
coaxing the acorn to become the oak
that will be felled to carve the cradle
to rock the wise one
who will heal the world's wounds.

Tammy Nuzzo-Morgan

DOWN CORDWOOD PATH

With an old cough
and a pain in my toe
I descend Cordwood Path
in an autumn so gentle
it erases all distress,
where tulip trees rise
so tall from the gulley
they lift me out
of this embrace of hills
and fermenting mulch . . .
A sudden silhouette
of red leaves shimmers
in dappled light
like a lone woman haunting
these woods with her
frivolity, a reminder
of the need for luxury.

Claire Nicolas White

Frank Muller

October 18

INSCRIPTIONS: SONG OF MYSELF #31

I believe a leaf of grass is no less than the journey-work of the stars,
And the pismire is equally perfect, and a grain of sand, and the egg of the wren,
And the tree-toad is a chef-d'oeuvre for the highest,
And the running blackberry would adorn the parlors of heaven,
And the narrowest hinge in my hand puts to scorn all machinery,
And the cow crunching with depress'd head surpasses any statue,
And a mouse is miracle enough to stagger sextillions of infidels.

I find I incorporate gneiss, coal, long-treaded moss, fruits, grains, esculent roots,
And am stucco'd with quadrupeds and birds all over,
An have distanced what is behind me for good reasons,
But call any thing back again when I desire it.
. . . .

Walt Whitman

Laura M. Eppig

October 19

MOON

Out of the reeds the bay the ocean sky
At once
The orange moon
Is on the porch.

Whiting, it plies steep far in purple blue
Above the fireplace, the firs
To reign over the guest room.

High in the night it governs
Moving still
Late spilling a cream dusk on the lawn, the woods
Its self seeps through the blinds
Staying the house our sleep
Is
Light.

Kay Kidde

October 20

Larry Landolfi

FIRE ISLAND: OCEAN BEACH

The little town is basic wood box shapes,
Gray, blue-green shingles, low
In the prevailing marsh,
Rife with birds
And walkways to the dunes.
A stag is watching from an autumn yard.

Then coming on the rise of morning
That old surprise
The sovereign sea.

Stone pilings wait
As the ocean lifts for them, then backs away.
A fisherman lofts his lure
To hang on a glinting crest before it plunges.

A tired monarch butterfly breathes on the beach
A fragile lady in a red-brimmed hat
Stops to mark
The geese that are pumping south.
The milling waves accept
An upturned faintly pawing crab.

A creature that falls here
May emerge
With sand
With water
Air.

Kay Kidde

Gil Weiner

October 21

AT THE EDGE

1.

A warm October: goldenrod lights
the dunes, the sky a prism
of lightnings.

2.

Fishing fleet on the horizon—
gray necklace of fat metal beads—
but what they trawl for, the rich ore
of ocean, is almost gone:
the striped bass my father cast for,
diminished, the sea *harvested*,
robbed of its blood.

3.

Wind lifts the waves,
a soft lace rustle.
Beautiful things tumble
out of those sleeves:
battered twists of drift-
wood, bottle glass
ground to green or purple
splendor, this trailing hem
of the sea, an instrument
a thousand miles long: clatter
of cracked clam shells, mutterings
of smoothed stones.

4.

What are we here for
if not to know beauty,
to taste the last sweetness
of being, to find the last
scatter of bones?

Charles Adés Fishman

Aija Birzgalis

TALKING TO LONG ISLAND

Hello, Long Island.

I met you on Crane Neck Beach
  Where pebbled, slushy stretches lay
    With whitened, chalky, soft-shelled clams.

I've seen you in the Pine Barrens woods
  Where crunchy beds of Low Bush Berry are hung
    With Pitch Pine needle tripods.

I met you in the meadow at Hempstead Plains
  Where grasses wave in winds
    And a Meadowlark wings off on a tight curve.

I've seen you on the Nissequogue River
  Where tall reed grasses crowd muddy banks
    Edged with Mallard Ducks.

I met you at Flax Pond salt flat edges
  Where Fiddler Crabs drop into holes
    On a lowering tide.

I've seen you on the moraine in Manorville Hills
  Where a red-tail hawk glides by
    With views of the ocean and bay.

I see you at a pond in Manorville
  Where placid waters reflect Swamp Maples
    And caterwauling Catbirds call from brush.

I've seen you on Fire Island
  Where wind has shear-shaped Shad Blow trees
    And Beach Plum branches blacken sand blowouts.

I met you at Orient Point
  Where wave motion tumbles beach stones
    And Horse Mussels lie strewn in wrack.

I've seen you at Connequoit Park Preserve
  Where trout spear water
    With quickened tail flicks.

I've seen you along the Great South Bay
  Where beaches blush with swaths of garnet sand.

Tom Stock

Jyoti Ganguly

THE NESCONSET CRICKETS

Either the crickets stopped,
or I fell asleep as they kept on.

But sometimes I'd count their song
all night, when I couldn't sleep,

or dreamed I couldn't sleep, or dreamed
from under grass that I helped them sing.

William Heyen

Pauline Southard

October 25

THE SPARROW'S DREAM

I see myself invisible
a bit of heaven
camouflaged as earth

I move among the brightness
safe and sweet
so small, so busy with my joy
they think they are imagining my song
they think I am a leaf

I watch myself efface
eat specks of grain
weave flecks of straw into my nest
What's inconspicuous works best

There in that bush
I teach my young to be obscure
As they begin to disappear
I think: *If they are meek enough*
They will inherit the sky.

Susan Astor

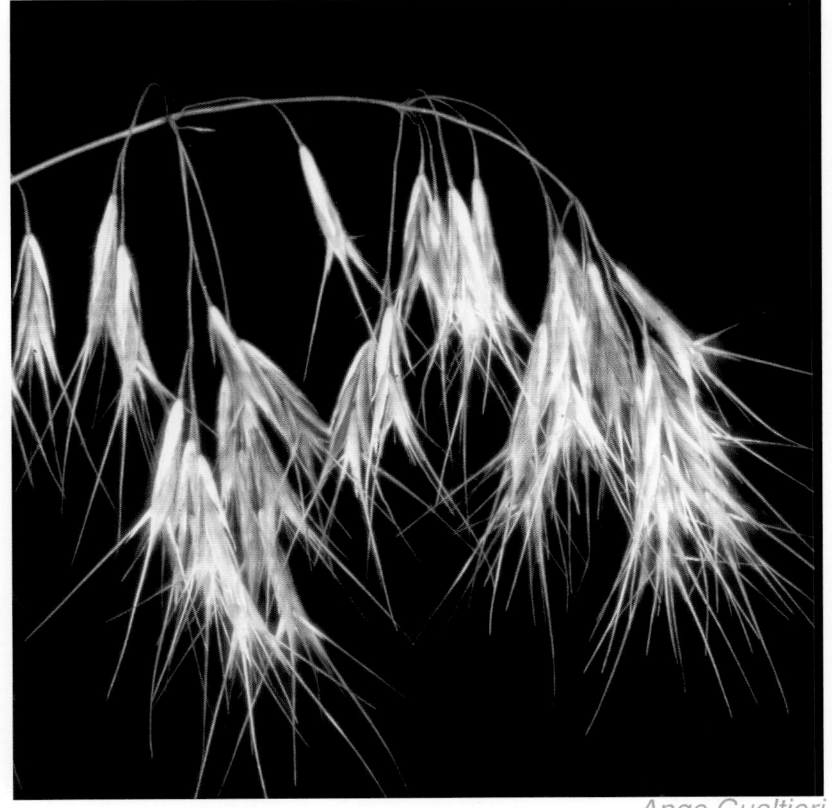

Ange Gualtieri

October 26

EARLY FALL

A weeping willow leaf
lazy tumble-falls
slow spiral round,
free-fall pinwheels,
zig-zags
to the paper texture pond.

Adam D. Fisher

Linda Russo

October 27

from
INSCRIPTIONS: SONG OF MYSELF #9

The big doors of the country barn stand open and ready,
The dried grass of the harvest-time loads the slow-drawn wagon,
The clear light plays on the brown gray and green intertinged,
The armfuls are pack'd to the sagging mow.

Walt Whitman

Ange Gualtieri

October 28

MARY'S ISLAND

A dreamer of things,
That can only be found
Where the sound
Of the angels is heard by the lark,
Once came from a city
Too small for his dreams,
To an openland pretty
With rillets and streams
In Massapequa.

There by the shore
Of a sky-spotted lake,
Gulls shake
From their pinions the salt of the sea,
And there with emotion
I lingered, the while
These birds of the ocean
Flew over an isle
In Massapequa.

Above Mary's Isle,
They appeared to the bard
Like the guard
Of swift angels the larks often meet
Beyond Kerry's valleys
Or over Lough Erne;
But the lark never dallies
O'er meadow or burn
In Massapequa.

The waters were filled
With a sky's fallen blue,
And the view
Of that island was dreamily fair
To one who could wander
Away in a thought,
While he grew all the fonder
Of what his dreams brought
In Massapequa.

O! fair was that isle,
As it waited at noon
For the moon
With her island to mirror its form;
But fairer than islands
In lake or in sky,
Were the heather-clad highlands
That seemed to be high
O'er Massapequa.

For a dreamer of things,
That can only be found
Where the sound
Of the angels is heard by the larks,
Still dreams; but the shadows
Of cities now blur
The mystical meadows
And things as they were
In Massapequa.

Francis Carlin

Robert Harrison

BRIEF CANDLE

Made vague by fog,
my house
is a blurred pumpkin.

Its glass smile
sprays the sky
with orange breath.

The night is cold,
and gaunt trees loom
before the distant
glow of home.

I will pass them,
find my door,
and, bathed
in gold awhile,
savor light.

Marcia Slatkin

Drew A. Pantino

I BROKE THE SPELL THAT HELD ME LONG

I broke the spell that held me long.
The dear, dear witchery of song.
I said, the poet's idle lore
Shall waste my prime of years no more,
For Poetry, though heavenly born,
Consorts with poverty and scorn.

I broke the spell—nor deemed its power
Could fetter me another hour.
Ah, thoughtless! how could I forget
Its causes were around me yet?
For wheresoe'er I looked, the while,
Was Nature's everlasting smile.

Still came and lingered on my sight
Of flowers and streams the bloom and light,
And glory of the stars and sun;—
And these and poetry are one.
They, ere the world had held me long,
Recalled me to the love of song.

William Cullen Bryant

October 31

Marlene Weinstein

WHAT TAKES HER BREATH AWAY . . .

days

when nothing *at all* happens—
the sun rises on the horizon and
licks with light the trees on the back hill;
a bird on a branch
sings
an ordinary song.

What takes her breath away is
digging dirt in her garden,
raking rust-colored leaves,
sautéing greens in hot oil,
purchasing toothpicks and Greek olives and
vine-ripened tomatoes.

It takes her breath away to sit
with a book
—even when her mind stray—
and turn the pages
willing words alive
before sleep.

And in her
daily dusting of small treasures,
in running her aged dog in a schoolyard,
preparing
meals at dusk,
belief threads through the hours

and she is grateful
for the liberty
to exhale.

Kate Kelly

Vidal Al Martinez

ALL SOULS' DAY ON LONG ISLAND

This is the time again when those that were return
and do not greet us, and go about their work
with the authority of precedence and age.
We are mere ghosts of those who came before,
who bartered not their land as we our loves
and knew the worth of being planted here.
Ah were we but the roots of such a tree
and not the leaves that glitter, fall and die.

Triumphantly
Aunt Bessie stalks along the bluffs, the Sound
a soft silk scarf of blue, lined with a strip
of taupe, the faded sand. I see her wave
her cane to chase the gulls, to poke the clams.
She picks the beach plums which are hard and sour.
She conjures up her woods, her wilderness
and fallow fields with purple weeds that roll
down to the brackish rivers, inlets, ponds
where the blue heron with folded foot long stands
and shrieking pheasants rise, and wild geese fall
in linear patterns. Wearing mended gloves
and a red woolen dress she shares with the moths
rises Aunt Bessie, autocratic and strong.
As far as she can see the land is hers.
"I am, I am!" she cries, and knocks her cane
on the dull ground, and smiles with innocence.

Come walk along the roads, dispel the ghosts
along Shep Jones's Lane, Three Sisters Road,
from Smithtown to St. James to Stony Brook,
of glaring, glossy, brittle little homes
that litter the once steaming, furrowed field.
Then let me meet you there, and we will try
to see it as the Mounts painted it once
with an erasing eye and lying hand,
till under tangled poison-ivy vines
we'll hear the Indian heartbeat in the shade,
where unshod feet left not a trace behind.

Claire Nicolas White

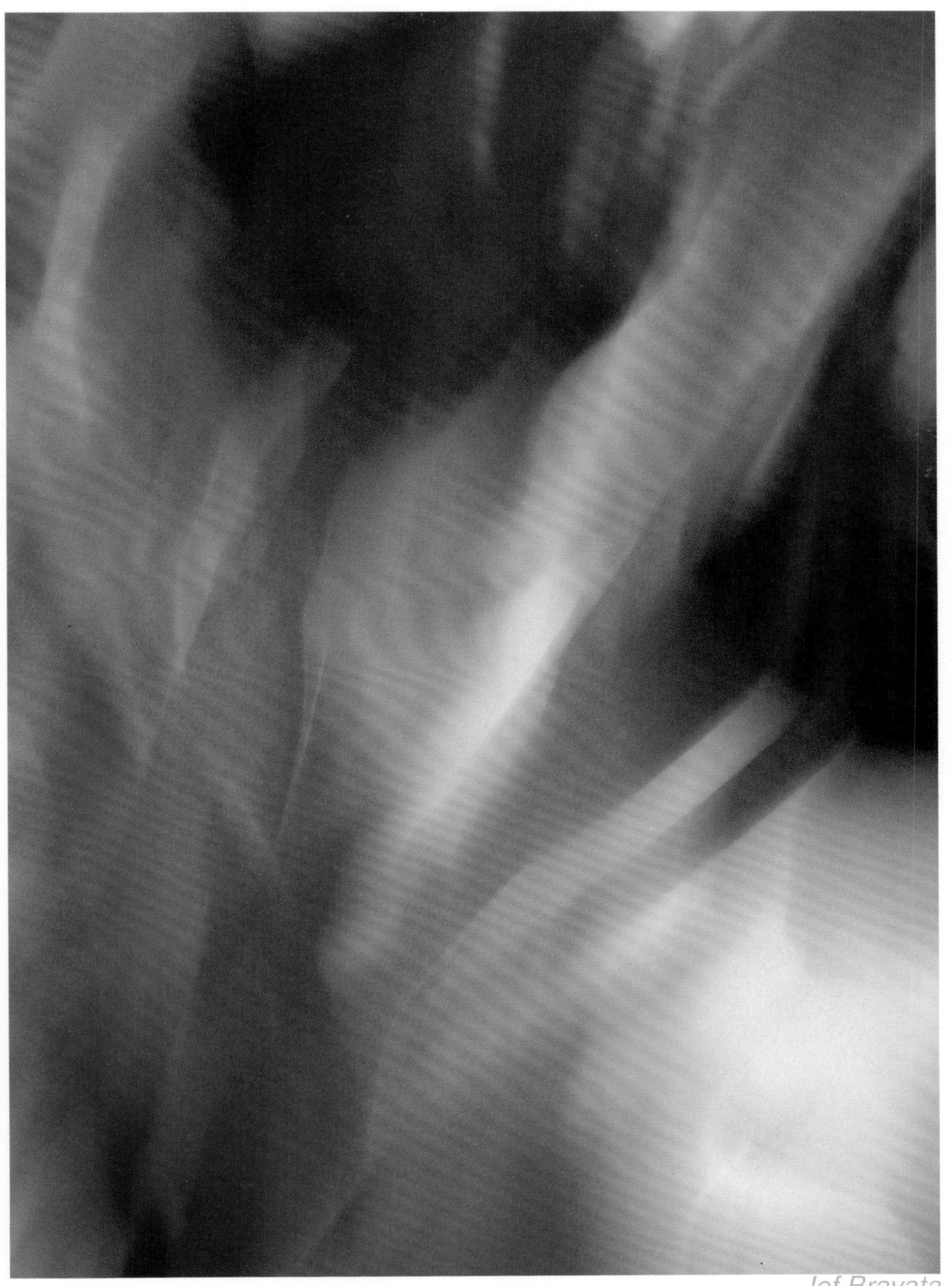

Jef Bravata

MILKWEED

Milkweed pods settle
on my mind
like sleeping birds.

Curled on branches
gray thoughts
wait for wind.

I pry one open.
Angels unfold
and take wing

flaring to orange
as if each dark seed
were the tip of a match.

While filaments fly
claiming the Earth
with milky light.

Orel Protopopescu

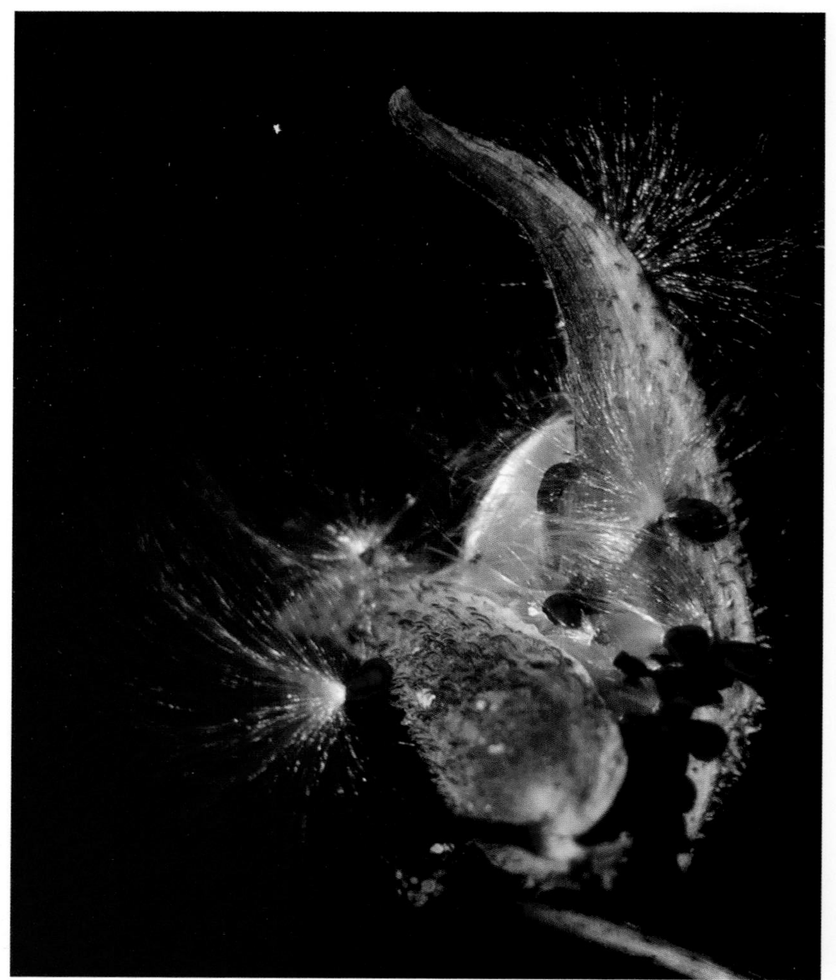

M. James Pion

November 3

CARDINAL

Some trick of vision,
refraction of light, familiar
branches etched against blue sky
prompted his choice
of the lower path, most direct,
straight into barrier glass.

He dropped like a flaming stone,
lay stunned on a world of leaves,
attempting to regain his breath of life.
The glory of a few bright feathers
waved lazily on the pane.

I carried him, trembling, through
a house he had never entered,
to a leafy shelf outside,
placed branches for his feet,
said a few soft words. His black
eyes glittered into mine.

Never mind all the others, flying,
chattering at feeders. I wanted
that bird to live—the one I had
held like a sacrament in my hand.

Suddenly, alert, he was off
to the nearest tree, leaving behind
a sound like happiness, the fire
of being alive.

Lynn Kozma

Sheldon Pollack

EELS

Before I was who I am now
the Nissequogue opened its mouth
to the Sound, where mussel bars
burn blue in the sun
& legions of crabs saluting
the sky dizzy the eye

I lived by that tide
dove at its flood
from a plank wedged in dune
dug worms with a shell
My blood was that brine

I've broke from that time
remember a woman, dress like a sail
changing her shape, dancing
barefoot with bucket & spear
on barnacle rocks, singing
could it be, of her life
as a bird, as a fish
in that world out of which
we are born

Drop-lines wrapped in her fists
she reins a wind in the water
seasons deep, snags & anchors me
to that other life

to what I was & yet may be

where she raises
triumphant wrists twined
with greenblack bracelets of slime

Dan Giancola

Vincent M. Noto

EAST OF JULY

for Emily

        somewhere east of july
where summer keeps
starting and restarting
my arms
        are the oars
of your rudderless
boat, my hair
        the main sail,
my eyes suffused
        with a light
        that peels free
        & bleaches
the waves
        of the shallow peconic
        flattening cornfields
        silvering vineyards
in mattituck
cutchogue
southold

        we have freed
the corn of their
        silken
husks
        we have loosened
the grapes
        from their vines,
        my legs encircling
your torso,
        we have fought
the flight
        of the tides . . .

Joan Carole Hand

John DeLorenzo

SHELL-PICKING IN AUTUMN

I like to see what the shore has gathered
on a fall morning, before the first frost.
A sudden march of blue mussel shells, the tattered
victims of an underwater storm, or in the lather

a bright yellow balloon some child evidently lost
and must have bothered mommy for, halfway home.
They say that autumn is the cost of having
lived so marvelously in summer—as for me,

forced by the inevitable rotation of the fickle sun
to roam in cool shell-picking time, I'm not
complaining. There are those of us who own
a temperament more suited to the splashing

struggle in the foam, the daring lunge
into the hot sea, the strong body straining
against the waves—or even how to tempt
that "kiss me" pout from pretty girls

as they go strolling past. It is my fate,
or misfortune, to be one more suited to this
short season's claim—the wistful recollection,
as the sun heads South. The great settling out.

George Wallace

Peter Brink

November 7

PATCHOGUE LANE

The road is level as a floor,
The fields yield choicest grain;
As yet no word was ever penned
In praise of Patchogue Lane.

Our peerless Bay abounds
With shellfish of all kinds;
If other kinds are in the sea
They are scarcely worth a rhyme.

The Bay of Naples is rather fine,
But meager in many a way.
Poets that used to laud it
Knew not of Patchogue Bay.

When on Vesuvius' lofty height,
As I viewed the Alpine way,
I thought the scene was not so grand,
As from Watch Hill across our Bay.

The fleetest yachts are brought
To compete upon its waters;
Gallants oft win silver cups
And present them to Eve's fair daughters.

Not Venice with all its splendor,
And watery streets of fame,
Could make me for one hour forget
The foot of Patchogue Lane.

Youngs land on the North,
With its hills of Coram sand,
Is hailed with joy by mariners
When nearing Freedom's land.

There is one lovely spot
As yet unknown to fame:
No stately pile in ruin lies
At the foot of Patchogue Lane.

The meadows are dressed in green
With many and various hues
And our noble Bay appears
In blue, etheral blue.

Betsey Ann Smith Roberts

INDIAN SUMMER

The sea winds blow a message
Up the bay of daffodils
That bloom in southern springs.
Reflected in the winter sun
The crimson breezes breathe
Aromas from the jungle shores.
This languid, airy tropicale
Of melodies that slowly sift
About the winter pavements
Keeps the summer's fortune
Frolicking about the trees.
The branches see the tainted leaves
And sigh, trembling, to ask
What is gone to come once more,
And then the leaves are in the wind.
The wind has changed;
The distant jungle lands
Have lost their spell once more,
While Arctic emptiness
Has built a corridor of cold.

Gregory Rabassa

Pauline Southard

AT THE DOCK

All I need to do
is be still, and the answer
will come. Weightless, I listen
for some profound reply
to a question that cannot be named.
In the hush of changing light
rafts of eelgrass drift by
on incoming tide. A tern drops
like a stone into flashing water,
emerges with its silver prize.
Mallards float soundlessly
toward the bay.

Lying flat on old weathered boards
I stare at flying clouds until
it seems the dock and I are moving.
I hold onto the piling, afraid of
falling off the earth's edge.

Cicadas have ended their chorus
for the day. Fireflies blossom into
sparks. An occasional plane drones
overhead, so high it might be a visitor
from another planet. A setting sun
drains the last light away, and the dark
bowl of sky is pricked by early stars.

Still I lie there in some deep
state of peace, treasuring each moment
as though it will never come again.
And it never will. And that is the answer
I have waited for, given silently,
flowing inward like the tide.

Lynn Kozma

Jyoti Ganguly

PERSPECTIVE

I draw a squirrel
it looks like
a pot-bellied man
squatting
under a sick palm tree

When I shut my eyes
I see
the small gray squirrel
sitting still
blue
glinting in his short fur

Bushy tail swishing
high above ever-watchful
eyes
paws poised high
cautious

I look again
at my drawing
wonder what happened
from eyes to hand
to paper

I write a love poem
see her in full detail
taste her throat

We are lying together
in a forest
on sweet grasses
watched by a small squirrel.

Louis Bussolati

Robert Harrison

AUTUMN ETHOLOGY

Our hackberry tree is on fire with autumn:
the leaves are flaming like your lips;
on every branch, in clusters, yellow gems—
dancing yellow flags—warblers are back,
heading south, they stopped here, in our tree.
Look (I want to say), warblers everywhere!
The tree is full of them—you say nothing.
I watch from the kitchen, trapped inside,
while out there birds are gorging on berries,
advertising their golden paint. I cannot
believe this, but it is happening, it really is.
Look! I call to you, my mouth is a big O,
but nothing comes out. All is silent, yellow.

Bob Schmitz

Mary Kennan Herbert

November 12

NOVEMBER ROAD, LATE AFTERNOON

I bike the orange yellow road to town.
The bridge, blue bay, deep red azaleas on the lawns
Have been absorbed,
Are home.

But heading back across the bridge at night
I come upon
The moon
Bouncing lightly with two stars
At the bottom of the bay.

Although I trust the shadow dappled way,
Its pitfalls in me down the years,
Each stretch now hides a mystery . . .
Withered leaves have come alive.
I memorized this lane in light before
In dark I find I'm learning more.

Kay Kidde

Sheldon Pollack

BIG FALL
Stony Brook

The maple leaves turn strawberry
every cold new day; this air
gaudies the trees, the yellows hiding
under sprinklings of green
vanishing utterly, and then there's amber
varnishing all the oak leaves, and
the brightest buckthorn berries
frost the cheeks of school kids.

Richard Elman

Stuart McCallum

November 14

SANDS AT SEVENTY: THE VOICE OF THE RAIN

And who art thou? said I to the soft-falling shower,
Which, strange to tell, gave me an answer, as here translated:
I am the Poem of Earth, said the voice of the rain,
Eternal I rise impalpable out of the land and the bottomless sea,
Upward to heaven, whence, vaguely form'd, altogether changed, and yet the same,
I descend to lave the droughts, atomies, dust-layers of the globe,
And all that in them without me were seeds only, latent, unborn;
And forever, by day and night, I give back life to my own origin, and make pure and beautify it:
(For song, issuing from its birth-place, after fulfillment, wandering,
Reck'd or unreck'd, duly with love returns.)

Walt Whitman

Bob Schmitz

HAIKU

The rocking horse, pushed
        by the breeze that blew the shades . . .
Echoing laughter.

Along the treadmill
        stuff of earth, the turtles crawl . . .
Look at the children!

Out of the cat's claws,
        the ashleaf blurts his story—
Oh, the screeching birds!

Soldiers in the grass,
        broken for . . . oh . . . twenty years . . .
Rusting in the sun.

A bench in a park;
        leaves gather and blow away . . .
Will spring come again?

Crimson maple leaves
        falling from the Harvest moon—
A cardinal cries!

Stanley H. Barkan

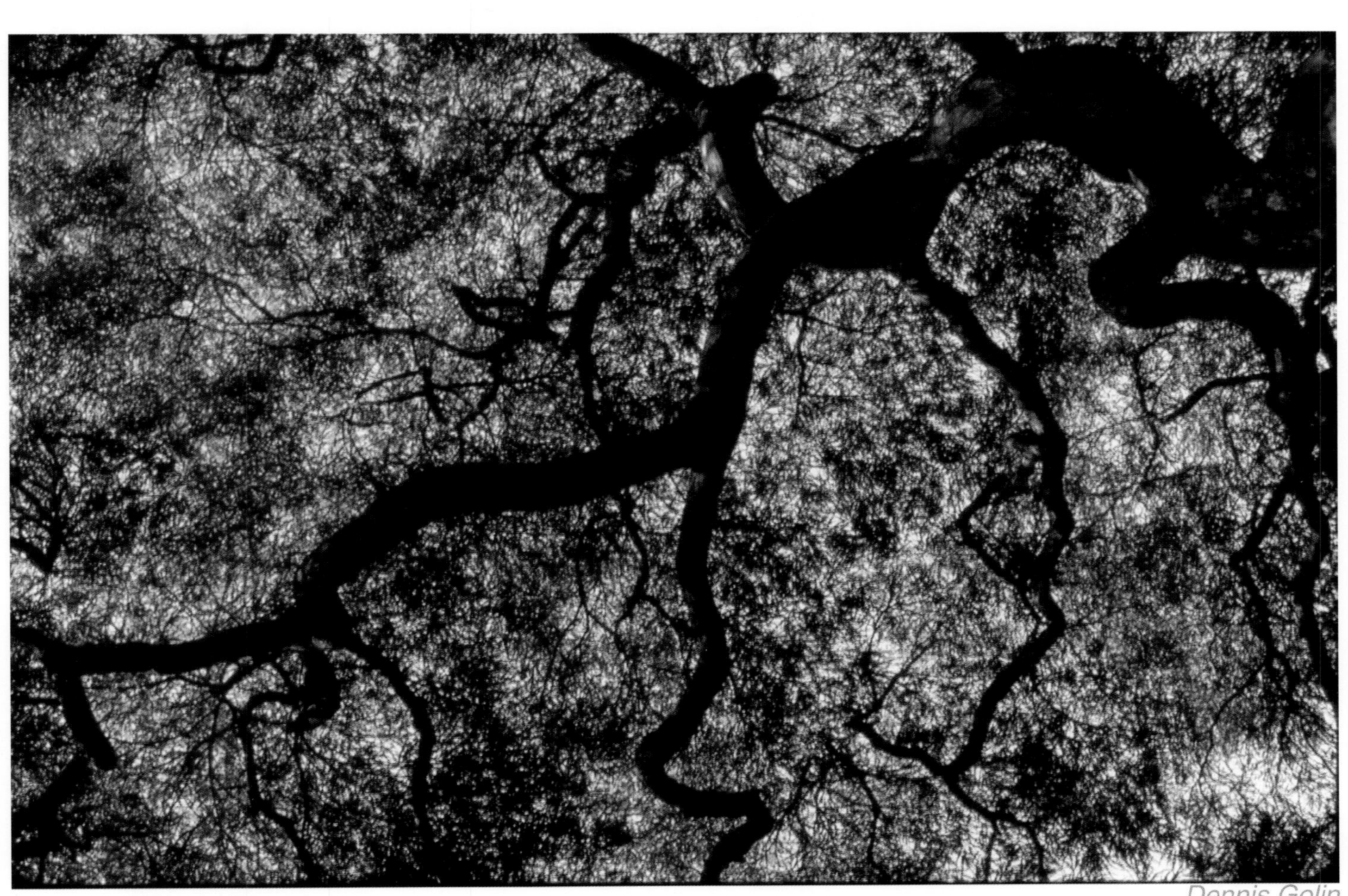

Dennis Golin

QUIETLY GOING NOWHERE

Sunlight lies
like a blessing
to be revoked

on the few leaves
that still cling
to boughs lifted

and lashed
by wind from
the northeast

as I listen
to the calm strings
of Pachelbel

in the background
and cars sizzle
past over shadows.

I look out
my window
at this moment

a man
quietly going
nowhere

and turn
and drift with
leaves and notes

and this light
that always finds
the right spots

to intensify
briefly before
fading again

Norbert Krapf

November 17

FLUSTERED MAPLES . . .

flustered maples
lose their blues to early snow
shimmy yellow silk
over sequined streets

Weslea Sidon

Marlene Weinstein

November 18

A GIFT OF BIRDS
for Maxwell Corydon Wheat, Jr.

The gold leaves of the maple
have turned cold.
Under their wintry dim
I walk as if toward you.

The sky is milky
like an eye half lost in sleep.
Already it is dreaming about snow.

November dozes
and begins to close.

And they come

winged messengers
delivering themselves out of
the stupefaction of the day
quick miracles
nobody thought to pray for:

cardinals and jays so bright
their colors ring out in the stillness,
juncos softening the ground
with their small fur,
dove, starlings, chickadees,
a mockingbird, his tail an exclamation,
a pheasant, festively arranged.

This is a holiday without a name
in celebration of some secret joy.

A woodpecker, like an inventive toy
begins to work,
a perfect, painted replica
of what he is.
Nuthatches, upside-down
look quizzically on.

High seagulls, sailing in,
cry out across
the white-capped distance of the sky.
Inside me, something rises
and prepares to fly.

Out of a nearby hedge,
dead until now
a flock of sparrows
bursts like generosity itself
and for a moment
I am overcome
not sure if
I am giving or receiving.

Susan Astor

Richard Hunt

TO AN OLD FRIEND AT A POETRY READING

for R. B. Weber

A small leaf settled on your shoulder,
stuck to the threads of your sweater.
I was about to pick it off, but you bent forward,
suddenly attentive to the speaker,
and your wild gray hair flapped and rustled about your head
as if in a wind.
I thought how much like an old tree you had become,
and I would not remove your only leaf.

Sandy McIntosh

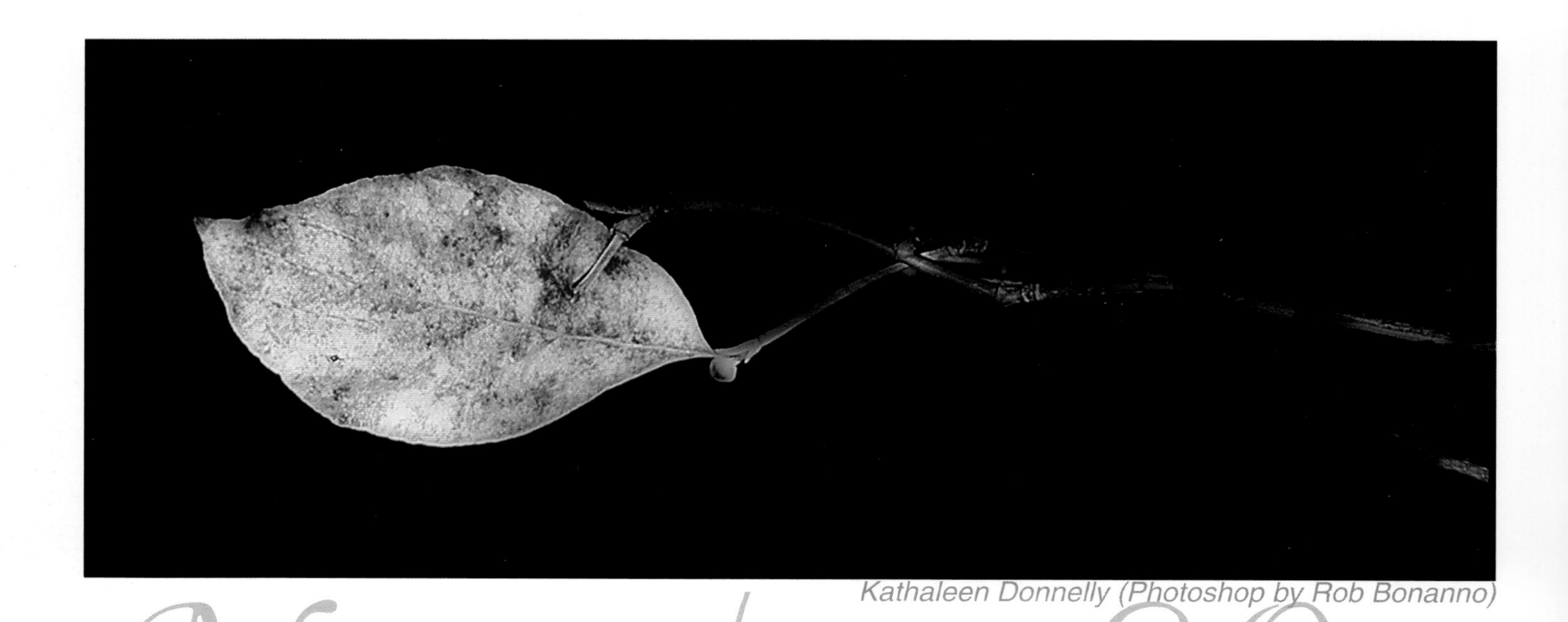

Kathaleen Donnelly (Photoshop by Rob Bonanno)

November 20

LOST IN AUTUMN

Dry leaves
crackle underfoot
in a forest of
fallen songs.

Gray clouds
hover overhead
in a sky of
remembered dreams.

Morning rain
brightens tired browns
in a puddle of
spoken words.

Misty drizzle
lingers mid-air
in a sea of
thoughts undone.

Kathaleen Donnelly

Richard Fiedorowicz

THE PINES' THOUGHT

Within the shadow of ourselves we stand
And see a thousand brilliancies unfold,
Where Autumn woods, in gorgeous ruin, hold
One late, last revel. Upon every hand
Riot of color,—death in pomp and state,
Decay magnificent inconstant blaze,
We have no past or splendor in these days;
They shall be changed,—we are inviolate;
Their voices shall be hushed on every hill,
Their lights be quenched, their color fade and die,
And when they stand like spectres gaunt and still,
With naked boughs against the far, cold sky,
Lo! we shall hide the flying moon from sight,
And lead the wind on many a roaring night.

Juliet Isham

November 22

Donald Case

BEFORE THE FROST

These are the nights
When every cricket sings
When in the dark around us
There is a flowering
Jubilant continuous
Festival of crickets

They sing together all night long
Drawing a pulsing
Chiming joy
Out of the dryness
Of their tiny bodies

The sky
Is black and clear tonight
Stars in their mountain villages
Glitter in silence

But in the trilling crickets
Among the autumn grasses
The stars
Have found their voices.

Anne Porter

Eric Lohse (Montage with Larry Landolfi)

THE OLD OVEN

A few days ago, I beheld an old oven,
With an entrance decayed and a fractured wall—
Its side by the steel of old time had been riven,
But the charm of its age on my spirit did fall;
It recalled the delight of the maiden and mother,
Surrounded with neighbors and relatives gay,
Delighted again to partake with each other,
The good things of life on a *Thanksgiving day*

It recalled to my mind the bright days of good living,
Of abundance and peace, which our forefathers saw
When the plough in the earth was contentedly diving.
And men *went to church* without *going to law*—
It brought to my mind, too, the young, blushing *creatures*,
So plump and so fair, yet so modest and shy,
With the bright bloom of health overspreading their features,
And a smile on their cheek and a dove in their eye.

The table arrayed in the beautiful order,
Our grandmother used in the last century—
The dimity cover and tasseled border,
With plates made of maple and fine hickory—
The old silver tankard, with cider o'erflowing,
The poultry that seemed "come and eat me" to call,
The duck and the rooster, that yet seemed a-crowing,
And e'en the old gobler, the prince of them all.

Oh! when shall I revel in rivers of gravy,
Of butter and honey, as they did of yore—
Or such oceans of fat as would float a small navy,
When the pots groaned "enough," and the kettles "no more"?
Ah, me! Will there never arrive a re-action,
When ovens no longer shall "emptiness" cry,
Nor tables be spread with a "mental abstraction,"
The stomach to mock, and the teeth to defy?

Alas! will there never again be presented,
The holyday pudding, and christmas-day pie,
And the gingerbread loaves, all with cinnamon scented?
I asked the old oven, and heard the reply:
"So long as the dandy, the driv'ler and sloven,
Half-baked, round the country are suffered to drone,
And the plough is neglected, the distaff and oven,
You may ask of me bread, and I'll give you a stone."

Then repair to the plough, and repair to the oven,
I said to myself, as I mused returned—
'Tis the way to recover the blessings of heaven,
So gracelessly lost, and so foolishly mourned:
Then the days of abundance, and mirth, and good living,
Our fathers enjoyed, will again re-appear,
And the ox and the fatling again be seen thriving,
To crown the *thanksgiving* the end of the year.

John Orville Terry

Marlene Weinstein

NIGHT

night has been brought down to all the trees
to test them   and reprieve
in giving back
what day breaks into particles
the discretion of wheels   wires
bridges   conflict

draw a mist over these

let there be
an intermediate peace
between us and orion and hesperus
here on this beach wooded into the night

D. H. Melhem

NOVEMBER

Yet one smile more, departing, distant sun!
  One mellow smile through the soft vapory air,
Ere, o'er the frozen earth, the loud winds run,
  Or snows are sifted o'er the meadows bare.
One smile on the brown hills and naked trees,
  And the dark rocks whose summer wreaths are cast,
And the blue gentian-flower, that, in the breeze,
  Nods lonely, of her beauteous race the last.
Yet a few sunny days, in which the bee
  Shall murmur by the hedge that skirts the way,
The cricket chirp upon the russet lea,
  And man delight to linger in thy ray.
Yet one rich smile, and we will try to bear
The piercing winter frost, and winds, and darkening air.

William Cullen Bryant

Ed Muller

GULL IN GREY WATERS

for Marie

Silent, stoic
in the stillness that is now,
announcing his place
in this world,
scavenger wading, waiting
for whatever
fish will fill his belly.
He does not fear
his own reflection.

Atlantic oceans
have made their pact
with the wind.
Water dense as deafness
breaks open,
wraps itself around
the spindly stems of him.

His wings lie closed
like the variegated leaves
of the prayer plant
in the hazy darkness
of this morning.

I remain rooted in sand,
pondering my place
in the order of things.
I wait for what will fill me,
wait for what is next to come
learning to love this moment.

Yolanda Coulaz

Richard Hunt

NOVEMBER

The big dipper sits full
on the moonlit line of pines
a chill rides the air

Once, deer stood these bright barrens
sniffed the air for scent of snow,
no human dreams worried them

The pool of stars snaps
—unnamed, nothing makes sense

Day's grey tarp
stretches all the way
to February

Graham Everett

Art Simendinger

November 28

A SONG TO NOVEMBER

The deer,
who posture upon
this slope of lawn,
have found their
treasure and sustenance
in the bitter scatter
of hickory and white oak.
The woods become
pastel and bare.
Sky and a moistened morning
herald a certain frost.

They emerge
from the vanishing green,
carrying the enigma
of the summer forest.
Their caution
strides light and silent
from beyond the veil
of the hidden places.
Somewhere the red fox
sleeps shunning daylight.

A million creatures
take to the air or earth.
Tomorrow the deer
will accept what is given,
drink while this
pond still reflects
the arc of this world,
and listen to the wind
as it chills
and then first whispers . . .
snow.

Daniel Thomas Moran

NOW

November. The sky whitens and waits.
The leaves are on edge.
The wind holds still.

You fold up your appointment book,
Take off your shoes,
Pad through the room to let me in:

We close before the door does.

Clouds lower snow across
The shoulders of the oaks
And down the curving
Rows of fencebones:

Against the shingles of the house,
The wind leans in.

Susan Astor

William Duryea, Jr.

WINTER ROSES

Their long necks reach for sun
climbing above the hedge,
their heads, tight-pointed buds,
sheathed bird beaks
streaked with faint promise.
I take them in. The house heat
unclasps one to spread
its skirts, voluptuous scent.
The others, reticent,
loosen pale fluttering tongues
then shrivel. Now I cling
to these ghosts out of season
with hirsute stems
and tri-part dark green leaves
more poignant than
easy outbursts of summer.

Claire Nicolas White

Vidal Al Martinez

December 1

. . . IN LATE AUTUMN

after the blizzard
jasmine blooms
in my bedroom

one white flower
at the tip of a bough
of green leaves

fragrance floating on the air
exotic night flower
blooming insider while outside

snow-laden pines bow
weighed down
by fierce wind-driven snow

branches cracked off
old trees   fractured arms
reaching out of snow-banks

elegant dark sculptures
in white snow
I am hemmed in

by the high drifts
hurt by the cold dry air
my separation form him

yet I cannot deny
the fragrance
of one jasmine blossom

Barbara Hoffman

Robert Harrison

TRANSFORMATIONS

The green world
modulates to white.

Trees streak the primed canvas;
goat-pits dot ice like sheet music;
wisps of straw seem gold veins
woven through the snow.

Ducks are changed
from chalky-white
to mayonnaise, within
bright cold. Cream pelts
have subtle sepia stains.
Dark hens look blue
beside stark snow.

All background space
grows clear
as easy breathing.

A touch
transforms
everything we know.

Marcia Slatkin

John Renner

GREENPORT, L.I.

Where good old Suffolk spreads her arms,
A lovely bay presents its charms,
All spangled o'er with sails;
By night, and day, the spacious bay,
Business and life, and wealth display,
And gallant vessels, trim and gay,
Wafted by island gales.

Its waters smooth as melted ore,
Securely kiss its peaceful shore,
Skirted by isles around;
And isthmuses, and bars and shoals,
That as the great Atlantic rolls,
The rushing giant safely holds
Within the proper bound.

First, Gardner's Island, like a rock,
Breaks off the sea, from old Montauk,
A pier, by Nature planned.
And then Plumb Island locked between
The sound, and bay, doth intervene,
Just like an emerald bright and green,
Upon a lady's hand.

Near where old Sterling's hamlet stood,
In sweet and happy solitude,
Behold our city rise!
Destined in future times to be
The mart of every land and sea,
And distancing all rivalry,
In wealth and enterprise.

A channel from the ocean tide,
Deep, safe, and beautiful, and wide,
Meanders at her feet;
And winding onward still its way,
It finds the smooth, Peconic bay,
Where Robin's vocal isle doth lay,
And rival waters meet.

Five hundred ships may safely ride,
Abreast her green, ascending side,
And storm and wave defy;
And listen to old Neptune's roar,
If he his wrath indignant pour
Upon Easthampton's fated shore,
In calm security.

Brooklyn from her majestic height,
May well look down upon the site
Of this young sister fair!
And fondly take her by the hand,
And by a double railroad band,
Her rising usefulness command,
And wealth and grandeur share.

Then see Long Island; pleasant line,
Resplendant with improvement shine,
Between its cities bright,
For each a rural paradise,
Where wealth pours out his golden prize,
And towns and villages arise.
And mansions of delight.

John Orville Terry

Ed Muller

HOUSE

house   through whose moonlit windows
I watched the trees   blue snow like a widening
mind bordered by water   and the deer

suggested in shadow
under black branches

a room   unvisited except in
a quiet time   brain laden like
a summer tree   its fruit
warming the skin

taste   on an empty tongue

D. H. Melhem

Frank Muller

WALKING THE GLACIER'S WAKE

Early morning

the rising sun at my back
  painting my extended shadow on the sand

I walk the edge of the path a glacier took
10,000 years before
  an icy finger ploughing up Paumanok in its wake

dropping these giant stones
four times my height
  like pebbles.

Russell Cameron Perry

Russell Cameron Perry

LOOKING AT THE SKY

I never will have time
I never will have time enough
To say
How beautiful it is
The way the moon
Floats in the air
As easily
And lightly as a bird
Although she is a world
Made all of stone.

I never will have time enough
To praise
The way the stars
Hang glittering in the dark
Of steepest heaven
Their dewy sparks
Their brimming drops of light
So fresh so clear
That when you look at them
It quenches thirst.

Anne Porter

Larry Landolfi

December 7

POETS FISHING

Who among us can deny
there is something beyond
the superficial world?

Pen in hand
we cast our poets' lures into it
        sometimes with intention
        sometimes simply trolling

waiting for a tug on the line
the signal that something has hooked us.

Russell Cameron Perry

Ralph Pugliese, Jr.

DECEMBER STORM, 1993

The storm begins with light
innocent snow, evolves into
sudden sleet, howling winds
leveling trees, sting of ice
against windows, dark and sodden
skies. Tides rise, inch by inch,
claiming the dock, the walk,
the patio. A swollen bay
finds its way to a rendezvous
with an arm of itself
on the disappearing street.
Barometers plunge.

We tape windows, fill oil lamps,
search for candles, fill the firebox
with logs, feel the cold clutch
of fear—pretend indifference.

When the driveway disappears
I shall sit in the shower stall,
close the door,
and sing.

Lynn Kozma

Barbara Imperiale

SNOWED IN

Pale light
and the bedroom curtains—
at last we are content indoors.

Nesting
on new fat pillows
stuffed with gosling feathers

we lie
in warm wait
for the snow's fine hissing

against the roof
and aluminum siding
to start.

This book I shall read
if it takes all night.
With any luck

we'll be snowed in by morning.

George Wallace

Ann Glazebrook

December 10

CURRENTS

A gray gull
from Hempstead Bay

glides in the currents
of a gray sky

high above this
small house

at the bottom
of a hill

where I kneel
tying boxwoods

for the winter.
I blink, it banks

and its white
breast feathers

blaze with a light
whose source

I cannot see.

Norbert Krapf

Bob Schmitz

December 11

OUT HERE

constable sky
carpets of vacuumed sand
the south fork of fish-shaped paumanok

swirls   twists in
northwest wind

out here
the land absorbs us
we are penciled in
flutter of footprints
bits of blown hair
feather brushed

out here
no wine makes the head spin
no joint raises spirit to gull

out here
nothing cleaves us to earth

Beverly Pion

Marlene Weinstein

December 12

THROUGH DARK LEAVES

A silver full moon
rides with me
to a wide beyond

beyond my glowing
cigarette-tip
captive under skies

skies slow to awaken
glows quiet
an unruffled snow

hides animus
like a hint
a barbaric claw

or eyes hold captive
why travel
moon-skin on black leaves

leave roads, abandon
essence for
a naked flamboyance

Pramila Venkateswaran

Russell Cameron Perry (Montage with Larry Landolfi)

DECEMBER

As inevitable as death,
December comes
with snow and ice
covering
rooftops, eaves,
crowns of trees,
mountaintops,
valleys.
The moon is wafer,
the sky black
with chalk-scrawled stars.
All the lakes frosted—
everyone can
walk on water.
Only the evergreens
retain their fierce grip
on the stuff of earth,
stretching towards Heaven.
White feathers fall—
geese arrow south,
honking. "Tomorrow!
Tomorrow!"

Stanley H. Barkan

HOMAGE TO WRAPPED PEAR

Gladys has prepared
pears
in tart pastry.

She puts them
in blue-patterned
bowls on the kitchen
counter where
the sun paints
pictures of orange
and late autumn
of purple and the coming
of evening.

We slice the pears
open ourselves up
to the parting
of past and present
the perfect
plu-perfect
of pear.

Ginger Williams

Victoria Twomey

WINTER WHITE
for my daughter, Rachel

like ermine you cover
the body's ground
filling in the contours
clinging to the curves
giving every hardened surface
a softness and uniformity.
everything of color
now white. the earth's
skin powdered
like a woman's face.

Arleen Ruth Cohen

William Duryea, Jr.

SNOW

I am perfect here in the snow,
within the whiteness.

If I keep my eyes shut long enough,
and tilt my face just so,
I could be enveloped, reabsorbed into
the beginning, the end.

In this crystal blanket
woven one flake
at a time
there is no dread,
no desire,
no need to be better,
anything other than myself.

I have no need for company,
nor for rescue.
I do not need to be called in from the cold.
I am one with the pureness of the day.

Tammy Nuzzo-Morgan

EASY AS WIND

Easy as wind that lifts white pine
and blows for flowers, showering rose
petals on cold marble statues,
we touch and separate.
I am familiar
With water burning the land,
turning catbrier to red-brown wire,
clinging to live. I have seen flame
waiting to burn, altering shadows,
striking rectangles beyond the trees.
Even the sea collects its powers and strikes,
baffling the sand's composure.
But now, suddenly,
wherever I look I see wind
I cannot see, touching nowhere, everywhere.

Grace Schulman

Frank Muller

GATHERING PEACE

If I could walk on clouds,
I'd fall through snowy mountains
on cities stirring where once I tread.
I'd sink in foamy seas,
rapturous, white
billowing in moonscape pillows
flowing where sunset sears
across the sky.

We are orphaned from ourselves
till we harvest clouds
gathering peace in metered time.

James P. Friel

TO BEGIN WINTER

Two squirrels
chase the last
hours of autumn
through a mantle
of brittle leaves.
A black flock
alights like snow
over the willow
beside the pond.
The sun lies
down for the night
in late afternoon.

Tonight
a warm touch
will be welcome.
A soft lamp
in a window.
A leap of flame
in the throat
of a stone hearth.
And perhaps,
a single
green thought
of spring.

Daniel Thomas Moran

December 20

Jan La Roche

SOLSTICE

It is December, and a half-moon
is suspended in the dusk.
If I could stretch my arm
that impossible distance,
breaking the membrane of space
and light to its pale, pitted surface

my hand would cup its roundness,
powdery and scarred,
cold to the touch but glowing
from where I stood,
basking in its ethereal veil.

It is winter, but I believe in love,
my feet seeking the soft grass
matted by gloss to the hardened ground
though stones and frosted reeds
knuckle under the soles of my shoes.

I am taking neither root nor flight,
but feel the shiver of longing
for the fire deep in the earth,
reaching beyond gravity's pull
to the luminous mirror of desire.

Mindy Kronenberg

Kate Kelly

December 21

SUCCESSION

I do not mind so much the blank look
on the face of dawn over the brittle fields,

the grass covered with white stipple. But when
first frost comes to the late-blossoming daisies,

I recognize what it means to be summarily tossed
aside by the season, as something irrelevant—

a thing designed for an undemanding season,
like spring, possibly even summer. This is winter:

the days of frozen birch have come. All
that was gentle is lost beneath a fine frost.

Now the wise old squirrel hides himself
in the cracked ribs of trees, or underground.

We will not see him again before the thaw,
when he comes out to consider the latest realities—

like who gets to nest in the maple,
and where are those acorns hidden?

George Wallace

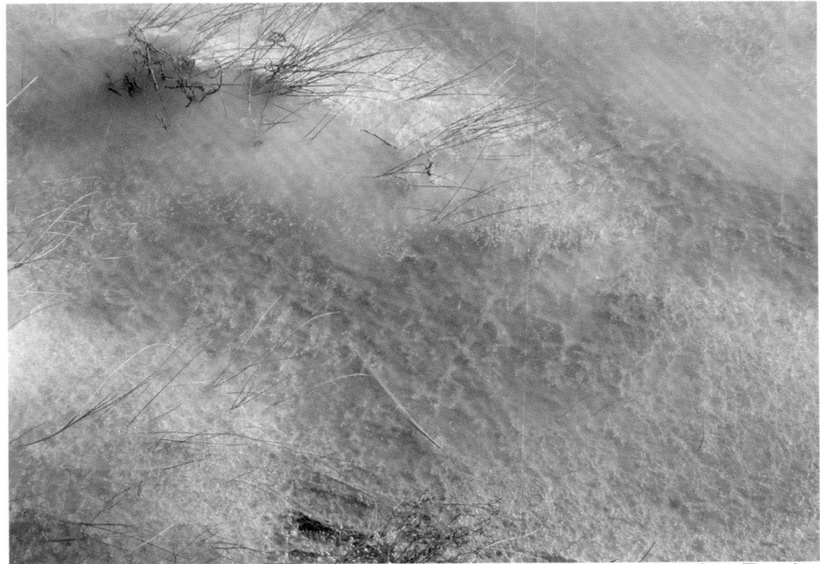

Jan La Roche

December 22

SMITHTOWN, LONG ISLAND

for William Heyen

If we wrote it all with skates
on Miller's Pond, if all
this time we'd shoveled upstate
soil off Highway Department trucks, stayed
in our boyhood houses
with next-door girls in blouse and apron,
never went to college but studied
in the circle Bull Smith rode that day—

combed clams out of the basket
of St. James Harbor, yanked flounder
and trout out of the Nissequogue—

never cradled many books,
never published anything except
our faces in the Island light,
our voices in the yoke of oars
would we be happy men?

Are all our poems a way of lacing
those old skates again?

John Kaufman

Ann Glazebrook

December 23

CLAMS FOR CHRISTMAS CHOWDER

In a room above my head,
I hear my brother.
He has dressed himself
in fleece-lined pants
and orange-flapped hat.

I hear him first in stocking feet
and then the green weight of waders
pacing with impatience,
waiting for me. I know this
as a special day and dress quickly.
Low tide is at noon and gulls
wait for us in shallow pools
warmed by a December sun.

Soon with some deliverance,
we will walk the snow edge of
crab meadow, crossing over rocks
hung with the snap weed of summer.
The gatherers before us will be few.
It is very cold and words
spoken hang like frosted pearls,
before they crash
themselves against the brine.

The day before Christmas
and I have clothed
myself as a pilgrim and
walk by my brother's side
yellow bucket in hand.

The sound of steel against rock
and the suck of black mud
as it yields to the fork.
Quickly I pick the sweet clams
in their blue-gray shells, quickly
before the iced sea finds its way
to the hole and reclaim its
children.

It is here in the rhythm of pitchfork
and shovel that I learned to hear the
stillness of time and joined the gatherers
before me, harvesting memories and clams
for Christmas chowder.

Gladys Henderson

DECEMBER

Out in the middle of the lake
Some men who work for the village
Have moored
A floating Christmas tree

At night I see it
From my bedroom window
It rocks a little
Drifts a little
In the wind from the ocean
A fiery cone of jewels.

Anne Porter

Linda Russo

WINTER AT SEVEN A.M.

At the base of a dark wall of trees
a fire burns, flameless and still
glows like a single hot coal—
a jewel dropped by a giant in my woods.

As I watch it grows, gains inner light.

My eyes lose focus, yet cannot resist
but look, glance off, look back
until the brightness overcomes my
power to see.

I cannot walk away, but stand
close by my window
which frames a dull sky, pink clouds
dark trees over cold snow
and that round fireball, rising.

Charlene Babb Knadle

Kate Kelly

DECEMBER

I follow footprints frozen
in the snow, each step by step;
then facing my own night,
they abruptly end. Frozen
water is moonlit & unbroken.
I go no farther.

Crystal night: iced imagination
fixes nothing,
stitches no figures in
the shiver of unlinked stars.

Wanting a grace & hoping
failure be buried here,
I get more wood for the fire.

Dan Murray

Barbara Keenan

December 27

WINTER

Dressed not in her green dress,
nor yellow,
nor red.

Nor the lake blue of a swimsuit—
skin gold
with the sun.

But comes instead in nothing
but a T-shirt,
white and snug;

an angel with frozen wings
in the stillness
of love.

Bill Graeser

Eric Lohse

December 28

DECEMBER 29TH

It's two days till the new year and August still hangs
on the calendar upstairs. The window's light
turns shadowless. Empty trees look old, dried up,
easy marks for huckster wind gusts off an ice cap
as imagination makes weird mistakes
tricking us into seeking meaning at year's end.

Let's not revel in the fact that we didn't wash
or wax the car once last summer. Let's ponder
the idea that soon winter draws to another close
and spring comes again. What is it we have to do?
Have we not been busy doing the best we can?

Graham Everett

Eric Lohse

IN DECEMBER
for Keith

Autumn comes to an end
like an eyelid slowly closing.

Looking out into winter's night,
the field once overrun
with wild grasses and brush,
now a fine white silk sheet
under glittering stars,
distant moon.

Crushed snow records footprints,
leafless trees silhouette,
an ice puddle shatters like glass,
frozen branches snap,
echoing.

Taking a deep breath,
I open the storm door,
exhale steam
into bitter night air.

It's just a short stay,
I tell myself, and
accept winter on this island,
yet another year.

Kathaleen Donnelly

from

SEA-DRIFT: ON THE BEACH AT NIGHT ALONE

On the beach at night alone,
As the old mother sways her to and fro singing her husky song,
As I watch the bright stars shining, I think a thought of the clef of the universe and of the future.
A vast similitude interlocks all,
All spheres, grown, ungrown, small, large, suns, moons, planets,
All distances of place however wide,
All distances of time, all inanimate forms,
All souls, all living bodies though they be ever so different, or in different worlds,
All gaseous, watery, vegetable, mineral processes, the fishes, the brutes,
All nations, colors, barbarisms, civilizations, languages,
All identities that have existed or may exist on this globe, or any globe,
All lives and deaths, all of the past, present, future,
This vast similitude spans them, and always has spann'd,
And shall forever span them and compactly hold and enclose them.

Walt Whitman

NASA

ABOUT THE POETS AND PHOTOGRAPHERS

Paul Agostino [Holbrook] is the author of a textbook about writing poetry: *Created Writing: Poetry from New Angles*. He has published two volumes of poetry: *The Tourist Heart* and *Engagements and Disengagements*. He teaches at Suffolk Community College and is in the Wiffleball Hall of Fame in Holbrook.

Terry Amburgey [Massapequa] is a fine art photographer, based out of New York and known for his scenic work, black & white being his favorite, which is normally placed on fine art paper as a Giclee. Also known as a haiku poet, a book combining his poetry and his photography, Nature's Cathedral, is due out soon. Website:www.terryamburgey.com

Marjorie Appleman's [East Hampton] poems have been published in many journals and anthologies, and in her chapbook, *Against Time* (Huntington, NY: Birnham Wood Graphics, 1994). She is also a widely produced playwright—in New York at the Manhattan Theatre Club, Playwrights Horizons, and around the country and abroad.

Philip Appleman [East Hampton] is the author of seven volumes of poetry, including his *New and Selected Poems, 1956–1996* (University of Arkansas Press, 1996), three novels, including *Apes and Angels* (Putnam, 1989), and various non-fiction works, including the Norton Critical Edition, *Darwin*.

Susan Astor's [Mineola] poetry has appeared in over 100 magazines and journals. Her first collection, *Dame*, was published by The University of Georgia Press, 1980. Her second, was *Spider Lies*, in 2001 by Trimble Press. For 25 years, she has worked as a poetry teacher in the public schools and in private classes.

Fuad Attal [Brooklyn] was born in Palestine and immigrated to the US in 1984. He wrote his first book in Arabic in 1998, *An Immigrant's Thoughts*. His work frequently appears in a bilingual cultural magazine, *Dahish Voice and Arabic Faces*. His latest book, *Love & Memory*, was published by Cross-Cultural Communications in 2005.

David B. Axelrod [Selden], current Poet Laureate of Suffolk County, has published eighteen books, most recently, *Deciduous Poems* (Ahadadabooks, 2008). Recipient of numerous awards, including three Fulbrights, his poetry has been translated into fourteen different languages. Website: www.writersunlimited.org/laureate.

Jesse Ball [Port Jefferson / Chicago] has lived both in the US and in Europe. Hew studied at Vassar College and Columbia University and currently teaches writing at the School of the Art Institute of Chicago. Jesse is the author of *Samedi the Deafness* (Vintage, 2007), *Vera & Linus* (Nyhil, 2006), and *March Book* (Grove, 2004). His work has appeared in *The Best American Poetry* in 2006. A novella, *The Early Deaths of Lubeck, Brennan, Harp and Carr*, was recently published in *The Paris Review*. www.jesseball.com

Mia Barkan Clarke's [Long Beach / New Paltz, New York] poetry and art have been published in the *Paterson Literary Review*, by Cross-Cultural Communications, and in many other literary magazines. She is the author of *My Sacred Circle Mandala Journal*. Her paintings have been exhibited at the Paterson Museum and the Stage Gallery in Merrick.

Stanley H. Barkan [Merrick] is the editor/publisher of the Cross-Cultural Review Series of World Literature and Art. In 1991, Poets House and the NYC Board of Education of named him "Poetry Teacher of the Year," and in 1996, the Small Press Center awarded him, as editor of Cross-Cultural Communications, the Ben Franklin bust for "the Best of the Small Presses." His own poetry has been translated into 25 languages, some of which are included in his 15 collections. His latest book is *Strange Seasons* (Sofia, Bulgaria: Angoboy, 2009).

William Batcher [Calverton] considers himself a poet under construction. He is a retired teacher and leads a writers group in Riverhead. His poetry has been published in both national magazines and online collections, and has won several awards. A book of Easter poems, *Footsteps to the Resurrection*, was published in 2005.

Aija Birzgalis [Port Jefferson] is a photographer, born and raised on Long Island. Trained as a biologist, she works in the Department of Physiology at SUNY Stony Brook. Her photos reflect an interest in the color and architecture of nature in general and plants in particular.

Janice Bishop [Manorville] has poems in journals in America, England, Wales, and Ireland. As an actress, she has portrayed Emily Dickinson, and recently in New York City, she has appeared in Caryl Churchill's *Heart's Desire* and as Tiresias in *The Burial at Thebes.*

Cliff Bleidner [East Meadow] writes haiku, formalist, and free verse poetry. Co-founder and coordinator at PPA (Performance Poets Association), he is a retired pharmaceutical chemist, former long-distance runner, and substance-abuse counselor.

Robert Bonanno [Amityville] has lived on Long Island all of his life, and art has always been a part of it. Whether it be photography or guitar playing or the photo lab that he now owns, Color Images Laboratory, Inc. in St. James, "the arts are always at the core."

Jef Bravata [St. James] has been a professional photographer for 28 years, shooting portraits and weddings as well as commercial imaging. His personal work, appearing in this book, celebrates his passion for floral blurs. These poetic studies are gestural and, at the same time, inspirational.

Mary Brennan's [Quogue] residence, located in the magnificence of the East End, inspires her photographs. Cupsogue is her favorite beach.

Aldolfo Briceno [West Hempstead] is a winner of several Leonard Victor Awards, and has received a "27," the highest points, at PFLI, Photographic Federation of Long Island. For three years in a row, he has finished among the top five "All Stars" photographers at PFLI. He shares his knowledge with others by judging and teaching both digital photography and Photoshop. He has been instrumental in helping the PFLI start competitions with digital projectors.

Peter Brink [Setauket] is Chairman of the Department of Physiology and Biophysics at Stony Brook. He has a life-long interest in biology and physiology that includes marine organisms. He has been scuba diving for over 40 years. Some 20 years ago, he decided to use underwater photography to illustrate the beauty of the underwater world around us. He dives locally in the Atlantic Ocean but has also traveled extensively to far-flung places as New Caledonia and the Seychelles. His photos are featured on a number of websites both nationally and internationally.

John Brokos [North Merrick] is an International Nature and Pictorial Photographer Exhibitor, listed in the top 25 in the world by the Photographic Society of America. He has sold more than 1000 photos through galleries and private craft fairs. He has been photographing more than 50 years.

Arnold Brower [Oceanside] has been a member of the Wantagh Camera Club for several years and enjoys nature and wildlife photography. He is an officer and director at the Photographic Federation of Long Island.

William Cullen Bryant (1794–1878) [Roslyn] was a lawyer, journalist, editor, poet, and part owner of the *New York Post*. He moved to Roslyn in 1843 and lived there at his estate, "Cedarmere," until his death. William has been called the "Nester" of American poets because of his leadership in the early poetry movement in America. Most of his poems on nature were written at Cedarmere which is maintained as an historic site by Nassau County.

Lynn Buck's [Hampton Bays / Cockeysville, Maryland] poetry has appeared in many national journals and anthologies. She has published two books of poems, *Autumn Fires* and *Two Minus One*. She also has authored three novels—*Eccentric Circles, Amanda's House*, and *Final Curtain*. She currently lives near Baltimore with her cat, Shadow, who keeps a watchful eye on her work.

Olivia Ward Bush-Banks (1869–1944) [Sag Harbor] was born in Sag Harbor of both African-American and Montauk Indian parents. She lived most of her life away from Long Island but visited the East End frequently. Olivia published two books of poetry which include poems about Long Island. Besides being a poet, Olivia was a columnist, drama coach, and writer.

Louis Bussolati [Baldwin] is a thirty-plus-year resident of Long Island, who studied with Virginia Terris. Moderator of the Baldwin Poetry Group for 10 years, he has been published in several little magazines.

Francis Carlin (1881–1945) [Bay Shore], who was a native of Bay Shore, wrote his one book of verse in 1918 while being employed as a floorwalker at Macy's in New York City. The poem, "Mary's Island," based on his observations of Massapequa Lake, is from his book, *My Ireland* (New York: Henry Holt & co., 1918). Many poets, including Christopher Morley, have expressed their appreciation of it.

Linda Carnevale [Glen Head] is happily married and a stay-at-home mother of two wonderful sons. She is the author of Barrow's, *Hot Winds for the SAT* and *SAT 2400: Aiming for the Perfect Score*. A sought-after SAT Tutor, Mrs. Carnevale is a professional development trainer for the Teacher Resource Center of Nassau BOCES. She enjoys cooking, decorating, travel, and, above all, being a wife and mother.

Donald Case [Farmingville] grew up on Long Island and has lived here most of his life. He is 50 years old and travels to upstate New York and western U.S. in order to hike, camp, and photograph the landscape.

Diana Chang (1925–2009) [Watermill] was the author of six novels and five chapbooks of poetry. She taught in the English Department and the Program in the Arts at Barnard College for ten years. She was also a painter whose work had been exhibited at the Guild Hall in East Hampton and at Ashwagh Hall in the Springs.

George Lawrence Chieffet [Dix Hills], raised on a farm in Dix Hills, received an MFA in creative Writing from the University of North Carolina. He has published over 50 stories and poems. He is the co-author (with Paul Rajeckas) of *Notes to the Motherland*, cited by Theatremania.com as Best Play for 2005.

Heather Cirincione [St. James / Weaverville, NC], a recent graduate of Furman University, has received many awards and honors in photography. She was on the photography staff of Furman University and has had her work published in several magazines and websites. Additionally, she has participated in many solo and juried shows displaying works from her overseas travels. She is an active participant in the Photographic Federation of Long Island. Recently, she has been awarded a fellowship to the Savannah College of Art and Design in order to pursue an MFA in photography.

Vince Clemente [Sag Harbor], a SUNY English Professor-Emeritus, is a poet/biographer whose works include, *John Ciardi: Measure of the Man* and *Paumanok Rising*. Author of nine volumes of verse, his latest volume is *Under a Baleful Star: A Garland for Margaret Fuller* (Cross-Cultural Communications, 2007).

Arlene Greenwald Cohen [Bellport / Stone Ridge, New York] is a painter and poet, a former art teacher, now a resident of the Hudson Valley, where she continues her pursuits of painting and writing, exhibiting and publishing in her new surroundings.

Arleen Ruth Cohen [Hewlett], for over 60 years, has lived on Long Island. She is a graduate of F.I.T. and received a B.A and an M.S. from Queens College. She is a professional artist and ceramicist who has published over 250 poems. In the last 10 years, she has worked as a Real Estate Broker and Property Manager.

Christopher Corradino [Wantagh] is a diverse photographer with a passion for capturing nature's fleeting moments. His coverage of major news and sporting events has appeared on the front pages of well-known publications, including *Newsday*. To view more of Christopher's award-winning images, visit his online gallery at www.christography.com.

Yolanda Coulaz [Rockville Centre] is a poet, photographer, editor, and founder of Purple Sage Press. She teaches poetry workshops to middle- and high-school students throughout Long Island. She edited and published the anthology *For Loving Precious Beast* to help benefit Loving Touch Animal Rescue. Her first book of poetry, *Spirits and Oxygen*, has been selected by SUNY Stony Brook to be used in an advance course in poetry. Her second book is forthcoming.

Darlene Cunnup [Rockville Centre] has been a photographer for over twenty years. Originally from South Carolina, she has lived in Rockville Centre for eleven years. Her photographs are in many private collections and have been exhibited in local coffee shops and libraries. She is accomplished in all aspects of photography but prefers photographing nature and pets. "Blue Bottle" is published in *Endless Journeys* (2008) and *The Best Photographs of 2007* (International Library of Photography, 2008).

George DeCamp [St. James] is a Long Island-based photographer, whose images have appeared in various magazines, including *Audubon* and *Nature's Best* and in museums, including the Smithsonian Museum of Natural History in Washington, DC. His work revolves around nature and wildlife subjects. In October 2007, he was named a Highly Commended Winner in the Shell/BBC Wildlife Photographer of the Year awards in London, the largest and most well-respected contest of its type in the world. www.decamp.net

John DeLorenzo [Nesconset] lives on Long Island with his wife Sue. He received a B.F.A. in photography from the School of Visual Arts in Manhattan in 1987 and has been shooting for magazines professionally since then. He is also a Financial Advisor with an office in Kings Park.

Donna Demian [East Setauket], born in a Mennonite community in Ohio, and moved to Long island in 1974. She began writing in an adolescent diary, letters, and poetry when introduced to Ginger Williams's Unitarian Universalist Free Writer's group, of which she is a member. She is also a psychotherapist, specializing in work with children and families, as well as a classical pianist.

Joan Reilly DeRosa [Setauket] has lived on Long Island for most of her life. Here she shares the variety of the seasons with her husband and explores a wealth of ideas in poems with her friends. She reads, writes, and, in season, gardens with the butterflies and a curious catbird never out of her sight.

Red Diamond [Port Jefferson] is the 2004 winner of the Phi Theta Kappa Citation Scholarship for Poetry and the author of a book, "the title of which he prefers not to provide for reasons of FCC broadcasting protocols." He is currently writing a guidebook to the brewpubs of the Pacific Northwest. Readers are invited to his e-mail at mrreddiamond@yahoo.com. He presently lives in a motor home somewhere in Washington State.

Arthur Dobrin [Westbury] is the author of 20 books, including several full poetry collections and chapbooks, two novels, a book of short stories, a memoir, and other books on ethics, and anthologies, either as the sole author, editor, or co-author. *Seeing Through Africa*, a memoir (Cross-Culural Communications, 2004), is one of his recent titles. He is a professor of Humanities at Hofstra University and Leader Emeritus of the Ethical Humanist Society of Long Island.

Kathaleen Donnelly [Please see About the Editor.]

William Duryea, Jr. [Remsenburg] is a native Long Islander, born and raised in Old Westbury with summers spent in East Hampton. He has been photographing for fifty years from boats to racehorses. He received a B.F.A. in Photography at age 65 from the School of Visual Arts. He tries to bring out the abstract in reality and believes pictures can be seen anywhere if the artist can forget he is looking at the familiar.

Arlene Eager's [Smithtown] poems have appeared in the *Hudson Review, Atlanta Review*, the *Southern Review, Critical Quarterly, The Gettysburg Review*, several anthologies and other publications. She leads the advanced poetry workshop in the Round Table Program, SUNY Stony Brook. She and her husband Bill live in New York and Maine.

Ken Eastman (1943–2008) [East Northport] is a member of the Sweetbriar Nature Photography Club and the Syosett Camera Club. Ken loves bird photography "because birds make such perfect models."

Richard Elman (1934–1997) [Stony Brook] was a poet, novelist, and journalist. For a bibliography of his work see the website: Literati.net/Elman. His memoir, *Namedropping: Mostly Literary Memoirs*, is published by SUNY Press.

Carolyn Emerson [Setauket] has poems published in *Poesie-U.S.A.*, *Long Pond Review, LIQ;* and *Long Island Sounds 2007*. She's a founder of the Euterpe Poetry Group and has been appointed to the Suffolk Poet Laureate Selection Panel. She is a reference librarian at Emma Clark Library in Setauket.

Laura M. Eppig [Bay Shore], an award-winning Long Island born photographer, Laura photographs the majority of her images locally. As an ardent lover of nature, photography enables Laura to combine her passions for the environment, bird-watching, all living beings, hiking, and art.

Graham Everett [Sound Beach] is the Founding Editor of *Street Magazine* and Press and a Professor in the General Studies Program at Adelphi University. He is the author of 14 books of poems—the latest, *That Nod Toward Love* (2006).

Richard Fiedorowicz [Oakdale] is a retired teacher and life-long Long Island resident. With nearly five decades of B&W and color darkroom experience, for the last six years, he has concentrated solely on digital photography. He shares his love of photography with fellow members of the Island Photo Group.

Adam D. Fisher's [Stony Brook] poems have appeared in a wide variety of publications, including *The Long Island Quarterly, Manhattan Review*, and *North Atlantic Review*. His books of poems are *Rooms, Airy Rooms* and *Dancing Alone*. He won First Prize at the 1990 Westhampton Writers Festival, an Anna D. Rosenberg poetry award, and a Mid-Island Y poetry award.

Charles Adés Fishman [Bellport] was co-founder of the Long Island Poetry Collective and a founding editor of *Xanadu Magazine*. He created and directed the Visiting Writers Program (1979–1997) and the Distinguished Speakers Program (2001–2007) at Farmingdale State. His books include *The Death Mazurka*, a 1990 Pulitzer Prize nominee, and *Chopin's Piano*, a recipient of the 2007 Paterson Award for Literary Excellence. His anthology, *Blood to Remember: American Poets on the Holocaust*, was published by Time Being Books in 2007.

James P. Friel [Northport] was born in the Bronx and has taught and traveled around the United States. He is a tenured professor at SUNY Farmingdale. He writes poetry, fiction, philosophy, and plays and has published widely. His longest poem, 30 pages, is in honor of the artist, Joan Miró.

Jyoti Ganguly [Stony Brook] is a physician in private practice who has been a photographer for 30 years but is an avid shutterbug for the past seven years. He has taken a couple of workshops, but most of his pictures are taken during daily travels.

Mary L. Gardiner (1791–1860) [Sag Harbor], daughter of Samuel and Sally L'Hommedieu, grew up in this whaling community writing sentimental and personal verse about her observations and friends. Her second marriage was to the Rev. John D. Gardiner of the Presbyterian Church of Sag Harbor. She was ill most of her life but managed to travel across Long Island and wrote poems about what she felt and saw. While visiting the home of Joseph Moulton in Roslyn, she wrote one of her best remembered poems, "Hempstead Harbor." The Moulton House was later sold to poet William Cullan Bryant. At age 52, she published her book, *Collections from the Prose and Poetical Writings*.

Dan Giancola [Mastic] teaches English at Suffolk County Community College's Eastern Campus in Riverhead. "Vivarium" and "Eels" can be found in his latest book, *Part Mirth, Part Murder* (Street Press, 2006).

Ann Glazebrook [Port Jefferson] strives in her photography to capture the beauty and tranquility found in nature. She feels that, in our increasingly materialistic society, there has been an increasing dissociation from the natural world. She hopes her photographs stimulate recognition of the close connection between humans and the Earth and the moral obligation that we have to protect it. "Peace."

Dennis Golin [Fresh Meadows] is a past president of the Photographic Federation of Long Island. His photos have been published in Kodak calendars, on book covers, and in magazine articles. He was the Grand Prize Winner of the *Newsday* Annual Photo Contest, the Queens Tri-Centennial Photo Contest, and the North Shore Hospital Photo Contest.

John Gozelski [East Northport] was born and raised in the Northport area and has loved taking pictures from a very young age. By the time he was in high school, he wound up spending most of his time in the media center, instead of class. From there, his love of nature has aimed his lens. Though he does love to travel to other places, he feels Long Island is still one of the greatest.

Bill Graeser [Mastic / Iowa] was born and raised in Mastic, Long Island, and taught the Transcendental Meditation technique for 16 years throughout the Long Island area. He now works as a carpenter at Maharishi University of Management, Fairfield, Iowa. His poems are published in *Michigan Avenue Review, Lyrical Iowa, Chiron Review, Long Island Quarterly, Performance Poets, Dryland Fish, The Live Poets Society,* and *Punk Debris*.

Ange Gualtieri (1919–2007) [Centereach] attended the Germain School of Photography in New York City and was a member of Paumanok Camera Club. He used a Bronica ETR and Hasselblad 2000FCW to shoot landscapes, portraits, and macro photography.

Joan Carole Hand [Rocky Point], a resident of Long Island, has always felt that the subjects of most of her poetry are inspired by both the ocean and Long Island Sound. Ms. Hand did her undergraduate work at Bard College and is the recipient of a Master's Degree from The Johns Hopkins University's Writing Seminar, as well as a Master of Fine Arts from the University of Iowa's Writer's Workshops. She has authored three poetry collections—*Entrances to Nowhere, The Facts of Life*, and, her latest, *East of July* (all published by Cross-Cultural Communications).

Robert Harrison [East Meadow] is a poet, photographer, and playwright. His photographs have won over 55 awards, including a Folio Award. His poems have been part of a Grammy Nomination and have been printed in many anthologies. His plays can be seen in libraries across Long Island. He is listed in *Who's Who in America*.

George Held [Sag Harbor] has owned a house in Sag Harbor since 1971, and the East End of Long Island inspired most of the nature poems collected in *Winged* (1995) and *Grounded* (2005). He is a four-time Pushcart Prize Nominee and has published nine collections of poems, most recently, *W Is for War* (2006).

Gladys Henderson [Nesconset] is a poet, painter, and retired Macy's retail executive. Her works have been published in the following magazines and anthologies: *For Love of Precious Beast, Kaleidoscope, The Light of the City and Sea, Long Island Dreams, Long Island Sounds, Lyrismos, Midwestern University Quarterly, Poets in Performance, Primal Sanities,* and *Songs of Seasoned Women*. An award-winning poet, in 2006 she was a finalist for the Paumanok Poetry Prize. Her first poetry chapbook, *Eclipse of Heaven*, was published by Finishing Line Press (2008).

Mary Kennan Herbert [Brooklyn] is a Brooklyn resident, originally from St. Louis, Missouri. She teaches literature and writing courses at Long Island University's Brooklyn Center. Her work has won awards and has been published in over 20 countries around the world.

Kathleen Hervey [North Babylon] is a retired educator who taught for over 30 years and often used photography as a tool in her classroom. In addition, she enjoys traveling and photographing the many types of flora and fauna of many countries. She has participated in art exhibits and has been published in a number of journals. She has been a member and officer of the Sweetbriar Photography Camera Club.

William Heyen's [Nesconset / Brockport, New York] many books include, *Long Island Light, Crazy Horse in Stillness* (winner of the 1997 Small Press Books Award), and *Shoah Train: Poems* (finalist for the 2004 Natural Books Award). His *Home: Autobiographies* appeared in 2006. Contact: www.wheyen@rochestor.rr.com

Joan Higuchi [West Islip] is a lifetime Long Island resident and a retired Registered Nurse. A first-place winner in the rhyming division of the Writer's Digest Competition, she has won a number of local awards, and her publication credits include *LIQ, The Lyric, Aurorean*, and several anthologies.

Barbara Hoffman [West Babylon] is a poet, photographer, and artist. She was awarded a Fellowship to VCCA, Sweetbriar, Virginia,1995, and was the subject of the WLIW Channel 21 show, Originals—Arts on Long Island series.

Mary L'Hommedieu Gardiner Horsford (1824–1855) [Shelter Island] grew up on Shelter Island with her sister, Phebe, while their father was the minister of the Presbyterian Church. She enjoyed nature, religion, and writing verse. Mary married Eben Horsford in 1847 and later became the mother of their four daughters. In 1855, Mary's only book of poetry, *Indian Legends and Other Poems*, was published shortly before she died.

Florence M. Hughes (1924–2003) [Mt. Sinai], a long-time Long Island resident, was both poet and artist with interests in still life, nature, and portraits. Her paintings were exhibited on the Island. She earned a B.A. in Studio Art and Literature.

Richard Hunt [Levittown] has won over fifty major awards for his nature and wildlife images at the Photographic Federation of Long Island and at local photography competitions. He was awarded a fellowship at the PFLI in 2002.

David Ignatow (1914–1997) [Springs] has lived mostly in the metropolitan area. His poems reflect the varied aspects of his life. He was an editor of the *Beloit Poetry Journal* for ten years, served for a time as poetry editor of *The Nation*, and, from 1968–1997, had been co-editor of *Chelsea*. His poems have appeared in *Abraxas, The New Yorker, Poetry*, and the *Yale Review*, to name a few. He earned the Poetry Society's Shelley Memorial Award, a Guggenheim Fellowship, and an award from the National Institute of Arts and Letters.

Yaedi Ignatow (East Hampton / Arizona] now lives and works in Tucson, Arizona. Her poems are included in *Long Island Poets*, edited by Robert Long (Sag Harbor: The Permanent Press, 1986).

Barbara Imperiale [East Yaphank] is an artist who has achieved a B.F.A. in Photography and an M.S. in Art Education (B-12). She has been active in the New York art community for the past ten years and could never imagine living anywhere else than Long Island. She is a photographer who tries to bring more of an artistic feel to her photographs and to break away from the technical constraints of photography as a medium. She is an artist at heart and by hand, with a passion for teaching others what she has learned about her surroundings through her visual journeys.

Juliet Isham (19th–20th Century) [Shelter Island] was a famous resident of Shelter Island who began writing poetry as a young girl. When she was just sixteen years old, one of her poems was accepted by the *Atlantic Monthly Magazine*. In 1924, her poetry book, *Winds and Tides*, about Shelter Island's people and naturally setting, was well received.

John Kaufman [Smithtown / Wisconsin] was born in Flushing, Queens, in 1960 and raised in Smithtown. He has an M.A. in English from the University of Connecticut at Storrs and currently edits a new online monthly journal, *The Northern Agrarian*. He now lives with his wife and daughter in a suburb of Milwaukee, Wisconsin.

Barbara Keenan [Center Moriches] is a happily retired teacher who loves to travel and look at the world and create images with her camera.

Kate Kelly [Northport] is active in the arts community as a poet and visual artist. She has presented her poetry on WBAI and has read at the Heckscher Museum of Art Poetry Series. *Barking at Sunspots*, her first book of poetry, is available at the Book Review in Huntington. Her visual work has been widely exhibited in many galleries and libraries, including The Huntington Arts Council's Galleries and The Alfred Van Loen Gallery in South Huntington. In 2005, she was chosen by Senator John Flanagan to be NYS Woman of the Year in the Arts.

Gene Keyes [East Northport] was born and grew up in New York City. He attended the Manhattan school of music and received a Bachelor of Music Degree in Performance, as well as a Master of Music in Music Education. He has a varied musical background, having worked as a professional musician in the New York area since the age of 15 and includes some 30 years in Music Education. His involvement with photography covers a span of four decades. He has worked extensively in the areas of travel and child photography and in recent years in nature and wildlife.

Kay Kidde's [Westhampton Beach] poems have appeared in dozens of literary magazines and anthologies. Her poetry collections are *Home Light Along the Shore* (North Atlantic Review, 1994), *Sounding for Light* (Linear Arts Books, 1998), *Early Sky* (Writer's Ink, 2002). Ms. Kidde founded the Peconic Housing Initiative for the homeless on Long Island's East End.

Jeanette Diane Klimszewski [East Northport] is a graduate of New York University. She taught Physical Education for 38 years and coached various sports, specializing in Archery and Field Hockey, and was acknowledged by local and state awards. After retirement, Jeanette became a clown where she entertained groups of abandoned and abused children. These experiences found their way into her poetry. She began writing and has been published in poetry columns and small press periodicals. She has published one book, *Promise* (Fore Angels Press, 2002).

Charlene Babb Knadle [Dix Hills] wrote her first poem at fourteen, inspired by a thunderstorm, then neglected poetry for prose while working toward her doctorate, achieved at St. John's University in 1998. After many published stories and essays, her novel, *Paper Lovers*, appeared in 2006. She teaches at Suffolk Community College.

Lynn Kozma [West Islip] is a Registered Nurse and served in WWII. She is a poet who has written two books, *Catching the Light and Phases of the Moon*. She is also an artist using pastels and watercolor, and an avid reader who loves to garden.

Norbert Krapf [Roslyn / Indiana], emeritus Professor of English at Long Island University and Poet Laureate of the C.W. Post Campus, now lives in Indianapolis. His poetry collections include, *Bittersweet Along the Expressway, The Country I Come From*, which was nominated for the Pulitzer Prize, and *Invisible Presence*, a collaboration with Indiana Photographer, Darryl Jones. He was named the 2008 Poet Laureate of Indiana.

Bill Kreisberg's [Great Neck] photography has been cited in the Sunday *New York Times* Art Section and has appeared in numerous exhibits, including the SoHo Gallery in Manhattan, and the B. J. Spoke Gallery in Huntington, where his work is sold.

Mindy Kronenberg [Miller Place] is an award-winning poet, writer, and Mentor at SUNY Empire State College. She conducts the Writer's Space at the Babylon Arts Council and teaches extensively through Poets & Writers. Her publication, *Book/Mark Quarterly Review*, co-sponsors literary events and is listed with the American Humanities Index.

Larry Landolfi [Islip / New Hampshire] was born in Pomona, California, but has lived three quarters of his life on Long Island. He now enjoys his two hobbies, photography and astronomy, with his lovely wife, Donna, in Rochester, NH.

Jan La Roche [St. James], a native Long Island artist, chooses imagery from around her life and creates moving poetry and beautiful icons of nature with her pen and camera. Since receiving her M.F.A. from Pratt in 1982, she has been a business partner in "Imagehouse" with her husband, Jef.

Toby Lieberman's [Long Beach] work experience is mainly in hand-knit instruction and as a WWII Arc Welder in the Brooklyn Navy Yard. His contributions to the baby boom are two sons and a daughter. He is the Moderator for the Great Books Discussion at Long Beach Library. He has written daily in his diary since 1980 to the present.

Tom Lindtvit [Rocky Point], prior to retirement, was licensed to practice professional engineering, land surveying, and real estate brokerage. He has been seriously photographing for about fifty years with all kinds of cameras. He did all his own film/print processing and is now using digital equipment.

Eric Lohse [Holtsville], since retiring from teaching, has been actively pursuing his long-term passion for photography and the natural scene. Varied and lesser-known natural areas of Long Island have been a rich resource. He has been a judge at local camera clubs, the Best in Show at Brookhaven Arts Council members' show, producer of slide shows and DVDs, and, most recently, of the 250th Anniversary of the 1757 Siege of Fort William Henry, Lake George, New York.

Stuart McCallum [Ridge], native to Long Island, grew up in the shadow of Whitman. Vestiges of the 19th Century Hamlet of Melville still remain, a link to his time. He "learned his song and sings it still." Thirty plus years of photographs connect him to this island, a lifetime seeking of the essence of Paumanok. Dutch roots that have remained unbroken since 1673 also keep him connected.

Sandy McIntosh [Oceanside] is the author of eight books of poetry, his latest collection, *Forty-nine Guaranteed Ways to Escape Death* (Marsh Hawk Press, 2007). His Op-Ed columns have appeared in *The New York Times, Newsday, The Nation, The Wall Street Journal*, and elsewhere. "To an Old Friend at a Poetry Reading" was published in *LIQ.*

Ray Makofske (1919–1998) [Hempstead], son of Jacob and Victoria Makofske, attended Hempstead High School and received a football scholarship in 1942 to Columbia University, where he studied English Literature. After serving as a Lieutenant Colonel in the Marine Corps during WWII, on Saipan-Tinnean, he received an M.A. from Teachers College at Columbia University and had four children with his wife, Joan Beer.

Henry Mangels [Sound Beach] is an avid photographer on Long Island, capturing its natural world. His work titled *Blizzard 2005* is just one example of his photographic talent. Other examples are in *New York Alive, Ranger Rick, The New York Daily News,* and *Pulse Magazine*.

Mankh (Walter E. Harris III) [Selden] is a poet, essayist, and small press publisher. He is the author/editor of seven books, including, *Singing an Epic of Peace, Modern Muses*, and *Haiku One Breaths*. He is a Turtle Islander as well as a Long Islander. Mankh's literary website: www.allbook-books.com.

David Martine [Southampton] is the Director of the Shinnecock Nation Cultural Center and Museum. He is an artist working in oil paintings, illustrations, and woodcarvings. He is a member of the Shinnecock-Montauk Chiricahua Apache Tribes. He lives on the Shinnecock Reservation.

Vidal Al Martinez [Smithtown] is the former Chief Surgeon of St. Catherine's Hospital in Kings Park. He is now retired, but started photography at 13 years of age after finding "Old Browny." He later trained with photo-luminaries Adam Jones, Rod Planek, Arthur Morris, and Ed Sambolin. A member of the Sweetbriar Camera Club and P.F.L.I., he has won numerous awards including second-place finish for the Leonard Victor Award in 2004, and Second-place for P.F.L.I. in 2005.

D. H. Melhem [Springs / Manhattan] has authored seven poetry collections, the latest, *New York Poems* (Syracuse University Press, 2005); a novel, *Blight*; a biography, *Gwendolyn Brooks*; and, as editor, *Heroism in the New Black Poetry*. In addition, her musical drama was produced in New York City, and she has published over 60 scholarly essays. Honors include the American Book Award and an NEH Fellowship. Two new novels, *Stigma* and *The Cave,* were published in 2007 by Syracuse University Press.

Eddie Mooney [Islip], an award-winning photographer, has been taking photos since 1982, but only went public in 2002. His love of the city comes from his early years in Brooklyn. His dyslexia helps him see things in a different light. Eddie's love of the water and exceptional eyes help him capture some breathtaking moments. You can visit his website to share some moments in time: www.edwardmooneyphotography.com.

Daniel Thomas Moran [Shelter Island] is the author of six collections of poetry: *Dancing for Victoria* (1991), *Gone to Innisfree* (1993), *Sheltered by Islands* (1995), *In Praise of August* (1999), *From HiLo to Willow Pond* (2002), and *Looking for the Uncertain Past* (2006). He was Poet Laureate of Suffolk County, New York, from 2005–2007. He edited *The Light of the City and Sea: An Anthology of Suffolk County Poetry*, 2006. He is a Doctor of Dentistry.

Geraldine B. Morrison [East Setauket] is a native Long Islander. Her husband, son, and twin daughters share her love of natural wonders, tending gardens, and enjoying the bounty of the land around them. She has been part of a writing group that continues to inspire writing and creative work and has held together for many years.

Annabelle Moseley [Dix Hills] was Poet-in-Residence at the Stevenson Academy of Fine Arts in Oyster Bay. Her Poems have appeared or are forthcoming in such journals as *The Texas Review, The Lyric, The New Formalist, Ward 6 Poetry Review*, and *The Seventh Quarry*, among others. In 2005, Birnham Wood Graphics published a chapbook of her poetry, *The Moon Is a Lemon*.

Ed Muller [Port Jefferson] was on the Dean's List in 1963 as a Commercial Art major at John Brown University. In 1964, while aboard the USS Enterprise, he engaged in Navy Photo Intelligence. In 1968, he worked in New York City's Fashion Photo Studios, and, in 1970, became owner of Photo Studios in Port Jefferson for 35 years. He received awards from the New York Professional Photo Association and Mt. Sinai Art Guild. He is currently (for 20 years) owner of Harbor Model Agency.

Frank Muller [Bellport / Lansing, New York] is a home-grown Long Island photographer, which gave him a chance to become intimately familiar with the natural beauty this island has to offer. He has been capturing images of its wild places for over 30 years. His photography can be seen on Doubleday book covers and the Nature Conservancy ads and newsletters of the New York League of Conservation Voters, Pine Barren Society, and many other environmental organizations. He hopes his work will bring a greater appreciation of our natural world.

Dan Murray (1936–2000) [Matituck] published five poetry collections: *Short Circuits, The Calendar Poems, Casualty Claim, None of This Is on the Map*, and *Duck*. From 1968 until his retirement in 1992, he was Professor of English at Suffolk Community College where he was the recipient of the Chancellor's award for Excellence in Teaching. He was also the recipient of a Mellon Foundation Fellowship in Poetry.

David Napolin (1911–2005) [Port Washington], a retired English teacher who taught for many years in the New York City Schools, was a nominee for the Pushcart Poetry Prize both in 1999 and 2005.

Vincent Noto [East Patchogue] is a nature and landscape photographer who loves Long Island waters and parks. He has been interested in photography since the seventh grade when he won his first award. He is very active in the Suffolk Camera Club and the Photographic Federation of Long Island. He has been digital since 2004.

Tammy Nuzzo-Morgan [Southampton] is Founder and President of the North Sea Poetry Scene. She was a 2005 nominee for Poet Laureate of Suffolk County and is listed in Poets & Writers. In 2006, her book, *Let Me Tell You Something* (2006), was nominated for a number of prizes for poetry. Her other books and CDs include: *Between Willows and Cedars* (2003), *The Bitter, The Sweet* (2004), and *One Woman's Voice* (2005). Her new collections are *For Michael* and *Howling the Moon*. In June 2009, Tammy Nuzzo-Morgan was appointed Suffolk County Poet Laureate (SCPL) for the term June 2009-June 2011.

Marc Oliveri [King's Park], born in Brooklyn and raised in Suffolk County, has been photographing nature and animals especially birds, for over 25 years. His photographs have appeared on Channel 12 News.

Ron Overton [Lake Grove] has published four collections of poems, among them, *Hotel Me: Poems for Gil Evans* (1994), *Love on the Alexander Hamilton* (1985), and, the most recent, *Psychic Killed by Train*, published by Hanging Loose Press. He teaches at Stony Brook University and is currently writing on film.

Drew A. Pantino [Port Jefferson Station] founded Eye Scar Photography, Inc. to meet the needs of commercial and individual Clients in 2000. His emphasis on quality is achieved through communication with his clients and his passion for photography. Contact: www.eyescarphotography.com.

Russell Cameron Perry [St. James] is an engineer, inventor, photographer, artist, craftsman, naturalist, philosopher, and sometime poet, living in Nissequogue whose love of nature leads him to many sanctuaries on the Island to comb our beaches, fish and clam, and paddle his kayak in our rivers, bays, and harbors. He is the father of two, and the grandfather of four wonderful children, who often appear in his poetry.

Joe Pihas [Island Park] is a printmaker who uses woodcuts, the last was his son's three-foot Bar Mitzvah invitation. Now he uses the images from his camera to produce his prints on rice paper. He is informed and indebted to the works of Hokusai and Hiroshige and *Images from the Floating World: The Japanese Print Including an Illustrated Dictionary of Ukiyo–E.*

Beverly Pion [Little Neck] has written in one form or another since she was very young. However, it was only after she retired from teaching that she has had the luxury of giving her writing the time and effort it requires—and is "enjoying it all (even the frustrations!)." Beverly is listed in *A Directory of American Poets and Writers.*

M. James Pion [Little Neck], who studied with Dr. Helen Manzer in 1980, is listed in *A Directory of American Poets and Writers*. He developed an eye for photography and took advanced workshops in 2001 with Freeman Patterson, a Canadian photographer. He had a one-man show at the Louis Armstrong School in 1997 and is a past President and Salon Worker at Great Neck Camera Club and a lecturer on ornithology.

Allen Planz [East Hampton] has written ten books of poetry. He is a teacher, editor, and journalist and holds two NEA's and two NYCCA's. He is also a licensed captain of a fishing boat.

Sheldon Pollack [Levittown] is a 76-year-old photographer who has been taking pictures for over 60 years. His pictures have been published in *Newsday* and various magazines, as well as in *Fish and Wildlife Refuge on Long Island*.

Anne Porter [Hampton Bays], born in 1911 in Sherborn Massachusetts, began writing poetry when she was seven and has continued all of her life. She is published in *Poetry, Commonweal*, and smaller magazines edited by friends, and books published from Zoland Press in 1994 and 2006. She married the painter Fairfield Porter in 1932 and has five children.

Steve Potter's [Oceanside] poems and stories have appeared in print and in on-line journals, such as *Arson, Blue Collar Review, California Quarterly, Drunken Boat, LIQ*, and *3rd Bed*. He is the editor and publisher of *The Wandering Hermit Review.*

Elaine Preston [Halesite] is an award-winning poet and English professor at Suffolk County Community College. She has published in such national journals as *Confrontation, College English, Poets On, NYQ, Slant, Zone 3,* and *Tampa Review* and has authored a poetry collection, *Look for a Field to Land*, and poetry workbook, *Fishing Underground.*

Orel Protopopescu's [Miller Place] most recent book for children, *Two Sticks*, was published by Farrar, Straus and Giroux (2007). Her poetry for adults has appeared in *Spoon River Anthology, LIQ, Oberon*, and others, several winning prizes. *A Thousand Peaks: Poems from China* (co-authored with Siyu Liu) features her translations.

Ralph Pugliese, Jr. [Cutchogue] graduated the School of Visual Arts with a B.F.A. in Photography. His work has been published in numerous books and other publications. He self-publishes his own work in the form of calendars and cards. Website: www.RalphJr.com.

Clementine C. Rabassa [Hampton Bays / Manhattan], born on the famous isle of Manhattan, as a student as well as professor, has always found inspiration in aquatic surroundings. During her childhood years, she enjoyed forays to Brighton Beach. Now, as an adult, she still can savor the beauties and pleasures of Great Peconic Bay. She is a poet and translator. The latest book of her own poetry is *Pollock's Polka* (Cross-Cultural Communications, 2004).

Gregory Rabassa [Hampton Bays / Manhattan] is a distinguished professor of Hispanic languages, Queens College (CUNY); a translator of numerous notable books from Spanish and Portuguese; and author of his prize-winning memoir, *If This Be Treason: Translation and Its Dyscontents* (New Directions, 2006).

Barbara Reiher-Meyers [Ronkonkoma] is a Board Member of the Long Island Poetry Collective and has performed her poetry in many East Coast venues. She also curates a poetry calendar for www.poetz.com/longisland, and has coordinated events for the Northport Arts Coalition and Smithtown Township Arts Council. Her poetry has been published in print journals and online. She facilitates monthly workshops in Ronkonkoma, sends weekly e-mails of local poetry events, and has edited several volumes of poetry. *Sounds Familiar* is her first book of poems.

John Renner [Locust Valley] finds much pleasure in the art of seeing, capturing, and sharing his photographs taken frequently in his own backyard.

Craig D. Robins [Huntington] is an attorney and frustrated artist. Although trained in law, he has been filled with passion about fine art photography for over 30 years. He seeks to produce unique surrealistic images, sometimes unsettling, with dark overtones and a cutting edge. He has won numerous awards for his works, including from the Huntington Camera Club and the Huntington Arts Council.

Betsey Ann Smith Roberts [Patchogue] was born in Patchogue on March 22, 1828, and in her time was one of the richest women on Long Island. Roberts freely distributed her money as gifts to the poor of Patchogue and surrounding areas. Roberts was a known crusader for women's rights and prohibition and wrote poetry about these causes that were included in her poetry book, *Original Poems* (1894). She died on December 7, 1897.

Peter Rodriguez [Brentwood], born in Puerto Rico, he came to the United States at age nine. He has spent the last three decades of his life on Long Island taking photographs since his teens. He has been working at Color Images Laboratory, Inc. for the last thirteen years, photo finishing for the last thirty five. He particularly likes candid shots.

Linda Russo's [New Hyde Park] passion for creative photographs began about 15 years ago after attending photographic workshops with Freeman Patterson and Andre Gallant. Her "seeing" in creative montages time and again illustrates her journal of the edge of perception. Her camera is her harmonious instrument that leads her onto the visual journey of her natural world.

Judy Saccucci [Stony Brook] is a retired Haupauge kindergarten teacher, who writes poetry and paints. She has been published in *Arts Review, Descant, Poet Lore, Oberon, Street, Nimrod, Hyperion, Quoin, et al.* Her paintings have been exhibited at Gallery North and Franzi and Nells restaurant (now Pentimento). She makes jewelry, dolls, and quilts and builds furniture. She has lived in Stony Brook for 31 years.

Linda Sack [Port Jefferson Station / Florida], a Full Gospel Minister and Nursing Home/Hospice Pastor, she is mother of three and grandmother of three. Her drawing, "I Can Do It Myself," appeared on the front cover of *Lilith* (1988), an art magazine published annually by Suffolk Community College, and two of her poems and drawings also appeared in *Lilith* (1889). She enjoys singing and writes her own lyrics and melodies.

Linda Sanchez [St. James], graduate of Smithtown High School East, 2008. Talented at computer graphics, designed school logo. She attends Villanova University, majoring in Finance and Economics.

Carol Schmidt [Setauket] is an editor and contributing nature writer for a publication of Sweetbriar Nature Center. A retired teacher, she lives in Setauket and New York City. Carol has been a regular contributor to *Oberon*.

Bob Schmitz [Levittown] is a serious amateur photography for over 20 years. His concentration is on the natural world with many photos published in the *Conservationist*, the Audobon Calendars, and others. He is a regular at the Photography Federation of Long Island and is often asked to judge. He has dedicated his life to taking images of nature that record and honor our natural world.

Elinor Schoenfeld [Bayside, Queens] is a photographer and an epidemiologist at a medical school in metropolitan New York. Her photographs are available at BJ Spoke Gallery in Huntington. Together with her husband, Eric Gottesman, they are co-founders of Elke Images, a fine art and digital photoart company: www.elkeimagess.com.

Grace Schulman's [East Hampton / Manhattan] newest poetry collection is *The Broken String* (Houghton Mifflin, 2007). Her latest books of poems are *Days of Wonder: New and Collected Poems* (2002) and *The Paintings of Our Lives* (2001). Honors include a Guggenheim Fellowship, the Aiken Taylor Award, and the Delmore Schwartz Award.

Weslea Sidon [Roslyn Heights / Maine] is a poet and musician who left Long Island for Seal Cove, Maine, in 1999. While in NY, she was an Editor of *Xanadu Magazine*, active in the L.I. Poetry Collective, and an advocate for poetry in the schools. She teaches guitar and writing to people of all ages.

Art Simendinger [Stony Brook] is a retired software engineer who has had a life-long passion for photography. His photographic interests are seascapes, landscapes, and sports. He has been an active member of the Paumanok Camera Club for more than ten years. He lives with his wife in Stony Brook.

Marcia Slatkin [Shoreham], formerly a teacher and backyard farmer, now plays the cello, takes photos, cares for her 90-year-old mother (an Alzheimer's patient), and writes poetry, fiction, and drama. Her latest poetry books are *Kidnap My Mother* (Finishing Line Press, 2005) and *A Woman Milking* (Word Press, 2006). Her fiction writing won two PEN Awards; her one-act plays have been produced in small New York venues.

Pauline Southard [Freeport], owner of Lady Kat Photography, specializes in portrait, glamour, and landscape photography. Over the last 20 years, her images have won national awards from the Professional Photographers of America. Her newest work combines her love of metaphysics with photography. Websites: www.karmickat.com and www.ladykat.com.

Joseph Stanton's [Roslyn / Hawaii] latest book of poems, *A Field Guide to the Wildlife of Suburban O'ahu*, is concerned with the small island on which he now lives. His other poetry collections are *Imaginary Museum: Poems on Art, Cardinal Points,* and *What the Kite Thinks*. His poems have appeared in *Poetry, Harvard Review, LIQ*, and many other publications. He teaches art history and American studies at the University of Hawaii at Manoa.

Tom Stock [Manorville] is a naturalist, essayist, poet, journal keeper, puppeteer, artist, farmer, Pine Barrens enthusiast, book discussion leader, rattlemaker, long distance hiker, grandfather, proud father of two daughters, bee keeper, handyman, community activist, host of poetry parties, and a paper maker.

Gayl Teller [Plainview] is Director of the Mid-Island Y Poetry Series (NYSCA) and a faculty member in Hofstra University's English Department. She is the author of five collections of poetry, most recently, *One Small Kindness*, and, forthcoming in 2010, *Inside the Embrace*. She is the winner of the Edgar Allan Poe Prize, PEN Women Prize, and Peninsula Library Poetry Prize. She has had poems published in *The Journal of the E. E. Cummings Society, Poet Lore, Phoebe*, and *Paterson Literary Review*. In June 2009, Gayl Teller was appointed Nassau County Poet Laureate (NCPL) for the term June 2009-June 2011.

John Orville Terry (1796–1869) [Orient] (known as "J.O.T.") was born in the North Fork town of Orient. As a youth, John loved the stories and traditions of the people and heritage of this sparsely settled area. John signed up on a whaling ship out of Greenport once and based one of his poems on this experience. In 1850, John gathered up some 179 poems into his only poetry book, *The Poems of S.O.T.* (New York: G.F. Nesbitt, 1850), which told in verse about his thoughts and experiences on the North Fork.

Susan Tiffen [Roslyn Heights] grew up on Long Island, always taking pictures, went to art school, but never considered photography a serious expression of her artwork. Along the way, she found the computer and computer graphics. Chance brought her to a PhotoShop seminar and a meeting with two photographers. Her world as an artist changed; it all comes together through the lens of her camera.

J R (Judy) Turek [East Meadow] is in her eleventh year as Moderator of the Farmingdale Creative Writing Group. An award-winning poet, and author of *They Come and They Go*, she writes a-poem-a-day. She resides with her soul-mate husband, her dogs, and her extraordinarily extensive shoe collection.

Victoria Twomey [Northport] is an award-winning photographer, digital artist, and poet. Her work has been exhibited at various galleries and outdoor art shows around Long Island and is always on display at the Twomey Gallery in Huntington. Her body of work has been called "beautiful and organically powerful." To learn more about her books and fine art go to www.victoriatwomey.com

Pramila Venkateswaran [Setauket] is the author of *Thirtha* (Yuganta Press, 2002) and *Women Like Us* (Plain View Press, 2008). A finalist for the Allen Ginsberg Poetry Award, she has published in *Paterson Literary Review, LIQ, Nassau Review, Prairie Schooner, et al.*, and has performed her poetry at the Geraldine R. Dodge Festival. She has a doctorate from George Washington University and teaches English and Women's Studies at Nassau Community College.

George Wallace [Huntington] is a poet, journalist, and editor living and working on Long Island. He is author of 14 chapbooks of poetry and editor of Poetry Bay.com. In 2003, he was named the first Poet Laureate of Suffolk County.

Michael C. Walsh [Rocky Point] is graduate of Cleveland State University in anthropology, has published over 100 poems, and is the author of a chapbook, *Up Green Ladders*. He has been nominated for a Pushcart Prize, and, as a paleontologist, collects marine animals and writes about them and their Paleozoic ancestors.

Gil Weiner [Roslyn Heights], a former lawyer for a large Long Island company, in retirement, has given him the time to rediscover his childhood interest in photography. With an academic background in biology, he naturally leans toward nature photography, which has allowed him to experience the great natural diversity of Long Island.

Marlene Weinstein [Setauket] has been an avid photographer for over 20 years. Her images are inspired by the creative possibilities of everyday places and subjects. She is especially dedicated to preserving the memories of the vanishing Long Island landscape. Her work has been exhibited widely and has received numerous awards.

Ray Welch [Ronkonkoma] is a naturalist and a Professor of Biology at Suffolk Community College for forty years. From film to digital, a few years back . . . "drowning in images. Help!"

Maxwell Corydon Wheat, **Jr**. [Freeport] is a teacher for Taproot Workshops, Inc., writing for people 55 and older. He teaches a Continuing Education class, "You Can Write Poetry!" for the Farmingdale Public Schools. To build a body of poetry about Long Island wildlife and habitats, with poet-naturalists Tom Stock and Edgar Carlson, he is organizing poetry writing workshops in the Pine Barrens, on the Hempstead Plains and on the salt marshes. Many in the poetry community consider him to be Poet Laureate of Nassau County for 2007.

John Hall Wheelock (1886–1978) [Far Rockaway] was one of Long Island's most distinguished poets during his lifetime. John was born in Far Rockaway but, while he was an editor at Scribner's, spent most of his writing career between East Hampton and New York City. He won many awards for his poetry, including the Bollinger Prize, and was an honorary consultant in American letters to the Library of Congress.

Claire Nicolas White [St. James] is a poet and translator from Dutch and French, who has authored art criticism, plays, opera librettos, and many books, including a novel, *The Death of the Orange Trees* (Harper and Row), a memoir, *Fragments of Stained Glass* (Mercury House), a family history, *The Elephant and the Rose* (Vinyard Press), *Biography and Other Poems* (Doubleday), and five poetry chapbooks. She has lived in St. James since 1947.

Walt Whitman (1819–1891) [Huntington] is considered by many to be the greatest of American poets. He was born in West Hills (Huntington), Long Island, and, during his lifetime, was a teacher, painter, journalist, editor, clerk, and hospital nurse during the Civil War. His book, *Leaves of Grass*, was self-published in 1855 and has affected the writing of poetry ever since.

Ginger Williams [Setauket], writing, performing, teaching, facilitating workshops and classes, has been active in the poetry community for the past fifteen years. A former teacher in the Three Village Schools, she lives in Setauket with her poet-historian husband, John. *Restringing the Beads* is her first published book of poetry.

John A. Williams [Setauket] grew up in Wisconsin. He taught history at SUNY Stony Brook 1968–2006 and has studied poetry at the Frost Place in Franconia, New Hampshire. He is married to the poet, Ginger Williams. His book of poetry and lyric essays, *Skipping Stones*, was published in 2008.

ABOUT THE EDITOR

Kathaleen Donnelly [St. James] is a 1976 graduate of St. Vincent's School of Nursing in Manhattan who currently works at Stony Brook University Hospital on Long Island as a Nurse Practitioner in Cardiology. She earned an M.A. in Philosophy while working twelve years in the Surgical Intensive Care Unit and raising her son Keith. In 1981, she opened and maintained for twelve years (till 1993), Whispering Wonders Child Care Center in Port Jefferson Village. She is both a photographer, a member of the Sweetbriar Nature Photography Club, and a poet. Her poems have been published in *Literary Review: A Publication of Performance Poets Association*, *LIQ*, *Songs of Seasoned Women*, *Long Island Sounds*: *An Anthology of Poetry From Maspeth to Montauk and Beyond* (2007, 2008, and 2009), and *Oberon, a Poetry Magazine*. Her poems have also been presented at the Stevenson's Academy in Oyster Bay, selected by Annabelle Moseley and at Art Sites Gallery in Riverhead, selected by Tammy Nuzzo-Morgan, the North Sea Poetry Scene. Her poems have won prizes at the Princess Ronkonkoma Annual Poetry Contests—Honorable Mention (2006), Second (2006), and First (2007)— and at the Brookhaven Arts & Humanities Council, First (2008). Her latest publication is two poems in the Swansea, Wales-based international poetry journal, *The Seventh Quarry* (Winter 2008), edited by Peter Thabit Jones.

ABOUT THE ARTIST-DESIGNER

Stoyan "Tchouki" Tchoukanov was born in Sofia, Bulgaria, in 1970. In 1996, he earned his M.F.A. at The National Academy of Fine Arts in Sofia. Since 1993, he has had thirty-five solo exhibitions throughout Europe and the U.S.A. and more than sixty group exhibitions in Belgium, Bulgaria, England, Egypt, France, Germany, Greece, Holland, Italy, Japan, Korea, Macedonia, Poland, Romania, Serbia, Slovenia, Slovakia, South Africa, Spain, Switzerland, UAE, and the U.S.A. He was awarded the Grand Prize for Graphics, Third International Biennial Art of the Miniature, Gorni Milanovac, Serbia (1994), the Honor Prize for Achievements in Graphics, Fifth World Print Triennial, Chamaliere, France (2000), and several national prizes. His work is in numerous collections of national museums and galleries in Bulgaria, Japan, Romania, UAE, and the U.S.A. Tchouki is currently working in the fields of painting, printing, murals, and book design. For Cross-Cultural Communications, he has illustrated and/or designed books by Argentine, Chicano, Korean, Persian, Russian, Welsh, and American writers, including Pulitzer Prize winners, Stanley Kunitz and Henry Taylor.

INDEX OF CONTRIBUTORS AND TITLES

A

B

C

D

E

F

G

H

I

J

K

L

M

N

O

P

Q

T

U

V

W

Z

PERMISSIONS

Every effort has been made to trace the ownership of copyrighted material and to make full acknowledgment of its use. The editor and Cross-Cultural Communications regret any errors or comissions, which will be corrected in an attached page of errata, as well as in subsequent editions, upon notification in writing to the publisher. Thank you to the many editors, publishers, poets, and photographers who generously granted permission to print or reprint the poems and photographs in this volume.

Paul Agostino: "Miracle on Avenue D," *LIQ.* Reprinted by permission of the author.

Terry Amburgey: "Dawn in the Cove," " Fire Island," published by permission of the author.

Marjorie Appleman: "Long Island Magic," from *Against Time* (Northport, NY: Birnham Wood Graphics, 1994). Copyright © 1994 by Marjorie Appleman. Reprinted by permission of the author.

Philip Appleman: "Thin Ice," from *Margie: The American Journal of Poetry* (2006). Copyright © 2006 by Philip Appleman. Reprinted by permission of the author.

Susan Astor: "A Gift of Birds," "Ocean of Snow," "The Sparrow's Dream," "Spider Lies," from *Spider Lies* (Mineola, NY: Trumble Press, 2001). Copyright © 2001 by Susan Astor. "Circa July," "Four Spacious Skies," "Night Rise," "Now," from *Dame* (Athens, GA: University of Georgia Press, 1980). Copyright © 1980 by Susan Astor. "Circa July," *Kansas Quarterly*; "Four Spacious Skies," from *New Collage Magazine*; "Night Rise," from *A Windflower Almanac*, Ted Kooser, ed. (Lincoln, NE: Windflower Press, 1980). Copyright © 1980 by Susan Astor. "The Road the Crows Own," *Outerbridge*; "The Sparrow's Dream," *West Hills Review*. Reprinted by permission of the author.

Fuad Attal: "Autumn," from *Love & Memory* (Merrick, NY: Cross-Cultural Communications, 2005). Copyright © 2005 by Fuad Attal. Reprinted by permission of the author and the publisher.

David B. Axelrod: "The Case Against Weeding," from *Deciduous Poems* by David B. Axelrod (Toronto/Tokyo: Ahadada, Books, 2008). Copyright © 2008 by David B. Axelrod. "The Old Couple," from *Random Beauty* by David B. Axelrod (Buffalo, NY: Amereon Press, 2001). Copyright © 2001 by David B. Axelrod. Reprinted by permission of the author.

Jesse Ball: "Anna's Song," *March Book* (New York, NY: Grove Press, 2004). Copyright © 2004 by Jesse Ball. Reprinted by permission of the author.

Olivia Ward Bush-Banks: "Oasis," from *The Collected Works of Olivia Ward Bush-Banks*, Bernice F. Guillaume, ed. (Oxford University Press, 1991). Copyright © 1991 by Oxford University Press.

Mia Barkan Clarke: "Autumn Equinox," "Winter Haiku," published by permission of the author.

Stanley H. Barkan: "At the Nassau County Museum of Art's Four Women Show," *Lips*. "December," "January," "October," from *Strange Seasons* (Sofia, Bulgaria: AngoBoy, 2007). Copyright © 2007 by Stanley H. Barkan. "Haiku," "Senryū," from *The American Hototogisu* (New York, NY: Copyquick, 1974). Copyright © 1974 by Stanley H. Barkan. Reprinted by permission of the author.

William Batcher: "Agritainment," published by permission of the author.

Aija Birzgalis: "Beach Jewels," "Beach Shells," "Beach Walk," "Evening Reeds," "Evening Sand," "Moonjelly," "Pebbles," "Snowdrifts," "Splash," "Watercolor," "The Wave," published by permission of the photographer.

Janice Bishop: "Awakening," *LIQ*. Reprinted by permission of the author.

Cliff Bleidner: "Haiku," "Haiku," published by permission of the author.

Robert Bonanno: "Etched Snow," "Ocean Reflection," "Sheltered by Branches," "A Single Leaf," "Sunlit Whitecap," published by permission of the photographer.

Jef Bravata: "Aurora Borealis," "For Georgia," "Melting Red," "Purple Movement," "Soil," "Thin Blue Ice," published by permission of the photographer.

Mary Brennan: "Cupsoque," published by permission of the photographer.

Adolfo Briceno: "Cosmo," "Orchid to Be," published by permission of the photographer.

Peter Brink: "Anemone," "Clam," "Coral," "Moon Shell," "Mussels," "Pipefish," published by permission of the photographer.

John Brokos: "Dew Drop on Green," "Swamp Maple Leaf," published by permission of the photographer.

Arnold Brower: "Sunrise Song," "Sweet Song Sparrow," "Thistle and Guest," published by permission of the photographer.

William Cullen Bryant: "The Gladness of Nature," "I Broke the Spell That Held Me Long," "March," "May Evening," "November," from *Poetical Works of William Cullen Bryant* (Whitefish, MT: Kessinger Publishing, LLC, 2003).

Lynn Buck: "Going Barefoot," *LIQ*. Reprinted by permission of the author.

Louis Bussolati: "Perspective," *LIQ*. Reprinted by permission of the author.

Francis Carlin: "Mary's Isle," from *My Ireland* by Francis Carlin (Orlando, FL: Henry Holt & Co., 1917). Copyright © 1917 by Henry Holt & Co.

Linda Carnevlae: "Daisies Grow on My Windowsill," *LIQ*. Reprinted by permission of the author.

Donald Case: "Emerald Meadow," "Flying Home," "God Beams," "Pine Forest," published by permission of the photographer.

Diana Chang: "Spellbound," "The Sphinx," "Things Are for Good," "Without Giving Notice," from *Earth Water Light* (Northport, NY: Birnham Wood Graphics, 1991). Copyright © 1991 by Diana Chang. "As Sky Come Undone," *LIQ*. *Dumb Beautiful Minister*. Reprinted by permission of the author.

George L. Chieffet: "Still Life II," published by permission of the photographer.

Heather Cirincione: "Diving Down a Country Lane," published by permission of the photographer.

Vince Clemente: "Black-Faced Lamb," from *Sweeter Than Vivaldi* by Vince Clemente (Merrick, NY: Cross-Cultural Communications, 2002). Copyright © 2002 by Vince Clemente. Reprinted by permission of the author and the publisher.

Arlene Greenwald Cohen: "City Visits," *LIQ*. Reprinted by permission of the author.

Arleen Ruth Cohen: "The Gull," *Newscribes* (The Newscribes Group, inc, 1981). Copyright © 1981 by Arleen Ruth Cohen. "Winter White," *LIQ*. Reprinted by permission of the author.

Christopher Corradino: "I've Landed," "Jones Beach, Field 10," "Lilies Reflection," "Livstrong Yellow," "Strike a Pose," published by permission of the photographer.

Yolanda Coulaz: "Gull in Grey Waters," published by permission of the author.

Darlene Cunnup: "Blue Bottle," published by permission of the photographer.

George DeCamp: "Black-Bellied Plover," "Calling for Mate," "Cardinal in Snow," "Deer Friends," "Grackle in Snow," "Jelly Fish," "Oystercatcher," "Snowy Egret in Mud," "Starling in Winter," "White Egret," published by permission of the photographer.

John DeLorenzo: "Bedell Vineyards," published by permission of the photographer.

Donna Demian: "The Wind off the Sea," published by permission of the photographer.

Joan Reilly DeRosa: "April," "It Rained," published by permission of the author. "This Day in May," *Oberon*. Reprinted by permission of the author.

Red Diamond: "An Apple Is a Poem," published by permission of the author.

Arthur Dobrin: "Next Door," "Westbury," from *Out of Place* (Port Jefferson, NY: Backstreet Editions, 1982). Reprinted by permission of the author.

Kathaleen Donnelly: "Lost in Autumn," from *Long Island Sounds: 2007, An Anthology of Poetry from Maspeth to Montauk and Beyond*, Tammy Nuzzo-Morgan, Lynn E. Cohen, J R Turek, eds. (North Sea, NY: North Sea Poetry Scene Press, 2007). Copyright © 2007 by Kathaleen Donnelly. Reprinted by permission of the author. "A Child Confronts the Sea," "Little Angel, Well, Sometimes," "Purple Crocus," "A Single Leaf," "Tall Trees," "Winter Tree," "Wisdom of the Grandmothers" and "In December," "Long Island Sound," "Warm Rain," published by permission of the author/photographer.

William Duryea, Jr.: "Blue Ice," "Egret Sentinel," "Light Bar in Wave." "Morning Reflections," "Snow Fence," "Swan in Branches," "Twilight Beach," "Varnished Bow," "Winter Curtain," published by permission of the photographer.

Arlene Eager: "The Dogwood," "Off Season," *Oberon*; "I Sit Very Still," from *Tar River Poetry*; "Levittown," *The Hudson Review*. Reprinted by permission of the author.

Ken Eastman: "Eagle," published by permission of the photographer.

Richard Elman: "Azaleas," "Mid May," "Natural, as Waste," from *Chontales: Selected New Poems and Sonnets* by Richard Elman (Sound Beach, NY: Street Press, 1980). Copyright © 1980 by Richard Elman. "Edible Landscape," "Big Fall, Stony Brook," from *Homage to Fats Navarro* by Richard Elman (Moorhead, MN: New Rivers Press, 1978). Copyright © 1978 by Richard Elman. Reprinted with the permission of the author's widow, Alice Elman, owner of the Estate of Richard Elman. "Dawn Fog," "Fall Light," "Just Before a Birthday," "September 9th," "This Harbor," published by permission of Alice Elman.

Laura M. Eppig: "Baby Mantis," "Catbird," "Connetquot Grasshopper," "Dahlia Bud," "Frog on a Limb," "Osprey in Flight," "Water Lily," published by permission of the photographer.

Graham Everett: "April 25th," April 30th," "August 20th," "December 29th," "February 27th," June 7th," "May 15th," "October 6th," "September 9th," from *Corps Calleux* by Graham Everett (Sound Beach, NY: Street Presss, 2000). Copyright © 2000 by Graham Everett. "Landless And," "November," "Uphill," from *Strange Coast* by Graham Everett (Brooklyn, NY: Tamarack, 1979). Copyright © 1979 by Graham Everett. "Summer, Sunday Night," *LIQ*. Reprinted by permission of the author.

Richard Fiedorowicz: "A Winter's Leaf," published by permission of the photographer.

Adam D. Fisher: "Early Fall," *Podium*; "Incandescence," *LIQ*. "Noon Garden Tour with My Granddaughter," from *Enough to Stop the Heart* by Adam D. Fisher (Sound Beach, NY: Writer's Ink, 2008). Copyright © 2008 by Adam D. Fisher. Reprinted by permission of the author. "Caleb Smith Park," "Feeling Fliers," "First Beach Day," "Suburban Street," published by permission of the author.

Charles Adés Fishman: "Opening," "Late Spring Quickens," "Jake Sleeping," from *Country of Memory* by Charles Adés Fishman (Seattle, Washington: Uccelli Press, 2004). Copyright © 2004 by Charles Adés Fishman. "Two Boys at the Seashore," "At the Edge," from *The Firewalkers* by Charles Adés Fishman (Greensboro, NC: Avisson Press, 1996). Copyright © 1996 by Charles Adés Fishman. "The Ice Poets," from *Mortal Companions* by Charles Fishman (Wantagh, NY: Pleasure Dome Press, 1977). Copyright © 1977 by Charles Adés Fishman. "Beach After Rain," *West Hills Review*. Reprinted by permission of the author.

James P. Friel: "Pebbles," "Gathering Peace," *LIQ*. Reprinted by permission of the author.

Jyoti Ganguly: "Backyard Repose," "Blydenburg Woods," "Early Snow," "Marsh Reeds," "New Mill Pond," "Summer's End," published by permission of the photographer.

Mary L. Gardiner: "Hempstead Harbor," from *Sounds and Sweet Airs*, Joan D. Berberich, ed. (Port Washington, NY/London: Kennikat Press, Inc., Ira J. Friedman Division, 1970).

Dan Giancola: "Eels," "Vivarium," from *Part Mirth, Part Murder* by Dan Giancola (Sound Beach, NY: Street Press, 2006). Copyright © 2006 by Dan Giancola. Reprinted by permission of the author.

Ann Glazebrook: "Autumn Leaves," "Childhood," "Ditch Plains," "Flax Pond," "Mill Pond," "North Light," "Orient Point," "The Second House," "Winter Window," published by permission of the photographer.

Dennis Golin: "Maple Tree," published by permission of the photographer.

John Gozelski: "Gold in the Fog," published by permission of the photographer.

Bill Graeser: "Whispering," *LIQ*. Reprinted by permission of the author. "Winter," published by permission of the author.

Ange Gualtieri: "Bales of Hay," "A Blade of Grass," "Clouds," "Little Pest," "Marsh Reeds," "Old Farm," "Oops," published by permission of the photographer.

Joan Carole Hand: "East of July" from *East of July* by Joan Carole Hand (Merrick, NY: Cross-Cultural Communications, 2004). Copyright © 2004 by Joan Carole Hand. Reprinted by permission of the author and the publisher.

Robert Harrison: "Checking It Out," "Mallard," "Morning Fog," "Winter Forest II," published by permission of the photographer.

George Held: "Montauk Chiaroscuro," from *North Atlantic Review* and *Grounded* (Georgetown, KY: Finishing Line Press, 2005). Copyright © 2005 by George Held. Reprinted by permission of the author.

Gladys Henderson: "Clams for Christmas Chowder," "Turtle for Graves' Pond," from *Eclipse of Heaven* by Gladys Henderson (Georgetown, KY: Finishing Line Press, 2008). Copyright © 2008 by Gladys Henderson. "However Today," from *Long Island Sounds 2006*, Tammy Nuzzo-Morgan, Walter E. Harris, Barbara Reiher-Meyers, eds. (North Sea Poetry Scene Press, 2006). Copyright © 2006 by Gladys Henderson. Reprinted by permission of the author. "Palm Sunday Hymns," "Riding in the Dory," "Transfiguration," "Understanding Heaven," published by permission of the author.

Mary K. Herbert: "Autumn Ethology," *LIQ*. Reprinted by permission of the author.

Kathleen Hervey: "Great Horned Owl," published by permission of the photographer.

William Heyen: "This Island," *Vanderbilt Poetry Review*; "The Nesconset Crickets," *Four Quarters*; "Clamming at St. James Harbor," *The New Yorker*. All three are also in *Long Island Light: Poems and Memoir, NY* (Vanguard Press, 1979). Copyright © 1979 by William Heyen. "The Crane at Gibbs Pond," from *The Host: Selected Poems* (St. Louis, MO: Time Being Books, 1994). Copyright © 1994 by William Heyen. Reprinted by permission of the author.

Joan Higuchi: "Psalm for a Winter Night," "Web," published by permission of the photographer.

Barbara Hoffman: ". . . In Late Autumn," "Quietude," published by permission of the author.

Mary L'Hommedieu Gardiner Horsford: "My Native Isle", from *Indian Legends and Other Poems* (New York: J. C. Derby, 1855).

Florence M. Hughes: "Afternoon in the Park," (Grist Mill, Stony Brook, NY)," "April Morning at the Lily Pond (Miller Place)," "The Island," *LIQ.* Reprinted by permission of the author.

Richard Hunt: "Bluejays," "Bumblebee," "Daffodils," "Her Inner Self," "Ladybug," "Landing Gull," "Lilies," "Majestic Butterfly," "Red Sunflower," "Seagull at the Shore," "A Swan's Reflection," "Woodpecker," published by permission of the photographer.

David Ignatow: "All Comes" and "Whistle or Hoot" from *David Ignatow Poems, 1934–1969* by David Ignatow (Middletown, CT: Wesleyan University Press, 1970). Copyright © 1970 by David Ignatow. Reprinted by permission of the author's daughter, Yaedi Ignatow.

Yaedi Ignatow: "Forest," from *Long Island Poets* (Sag Harbor, NY: The Permanent Press, 1986). Copyright © 1986 by Yaedi Igntow. Reprinted by permission of the author.

Barbara Imperiale: "Fallen Apples," "Winter Storm," published by permission of the photographer.

Juliet Isham: "The Pines' Thought" and "Return," from *Sounds and Sweet Airs*, Joan D. Berberich, ed. (Port Washington, NY/London: Kennikat Press, Inc, Ira J. Friedman Division: 1970). Copyright © 1970 by Juliet Isham.

John Kaufman: "Stump Pond," Fireweed; "Island of Longing," *Kentucky Poetry Review*. "Smithtown, Long Island," *LIQ*. "Small Craft," *Wisconsin Academy Review*. Reprinted by permission of the author. "Moon Shell," "Small Craft," "Smithtown, Long Island," "Stump Pond," published by permission of the author.

Barbara Keenan: "Carman's River," "The Hope of Spring," "Who Goes There," published by permission of the photographer.

Kate Kelly: "What Takes her Breath Away," *LIQ*. Reprinted by permission of the author."Angel Wings," "Circling Jones Beach," "Emerging," "Feather Dance," "Impossible Desire, " "Kite Dreams, " "Reflection," "The Rising," "Sowing Seeds," "Spring Storm," published by permission of the photographer.

Gene Keyes: "Hawk," "In Flight Over the Island," "Osprey," "Skimmer's Squadron," published by permission of the photographer.

Kay Kidde: "Moon," "Fire Island: Ocean Beach," and "November Road, Late Afternoon," "September," from *Early Sky: New and Collected Poems* by Kay Kidde (Selden, NY: Writers Ink, 2002). Copyright © 2002 by Kay Kidde. Reprinted by permission of the author.

Jeanette Klimszewski: "Centerport Concert," from *Promise* by Jeanette Klimszewski (Fore Angels Press, 2002).

Charlene Babb Knadle: "January, Seen," "Near View," "Winter at Seven A.M.," from *Dandelion Sleeves: Poems of Nature and Ordinary Life* by Charlene Bab Knadle (Melville, NY: Two Cardinals Press, 2005). Copyright © 2005 by Charlene Babb Knadle. "Fairway" and "Dedalia," *LIQ*; "Fox," *Long Islander.* Reprinted by permission of the author.

Lynn Kozma: "Animus," "Any Moment," "At the Dock," "Cardinal," "Courtship Dance," "December Storm, 1993," "Gray Day in Autumn," "One Morning in June," "Osprey," "Salvation," "Sound Effects," "Symphony," "Traveler," "Winter," from *Phases of the Moon* by Lynn Kosma (Papier-mâché Press, 1993). Copyright © 1993 by Lynn Kosma. Reprinted by permission of the author.

Norbert Krapf: "Arriving on Paumanok," "In the Time of Irises," "Long Island Crow," "The Politics of Weeds," "Sassafras," "When the Call Came," from *Bittersweet Along the Expressway: Poems of Long Island* by Norbert Krapf (Hardwick, MA: Waterline Books, 2000). Copyright © 2000 by Norbert Krapf. "Cardinal," "Currents," "Little Bug Man," "Quietly Going Nowhere," "The Sea Comes Calling," "The Visitor" *LIQ*. Reprinted by permission of the author.

Bill Kreisberg: "Cedarmere House," "Jones Beach," published by permission of the photographer.

Mindy Kronenberg: "Crocus," "Duck Walk," "Green," "The Nest," *LIQ*. Reprinted by permission of the author. "Solstice," from *Many Waters* by Mindy Kronenberg (SUNY, Empire State College, 2004). Copyright © 2004 by Mindy Kronenberg. Reprinted by permission of the author.

Larry Landolfi: "Earth & Sky (Montage)," "Frozen Sound," "Jupiter," "Milky Way," "Moonlit Night," "Moonrise," "Sea Heaving Full," published by permission of the photographer.

Jan La Roche: "Ars Poetica," "Late Afternoon in Autumn," "Marsh with Ice," "White Gate" "Strutting in Peconic," "There Is No # on the Road in Southampton," published by permission of the photographer/author.

Toby Lieberman: "At Lindell School Bulkhead," "Parting Gifts," published by permission of the author.

Tom Lindtvit: "The End of the Day," published by permission of the photographer.

Eric Lohse: "Earth & Sky," "Field of Gold," "Southold Rocks," "Winter Tree," "Winter Woods #1," "Winter Woods #2," published by permission of the photographer.

Stuart McCallum: "Gladiolus," "East End Oak," "Eaton's Neck," "Grass, Water, Sky," "Haiku," "Magnolia," "Maple Leaf," "Shinnecock Winter," "Tomatoes at the Window," published by permission of the photographer.

Sandy McIntosh: "To an Old Friend at a Poetry Reading," published by permission of the author.

Ray Makofske: "Stillness," *LIQ*. Reprinted by permission of the author.

Henry Mangels: "Blizzard 2005," published by permission of the photographer.

Mankh (**Walter E. Harris III**): "Haiku," "Montauk Haiku Sequence," "Saturday Spring Portrait–Selden, NY," published by permission of the author.

David Martine: "The Farmer," "Pictures of Great-Grandfather Habits," published by permission of the author.

Vidal Al Martinez: "Autumn Leaves," "Blossoms," "Deer," "Early Morning in Connetquot," "Fenced Beach," "Morton's Nature Preserve," "The Nest," "A Rose," "Spring Is Here," "Squirrel," "Surveying," "A Tree in Autumn," "Woodpecker," "Zinnia," published by permission of the photographer.

D. H. Melhem: "Absolutes," "House," "Night," from *Rest in Love* by D. H. Melhem (Brookville, NY: Confrontation Magazine Press, 1995). Copyright © 1995 by D. H. Melhem. "Poem for You," from *Poems for You: A Sequence* by D. H. Melhem (New York, NY: P& Q Press, 2000). Copyright © 2000 by D. H. Melhem. Reprinted by permission of the author.

Eddie Mooney: "Mother's Day," published by permission of the photographer.

Daniel Thomas Moran: "From the Porch in Summer," "A Side of Life," "The Swan in the Pond," "Traveling," from *In Praise of August* by Dan Moran (Sag Harbor, NY: Canio's Editions, 1999). Copyright © 1999 by Dan Moran. "If These Birds," from *Looking for the Uncertain Past* by Dan Moran (Salzburg, Austria: Poetry Salzburg at the University of Salzburg, 2006). Copyright © 2006 by Dan Moran. "An Encounter, "Sleeping Late," "A Song to Remember," "To Begin Winter," "Willow Pond on a Morning Before Spring," from *HiLo to Willow Pond*: *New and Selected Poems* by Dan Moran (Sound Beach, NY: Street Press, 2002). Copyright © 2002 by Dan Moran. Reprinted by permission of the author.

Geraldine B. Morrison: "Conversation with a Grasshopper," "One Swat," published by permission of the author.

Annabelle Moseley: "For the Hempstead Plains," "My Latest Goddess," published by permission of the author.

Ed Muller: "Autumn Snow," "Beach Biking," "A Gallant Vessel," "The Night," "Night Prowler,""Rice Paper Moon," published by permission of the photographer.

Frank Muller: "The Abandoned House," "Autumn Flowers," "Colored Glass," "Curious Child," "Dawn Reflection," "Dramatic Sky," "Egret in the Afternoon," "Fire on the Bay," "Flaming Sky," "Glorious Sunrise, " "Heron," "House Ignites," "Leaf Drops," "Lemon Wings," "Lily Ponds," "Maidenhair Ferns," "Moonrise," "Morning Fog," "Pitcher Plants," "Quiet Snow, " "Roaring Sea," "Sea Heaving Full," "They Know Which Way to Go," "The Watcher," "Woodland Wandering," published by permission of the photographer.

Dan Murray: "December," "July," "June," "Passamaquoddy Sunrise," from *None of This Is on the Map* by Dan Murray (Sound Beach, NY: Street Press, 1998). Copyright © 1998 by Dan Murray. Reprinted by permission of the author's widow, Jackie Murray, owner of the Estate of Dan Murray.

David Napolin: "Nightfall," published by permission of the author.

Vincent M. Noto: "Curves," "Orange Phragmites," published by permission of the photographer.

Tammy Nuzzo-Morgan: "Raking Leaves," "Snow," published by permission of the author.

Marc Oliveri: "Turtle's First Day of Summer," published by permission of the photographer.

Ron Overton: "Beyond Words," "Midnight," from *Hotel Me: Poems for Gil Evans and Others* by Ron Overton (Brooklyn, NY: Hanging Loose Press, 1994). Copyright © 1994 by Ron Overton. "Montauk" *LIQ*. "Getting to Know Your House," "The Reprieve," from *Love on the Alexander Hamilton* by Ron Oveton (Brooklyn, NY: Hanging Loose Press, 1985). Copyright © 1985 by Ron Overton. Reprinted by permission of the author.

Drew A. Pantino: "Crystal Willow," "Japanese Maple Tree," "Paschal Moon," published by permission of the photographer.

Russell Cameron Perry: "Frozen Sound," "Pebbles and Shell," "A Poem of Doors Unlocked," "Poet's Fishing," "Raised Panel Doors," "Rocks at Weld Sanctuary," "Walking the Glacier's Wake," published by permission of the photographer.

Joe Pihas: "Icy Swirl," published by permission of the photographer.

Beverly Pion: "Call 911," *LIQ*. "Daylily," from *Taproot Workshops, Inc.*, Philip W. Quigg, ed. (Stony Brook, NY: Stony Brook University Fine Arts Center, 1999). Copyright © 1999 by Beverly Pion. "Fish-Shaped Paumanok," "Out Here," from *East of Little Neck* by Beverly Pion (Fort Salanga, NY: Rana Press, 2002). Copyright © 2002 by Beverly Pion. Reprinted by permission of the author.

M. James Pion: "Crows," "Memories," "Ocean Waves," "Pod's Away," "Sands," published by permission of the photographer.

Allen Planz: "Winter Dawn" *Hanging Loose*; "Mola Mola," *Whelks Way Review*. "East End Archipelago," "Little Deep," "Peconic," from *Creaturely Drift* by Allen Planz (Sound Beach, NY: Street Press, 2008). Copyright © 2008 by Allen Planz. Reprinted by permission of the author.

Sheldon Pollack: "First Boat," "Great Egret," "Red and White Rose," "Road to Town, Massapequa," "Sandpiper & Reflection," "Stunned," "Tiny Spider," "White Crown Night Heron," published by permission of the photographer.

Anne Porter: "At the Shore," "Autumn Crocus," "Before the Frost," "Consider the Lilies of the Sea," "Cradle Song II," "December," "An Easter Lily," "The First of May," "Getting Up Early," "Houseguest," "In Storm-Watch Season," "Looking at the Sky," "The Neighboring Sea," "Winter Twilight," from *Living Things: Collected Poems* by Anne Porter (Hanover, NH: Zoland Books, 2006). Copyright © 2006 by Anne Porter. Reprinted by permission of the author.

Steve Potter: "The Awl That Through the Leather Pierces," "In the Winter Silence of the Woods," published by permission of the author.

Elaine Preston: "At the Seam of Everything We Are," "The Light in the Practice Area," "Long Island Sound, the First Day," published by permission of the author.

Orel Protopopescu: "Milkweed," "To Make a Poem," published by permission of the author.

Ralph Pugliese, Jr.: "Fire Island National Seashore," "Long Island Sound," "Queensboro Bridge," "Surf Fishing," "Turtle Cove, Montauk Point," published by permission of the photographer.

Clementine C. Rabassa: "Nautica," published by permission of the author.

Gregory Rabassa: "Indian Summer," from *A Cloudy Day in Gray Minor*, Cross-Culural Review Chapbook 35, by Gregory Rabassa (Merrick, NY: Cross-Cultural Communications, 1992). Reprinted by permission of the author and the publisher.

Barbara Reiher-Meyers: "Hidden Pond," published by permission of the author. "Local Tomatoes" from *Sound Familiar* by Barbara Reiher-Meyers (Bohemia, NY: Brooks Printing, 2004). Copyright © 2004 by Barbara Reiher-Mayers. Reprinted by permission of the author.

John Renner: "White on White," published by permission of the photographer.

Craig D. Robins: "Girl in Summer Shower," "Horse in a Foggy Meadow," "Max Running in the Cabbage Patch," "Walkers in the Fog," published by permission of the photographer.

Betsey Ann Smith Roberts: "Patchogue Lane," from *Original Poems* (Patchogue, NY: Patchogue Advance Print, 1894, Second Edition) and from *Sounds and Sweet Airs*, Joan D. Berberich, ed. (Port Washington, NY/London: Kennikat Press, Inc., Ira J. Friedman Division, 1970).

Peter Rodriquez: "Snow Blizzard," published by permission of the photographer.

Linda Russo: "Apple Orchid," "Berries in Winter," "Blue Iris," "Chicken Feathers," "Christmas Jewels," "Cleome," "Crows," "Dance of the Dogwood," "Early Morning Sunburst," "Ice Storm Montage," "Rhododendron," "Sassafras," "Under the Green Maple," "White Tulips," "Willow Leaf," "Winter Tree," "Zinnia Harvest," published by permission of the photographer.

Judith Saccucci: "The Ice Storm," published by permission of the author.

Linda Sack: "Fragmented Wings," published by permission of the author.

Carol Schmidt: "Seven Swans," published by permission of the author.

Bob Schmitz: "Bird's Foot Violet," "Blue Flag," "Cardinal," "Common Tern," "Dahlia," "Dahlia," "Dahlia," "Day Lily," "Dove Looking for Supper, " "Fireworks," "Green Buds," "Green Reflection," "Leaves," "Lesser Celandine," "Red-Winged Blackbird, "The Robin," "Seagull in Flight," "Stillness," "Snowy Egret," "Starling," "Swans," "Tulips," "Wet Maple Leaf," "Yellow Warbler," published by permission of the photographer.

Elinor Schoenfeld: "Stony Brook Fantasy," published by permission of the photographer.

Grace Schulman: "Easy as Wind," from *The New Yorker* and *Days of Wonder: New and Selected Poems* by Grace Schulman (Houghton Mifflin, 2006). Copyright © 2006 by Houghton Mifflin Co. Reprinted by permission of the publisher. "The Island," "The Swans," *Ontario Review*, reprinted by permission of the author.

Weslea Sidon: "Fog, " "Flustered maples . . . ," "In the afterlight . . . ," "Sweet May Rhyme," published by permission of the author.

Art Simendinger: "Foraging the Beach," published by permission of the photographer.

Marcia Slatkin: "Brief Candle," "Change," "Spring Cleaning, "Transformations," from *A Woman Milking* by Marcia Slatkin (Cincinnati, OH: Word Press, 2006). Copyright © 2006 by Word Press. Reprinted by permission of the publisher.

Pauline Southard: "Another Reflection," "Daffodil Curve, " "Fairy Lake," "Forsythia," "Lilacs," "Purple Sunset," "Seagull," published by permission of the photographer.

Joseph Stanton: "Edward Hopper's *Roads and Trees*," published by permission of the author.

Tom Stock: "April Wind," "Sewing Machine in the Pines," "Spring Outing," "Talking to Long Island," "Timeless Moment" and "Sand and Pebbles," "Unplowed Field," published by permission of the author/photographer.

Gayl Teller: "Cleomes," "Grandma's Prayer for Aviva," published by permission of the author.

John Orville Terry: "Greenport, L.I., " "Long Island," "The Old Oven," from *Sounds and Sweet Airs*, Joan D. Berberich, ed. (Port Washington, NY/London, Ira J. Friedman Division: Kennikat Press, Inc., 1970). Copyright © 1970 by John Orville Terry. Reprinted by permission of the author.

Susan Tiffen: "Almost Tulips," "Blue Flower," "Just Bee," "Peach Dahlia," "Pink Dancer," "Yellow Daisy Blue Center," "Yellow Lily," published by permission of the photographer.

J R Turek: "At the Death of Winter," "Jones Beach," published by permission of the author.

Victoria Twomey: "Strawberries and Flowers," "Two Pears in the Window," "Yellow, Pink, Teal," published by permission of the photographer.

Pramila Venkateswaran: "Futility," *LIQ*. Reprinted by permission of the author. "Night Vision," "Through Dark Leaves," published by permission of the author.

George Wallace: "Bird Wading," "A Dogwood Sapling Made Clear," "Forsythia," "I'll Take My Winters Cold," "Imprints," "It's Not Only in the Botanical Garden," "North Shore," "Old Fishing Village at Dawn," "On This Particular Morning," "Serious Spring," "Shell-Picking in Autumn, " "Snowed In," "Some Septembers," "Succession," "Summer Cultivation," "West Hills," from *The Poems of Augie Prime* by George Wallace (Selden, NY: Writer's Ink, 1999). Copyright © 1999 by George Wallace. Reprinted by permission of the author.

Michael C. Walsh: "Revisiting the Orchard," published by permission of the author.

Gil Weiner: "Gaillardia," "Lonely on the Beach," published by permission of the photographer.

Marlene Weinstein: "Black-Eyed Susans," "Leaf," "Leaf Dance," "May Beach," "Red Window," "Sandbar Sunset," "Spring Glow," "Still Life Melody," "Triple Reflection," "West Meadow Sunset," published by permission of the photographer.

Ray Welch: "Phragmites," published by permission of the photographer.

Maxwell Corydon Wheat, Jr.: "The Angler," *LIQ*. Reprinted by permission of the author. "Bird's-Foot Violets," "Cedarmere," "Haiku," "The Great Blue Heron," "Green Knows," "Tulips," "Marsh Evening," "Pond Lilies," published by permission of the author.

John Hall Wheelock: "Moon-Dawn" and "Sunday Morning Moment," reprinted with the permission of Scribner, a Division of Simon & Schuster Adult Publishing Group, from *Poems Old and New* by John Hall Wheelock. Copyright © 1956 by John Hall Wheelock. All rights reserved.

Claire Nicolas White: "Horse on the Loose," *LIQ*; "All Souls' Day on Long Island," "Autumn on the Sound," "The Roses of Queens," "Winter in Port Jefferson," from *Biography and Other Poems* by Claire Nicolas White (New York, NY: Doubleday, 1981). Copyright © 1981 by Claire Nicolas White. "Morning," "Red Sunflowers," "Winter," from *News from Home* by Claire Nicolas White (Northport, NY: Birnham Wood Graphics, 1998). Copyright © 1998 by Claire Nicolas White. "Romance," "Seduction," "Summer," "Winter on the North Shore," from *Riding at Anchor* by Claire Nicolas White (Great Falls, VA: Waterline Books, 1994). Copyright © 1994 by Claire Nicolas White. "Winter Roses," from *An Armful of Time* by Claire Nicolas White (Hardwick, MA: Waterline Books, 2005). Copyright © 2005 by Claire Nicolas White. Reprinted by permission of the author. "Afternoon at Short Beach," "Down Cordwood Path," "Easter," "Garden," "Geese," "Rhododendron," published by permission of the author.

Walt Whitman: "Crossing Brooklyn Ferry #9," "Good-bye My Fancy: Unseen Buds," "[I Am the Poet]," "INSCRIPTIONS: Song of Myself #2," "INSCRIPTIONS: Song of Myself #6," "INSCRIPTIONS: Song of Myself #9," "INSCRIPTIONS: Song of Myself #17," "INSCRIPTIONS: Song of Myself #21," "INSCRIPTIONS: Song of Myself #22," "INSCRIPTIONS: Song of Myself #31," "INSCRIPTIONS: Song of Myself #33, "INSCRIPTIONS: Song of Myself #46," "INSCRIPTIONS: Song of Myself #52,""INSCRIPTIONS: Starting from Paumanok #16 / Song of Myself #39," "Memories of President Lincoln: When Lilacs Last in the Dooryard Bloom'd #3," "SANDS AT SEVENTY: From Montauk Point," "SANDS AT SEVENTY: Paumanok," "SANDS AT SEVENTY: The Voice of the Rain," "SANDS AT SEVENTY: Soon Shall the Winter's Foil Be Here," "SEA-DRIFT: As I Ebb'd with the Ocean of Life #1," "SEA-DRIFT: On the Beach at Night Alone, "SEA-DRIFT: Out of the Cradle Endlessly Rocking, "SEA-DRIFT: Out of the Cradle Endlessly Rocking," "SEA-DRIFT: The World Below the Brine," "Song of Joys," from *Leaves of Grass: Comprehensive Reader's Edition*, edited by Harold W. Blodgett and Sculley Bradley (New York, NY: New York University Press, 1965).

Ginger Williams: "Perhaps I'm Seven," LIQ. "Homage to Wrapped Pear," "Notes from Porpoise Cove," "Reflections on a Swamp Maple in Autumn," "Total Eclipse of the Moon," "Walking to the Sea," from *Restringing the Beads* by Ginger Williams (Quaker Path Press, 2007). Copyright © 2007 by Ginger Williams. "The Great Blue Heron," from *Voices from Northwood*. Reprinted by permission of the author. "Green Knows," "Tulips," published by permission of the author.

John A. Williams: "April Snowstorm," from *Skipping Stones* by John A. Williasm (Quaker Path Press, 2008). Copyright © 2008 by John A. Williams. Reprinted by permission of the author.

BAYVILLE
LLOYD HARBOR
GLEN COVE
OYSTER BAY
NORTHPORT
FORT SALONGA
EAST SETAUKET
STONYBROOK
HUNTINGTON
EAST NORTHPORT
NISSEQUOGUE
MT. SINAI
JACKSON HEIGHTS
COLLEGE POINT
ASTORIA
WOODSIDE
PORT WASHINGTON
GREAT NECK
NORTH HILLS
EAST HILLS
SYOSSET
HUNTINGTON STATION
ELWOOD
CENTEREACH
ST. JAMES
TERRYVILLE
MANHASSET
UTOPIA
QUEENS
LITTLE NECK
GARDEN CITY
JERICHO
MELVILLE
DIX HILLS
SMITHTOWN
LAKE GROVE
CORAM
FOREST HILLS
HOLLIS
FRANKLIN SQUARE
EAST MEADOWS
PLAINVIEW
RONKONKOMA
FARMINGVILLE
FRESH POND
WOODHAVEN
ELMONT
UNIONDALE
FARMINGDALE
WEST BABYLON
DEER PARK
CENTRAL ISLIP
HOLBROOK
RIDGEWOOD
OZONE PARK
NORTH BELLMORE
BRENTWOOD
NORTH PATCHOGUE
HOWARD BEACH
BROOKLYN
BALDWIN
COPIAGUE
NORTH BABYLON
ISLIP
EAST ISLIP
EAST PATCHOGUE
ROCKVILLE CENTER
MASSAPEQUA
WEST ISLIP
SAYVILLE
FORT HAMPTON
ROCKAWAY POINT
BAY SHORE
WEST SAYVILLE
BELLPORT
OAK BEACH
FAIR HARBOR